The Stock Market: Bubbles, Volatility, and Chaos

The Stock Market: Bubbles, Volatility, and Chaos

Proceedings of the Thirteenth Annual Economic Policy Conference of the Federal Reserve Bank of St. Louis

edited by
Gerald P. Dwyer, Jr.
Clemson University *and*
Federal Reserve Bank of St. Louis

and

R. W. Hafer
Southern Illinois University at Edwardsville
and Federal Reserve Bank of St. Louis

Kluwer Academic Publishers
Boston/Dordrecht/London

Distributors for North America:
Kluwer Academic Publishers
101 Philip Drive
Assinippi Park
Norwell, Massachusetts 02061, USA

Distributors for all other countries:
Kluwer Academic Publishers Group
Distribution Centre
Post Office Box 322
3300 AH Dordrecht, THE NETHERLANDS

Library of Congress Cataloging-in-Publication Data

Economic Policy Conference of the Federal Reserve Bank of St. Louis
(13th: 1988: Federal Reserve Bank of St. Louis)
The stock market: bubbles, volatility, and chaos: proceedings of the Thirteenth Annual Economic Policy Conference of the Federal Reserve Bank of St. Louis / edited by Gerald P. Dwyer, Jr. and R. W. Hafer.
p. cm.
Conference held 10/21–22/88.
ISBN 978-90-481-5781-5
1. Stocks—Prices—United States—Congresses. I. Dwyer, Gerald P. II. Hafer, R. W. (Rik W.) III. Title.
HG4915.E33 1988 89-11150
332.63'222'0973—dc20 CIP

Printed in the United States of America

Contents

Contributing Authors

Bradford Cornell
Anderson Graduate School of Management
University of California—Los Angeles
405 Hilgard Avenue
Los Angeles, California 90024

W. Davis Dechert
Department of Economics
University of Houston
4800 Calhoun Road
Houston, Texas 77004

Behzad T. Diba
Department of Economics
Georgetown University
37th and O Streets, N.W.
Washington, D.C. 20057

Gerald P. Dwyer, Jr.
Department of Economics
Clemson University
Clemson, South Carolina 29631

Robert P. Flood, Jr.
Research Department
International Monetary Fund
700 19th Street, N.W.
Washington, D.C. 20431

J. Douglas Gordon
Office of Thrift Supervision
U.S. Department of Treasury
Washington, D.C.

David D. Haddock
Northwestern University Law School
357 East Chicago Ave.
Chicago, Illinois 60611–3069

R. W. Hafer
Department of Economics
Southern Illinois University at Edwardsville
Edwardsville, Illinois 62026–1102

Lawrence Harris
School of Business Administration
University of Southern California
Los Angeles, California 90098

Bang Nam Jeon
Department of Economics
Drexel University
Philadelphia, Pennsylvania 19104

Gregory Kusek
Division of Economic Analysis
Commodity Futures Trading Commission
2033 K Street, N.W.
Washington D.C. 20581

Kenneth Lehn
Securities and Exchange Commission
450 5th Street, N.W., Stop 6–3
Washington, D.C. 20549

Eugene Moriarty
Evergreen Financial Management, Inc.
Washington, D.C.

James B. Ramsey
Department of Economics
New York University
269 Mercer Street, 7th Floor
New York, New York 10003

George Wang
Division of Economic Analysis
Commodity Futures Trading Commission
2033 K Street, N.W.
Washington, D.C. 20581

George M. von Furstenberg
Department of Economics
Indiana University
Bloomington, Indiana 47405

Acknowledgments

The annual economic policy conference is the joint effort of many in the Research and Public Information Department of the Federal Reserve Bank of St. Louis. In particular, we would like to thank Linda Moser, Donna Getrost, and Daniel Brennan for their help with the many facets of planning and holding a successful conference. We would also like to thank Gary Santoni of Ball State University for his advice and suggestions during the early stages of planning the conference.

The Stock Market: Bubbles, Volatility, and Chaos

1 INTRODUCTION

Gerald P. Dwyer, Jr. and R. W. Hafer

The articles and commentaries included in this volume were presented at the Federal Reserve Bank of St. Louis' thirteenth annual economic policy conference, held on October 21–22, 1988. The conference focused on the behavior of asset market prices, a topic of increasing interest to both the popular press and to academic journals as the bull market of the 1980s continued. The events that transpired during October, 1987, both in the United States and abroad, provide an informative setting to test alternative theories. In assembling the papers presented during this conference, we asked the authors to explore the issue of asset pricing and financial market behavior from several vantages. Was the crash evidence of the bursting of a speculative bubble? Do we know enough about the workings of asset markets to hazard an intelligent guess why they dropped so dramatically in such a brief time? Do we know enough to propose regulatory changes that will prevent any such occurrence in the future, or do we want to even if we can? We think that the articles and commentaries contained in this volume provide significant insight to inform and to answer such questions.

The article by Behzad Diba surveys existing theoretical and empirical research on rational bubbles in asset prices. On the theoretical front, Diba asks whether bubbles that arise in simple dynamic linear rational expectations models also are found in general-equilibrium models. Assuming that wealth differentials among individuals do not exist, and allowing for population growth, Diba finds that bubbles can arise in a certain class of dynamic linear rational expectations models. The problem remains, however, that the appearance of a bubble may mean that the bubble has existed since the beginning of trading. This leads to the unpleasant notion that if one finds evidence of a bubble influencing today's prices, then stock prices always must have been overvalued.

Diba's analysis of the existing empirical evidence, while generally not very supportive of the rational bubble hypothesis, raises the important issue of whether the tests used are powerful enough to capture the presence of a bubble. In addition, the finding of a bubble's existence may reflect the test's inability to distinguish true bubble effects from behavior that is caused by the fundamentals. Since much of the work done assumes that the fundamentals model used is correct, could it be that reported empirical results reflect the misspecification of the underlying fundamentals model? Do we really know enough about the fundamental determinants of asset prices that empirical evidence will enable us to sort out one effect from another? As Diba notes, understanding the volatility of stock prices may best be accomplished by analyzing why returns from holding stock over long horizons appear to be more predictable.

Robert P. Flood's commentary points out that students of asset markets do not known very much about what determines these prices. The conditions to be met in theoretical models are often so constraining that the usefulness of such models is taxed. Flood notes that finding the existence of a bubble in observed asset prices does not rule out the possibility that the model is merely misspecified. In other words, since the fundamentals model to which the existence of a bubble is compared is not well specified in theory or practice, finding empirical evidence of a bubble is meaningless: One cannot reject the fundamentals model because one really does not know what it is.

Our article addresses a basic issue about the stock market: What determines stock prices? In this analysis, we first consider a model of stock prices based on "rational bubbles," self-sustaining increases in stock prices consistent with present-value maximizing behavior by informed agents. Tests for rational bubbles in the behavior of daily stock prices in the United States, European countries, and Japan in 1986 and 1987 find little support for the importance of rational bubbles. We also test a version of a hypothesis found in both the Brady Commission Report and elsewhere that increases in stock prices in one country spurred stock-price increases in others, a hypothesis that might usefully be called a "contagious bubble." In an extreme form, this hypothesis suggests that stock price indexes in various countries rose in lock step. Under an assumption that expected holding-period returns are the same everywhere in the world, we show that stock-price indexes generally do not rise in step: The ratio of any two stock-price indexes has a unit root if there are country-specific factors affecting stock prices. The data generally are consistent with the hypothesis that relative stock-price indexes do have unit roots, evidence which is inconsistent with the proposition that contagious bubbles are an important component of the data.

We then test a particular model of the fundamentals. The analysis uses cointegration tests relating the levels of stock prices to the levels of dividends and interest rates. Using monthly data for the United States, European countries, and Japan in the 1970s and 1980s, we find virtually no support for the fundamentals model with this particular test.

Because of the apparent failure of both bubbles and particular implications of the fundamentals to provide a characterization of stock prices, we then examine the relationship between monthly changes in stock prices, interest rates, dividends, and aggregate variables such as industrial production. In these regressions, changes in stock prices are associated with changes in long-term interest rates, but other variables generally are not important.

In their commentary, George M. von Furstenberg and Bang Nam Jeon suggest that because there is no good reason to assume constancy of the expected probability that a bubble will burst, the analysis of rational bubbles is not likely to be particularly informative. With a probability that varies over time, any time pattern of changes in stock prices is possible. As a result, without survey data on the probability a bubble will burst, the hypothesis of rational bubbles is effectively untestable. In addition, von Furstenberg and Jeon argue that even if a contagious bubble were an important component of the daily data on stock prices in 1986 and 1987, it could be swamped by the other factors affecting stock prices. In the last section of their commentary, the authors suggest that a more thorough analysis of changes in stock prices would have produced more informative results on the importance of various factors affecting stock prices.

James B. Ramsey sketches the motivation for a new way to analyze economic data and some results of recent research by himself, associates, and others. The motivation for this type of research, as Ramsey states, is that many current findings show that "the only information in economic time series is contained in the first two moments and those have been milked to little effect." Two currently pursued lines of attack on this unsatisfactory state of affairs are 1) to pursue anomalies in the data, such as weekend effects, January effects, and a host of other "effects" in the stock market, and 2) to soup up standard econometric models (for example, by modeling variances using statistical models.)

An alternative line of attack discussed by Ramsey explores the possibility that nonlinearities are an important aspect of economic data. The feasibility of such a venture has been enhanced by, among other things, a relatively new line of analysis in the physical sciences called "chaos theory." Ramsey argues that while certain aspects of chaos theory are useful in analyzing nonlinearities in economic data, a mindless transfer of the techniques in the physical sciences to economics is not useful. In particular, low-dimensional deterministic systems that are valuable in solving many physics and engineering problems are unlikely to be useful for completely characterizing economic systems.

Ramsey discusses a particular test for nonlinearities that he and coworkers have developed. The test statistic is designed to be sensitive to "time irreversibility," a particular aspect of nonlinear equations. Time reversibility, common in the stationary representation of economic models, exists when the joint probability distribution function of a set of data is independent of whether it is ordered with time running backwards or forwards. If a time series process is asymmetric in its predictable behavior—for example, increases occur slowly and decreases occur rapidly—then it is time irreversible. Using this test, Ramsey finds interesting evidence of time irreversibility in several economic series.

In his commentary, W. Davis Dechert suggests that a modeling strategy based on estimation of particular nonlinear models is not currently useful in economics. He suggests that a less ambitious strategy focusing on the discovery of nonlinearities and the effects of stochastic components on the data is likely to be more fruitful. As part of such an analysis, the BDS (Brock-Dechert-Scheinkman) statistic, based on the correlation dimension of data, can be used to test the hypothesis that the residuals (for example, from a linear time series model) are independently and identically distributed over time. Failure to pass this test, while it does not imply nonlinearity, is consistent with the hypothesis that nonlinearity is present in the data. Such a result provides a first step in characterizing any non-linear structure in the data.

The article by Eugene Moriarty, J. Douglas Gordon, Gregory Kuserk, and George Wang investigates whether the futures market led the cash market down during the October 1987 break. Some have interpreted the observed negative basis between the futures and cash markets during this period as evidence that the decline in the cash market was exacerbated by declines in the futures market. The authors argue, however, that this conclusion may well depend on how one measures the price series.

In this study, the behavior of the futures and cash markets is analyzed by constructing a proxy index for the S&P 500 that more accurately captures the trading actually taking place on the floor during the break. Even though the S&P index uses the most recent prices on the securities included, the type of erratic, discontinuous trading that took place during the break introduces a nontrading effect to the index. When stock prices are falling sharply, the index is biased upward since previous prices for trades of some stocks may be above the current equilibrium level when prices are falling. Using their proxy index, the authors investigate whether the observed lead between the futures market and the S&P 500 index is a function of how the cash index is measured.

Using data spanning October 12 through October 26, Moriarty et al. report two significant results. First, the removal of serial correlation in the S&P 500 index lowers the lead time observed between the futures and cash market from fourteen minutes to four minutes during the week of October 12 and to zero during the week of October 19. Second, using their proxy index, the authors find that actual trading on the floor of the exchange and in the futures market are more often simultaneous than an analysis of the futures and S&P 500 index would suggest. This result, they argue, reflects the nontrading effect inherent in thie S&P 500 index. Once this effect is removed from the cash index, the large basis difference between the futures market and the cash index observed during the break disappears. The authors conclude that behavior in the futures and cash markets during October 1987 represented "nearly simultaneous price discovery," not the futures market leading the cash market.

Bradford Cornell asks if this research answers the question of whether the futures market deepened the stock market crash. Cornell argues that it does not, especially when one examines the evidence from markets around the world. He notes that others have shown that the existence of a futures market does not seem to play an important role in explaining the depth of the stock-price decline. He also notes that differentials between futures and cash markets of the magnitude observed during the break surely would entice arbitrageurs to enter the market. This did not happen, Cornell notes, because of the problems they would have encountered in executing cash transactions and the difficulties they would have faced in attempting to take offsetting positions, especially when facing margin requirements in both markets and uncertainty in the timing of transactions. While the evidence suggests that the cash market's clearing mechanism could be improved, Cornell argues that comprehensive reform without a clear understanding of what happened in October 1987 would more likely interfere with the market's normal functioning than prevent another crash.

Lawrence Harris's discussion of the study by Moriarty et al. considers the technical aspects of constructing an index of cash market activity. With available time and price data for every trade, Harris notes that an index can be constructed that helps to eliminate the nontrading effect, referred to here as the problem of stale prices. Using such information, he says, would produce an index that more accurately reflects the actual trading activity on the floor. Citing his own earlier work, Harris finds that this approach and the one used in the Moriarty et al. article come to the same conclusion: Eliminating the nontrading or stale-price effect helps explain a large degree of the common basis between the futures and cash market observed during the market crash. Based on these findings, he aruges that reforms that increase the flow of information between the markets could ease the problems encountered in October 1987.

In the final article, David Haddock analyzes the regulatory recommendations of the Brady Report from a public interest perspective. Would the public's interest be enhanced if the suggested reforms were made? Haddock's answer is an emphatic no. One reason is the wrong-headed presumption in the report that regulators are able to perceive the activity of the market better than private agents; this invariably leads to regulatory reform after the fact. The question is: Will such reform prevent future breaks? Further, what if the reforms mandated by an event such as the October 1987 market decline are inappropriate for future market changes? Haddock's response is that private-market responses should be emphasized over those of regulators, and private-market responses are based on a profit calculus that regulators may not consider.

Should there be any regulatory reform fallout from the October crash? Haddock suggests that the decline may speed the market's modernization of certain trading activities. For example, the problems encountered during the crash stemming from the inability to cope with the flood of incoming orders may spur the exchanges to alter the ways information flows are handled. Since external regulations create rigidites in the functioning of the market, Haddock concludes with the hope that regulatory changes in the direction of less—not more—interference in the market place become the rule.

While agreeing with the general thrust of the Haddock article, Kenneth Lehn takes a more sympathetic view of the Brady Report. In his discussion, Lehn argues that Haddock's dismissal of the report's "one market" approach may be hasty. Using such a framework, Lehn argues, maintains the importance of the linkage between the futures and the stock markets.

Lehn also notes that while Haddock criticizes the report for ignoring private incentives to innovate, such reforms may also miss the mark. For example, in response to the October 19 crash, the New York Stock Exchange on October 20 suspended indefinitely the use of its DOT system that is used for index arbitrage trading. Lehn notes that such a suspension, although endorsed by the report as a barrier to program selling, also raised the cost of index arbitrage and removed a source of liquidity from the futures market. This "reform" may explain the disparity in futures and stock prices throughout October 20, Lehn argues.

Lehn also takes a different perspective on the inaction by Congress following the crash. Haddock asserts that the failure to act is consistent with rent extraction theory. Lehn suggests that it reflects the institutional structure of Congress, with different committees responsible for different markets. Another explanation is that following the crash, stock-price volatility subsided, thus reducing the incentive to act.

2 BUBBLES AND STOCK-PRICE VOLATILITY

Behzad T. Diba

2.1. Introduction

The possible contribution of speculative bubbles to asset-price fluctuations has long intrigued observers of financial markets. Economist, however, have not attempted to formally test for the existence of asset-price bubbles until recently, probably because a prerequisite for developing such tests was a compelling joint hypothesis about how asset holders' expectations evolve over time. The advent of the rational-expectations hypothesis furnished such a joint hypothesis and thus stimulated theoretical and empirical research on "rational" bubbles—that is, asset-price fluctuations that reflect extraneous factors and, yet, contradict neither the assumption of rational expectations nor the intertemporal equilibrium conditions implied by the model at hand.

I thank Robert Flood, Seonghwan Oh, and the participants of the Federal Reserve Bank of St. Louis Conference on the Stock Market for helpful comments on an earlier draft. This paper was partly written while I was an economist at the Federal Reserve Bank of Philadelphia. The views expressed here do not necessarily represent the views of the Federal Reserve Bank of Philadelphia or of the Federal Reserve System.

This article attempts an exposition and a partial assessment of a number of theoretical and empirical studies that seem relevant for assessing the possible existence of bubbles in U.S. aggregate stock prices. Section 2.2 presents my assessment of theoretical results about the possibility of rational bubbles in a general equilibrium setting. Section 2.3 discusses the problems of testing for the existence of rational bubbles in stock prices. Section 2.4 contains some observations about irrational bubbles and other potential causes of the apparent excess volatility of stock prices. Section 2.5 concludes the article.

2.2. Theoretical Results

Tirole [1985] examines the theoretical possibility of asset-price bubbles in a perfect-foresight general-equilibrium framework, with an infinite succession of overlapping generations of asset holders having finite planning horizons. In Tirole's model the market-fundamentals value of the asset is equal to the discounted present value of its future payoffs; if the asset's price is above market fundamentals, a bubble is present. Tirole shows that, as long as the growth rate of this economy is not less than the asset's required rate of return, the restrictions implied by perfect foresight and general equilibrium do not preclude the existence of a bubble. O'Connell and Zeldes [1988] derive the same result in a model with a growing number of asset holders with infinite planning horizons—thus, they show it is the potential infinity of asset holders, rather than the finiteness of planning horizons, that is central to Tirole's argument.

In the models of Tirole and O'Connell and Zeldes, a would-be bubble must grow exponentially at a rate equal to the required rate of return because agents would not hold an overvalued asset unless they expected it to be overvalued by a sufficiently greater amount next period. Moreover, these perfect foresight models imply that the existence of a bubble depends on a single initial condition: If there is no bubble on the first day of trading, bubbles cannot arise subsequently; if there is a bubble on the first day of trading, it will exist forever and will grow exponentially, causing a divergence of the asset's price from its market-fundamentals value.

The theoretical possibilty of explosive deterministic bubbles in perfect-foresight general-equilibrium models does not seem empirically relevant for understanding the fluctuations of U.S. stock prices; with any plausible definition of market fundamentals, the data would clearly reject the hypothesis that stock prices diverge from their fundamental value. Partial equilibrium analyses of dynamic linear rational expectations (DLRE) models, however, suggest the possibility of stochastic bubbles that seem empirically more plausible on a number of grounds (and more interesting) than deterministic bubbles.

Taylor [1977] shows that intrinsically irrelevant random variables can impinge on the solution to a DLRE model.[1] This finding implies that bubbles can contribute to the variance of asset prices and can cause asset prices to depend on seemingly irrelevant news about the economy, or to exhibit seemingly excessive reactions to relevant news. Shiller [1978] shows that no finite set of initial or terminal conditions would preclude the existence of a stochastic bubble term in the solution to a DLRE model. This result implies, in particular, that the price of an asset may coincide with market fundamentals for a long time before the inception of a speculative bubble. Blanchard [1979] shows that an existing stochastic bubble may burst at a random date. Thus, the existence of bubbles in DLRE models need not imply that prices will diverge from market fundamentals. Blanchard and Watson [1982] and Quah [1985] extend Blanchard's original specification to allow for stochastic bubbles that burst and restart repeatedly.

Can the empirically interesting stochastic bubbles arising in DLRE models arise also in a stochastic general-equilibrium model? The answer is not immediately obvious because the perfect-foresight general-equilibrium models of Tirole and O'Connell and Zeldes cannot be directly generalized to a rational-expectations framework. The basic complication is that wealth differentials between young and old agents introduce a nonlinearity into these general-equilibrium models, while the partial-equilibrium analyses of DLRE models presume a linear structure. To address the question, I will assume an allocation scheme that eliminates wealth differentials among agents in a stochastic version of the O'Connell-Zelds model. Although the scheme is highly arbitrary and unconventional, it provides a useful expositional device because wealth differentials do not play a key role in the existing literature, while population growth and a stochastic structure do.

Consider a competitive exchange economy with infinitely lived agents as studied by Lucas [1978], but let the number of agents grow over time. Specifically, assume that the population of agents evolves according to the deterministic process:

$$L_t = (1 + g)L_{t-1},\ t = 0, 1, 2, \ldots, g \geq 0,$$

where L_t denotes the number of agents at date t, and g the nonnegative growth rate of population.

Each of the L_0 agents born at date zero is endowed with e_0 units of a single perishable consumption good (fruit) and with a single share of equity (in a tree yielding the fruit) that entitles its owner to a stochastic dividend stream of d_t units of the consumption good at date t. Assuming nonsatiation in consumption and the existence of equilibrium, the price of shares in terms of the consumption good p_0 will adjust to clear the markets: Each agent will demand $e_0 + d_0$ units of the consumption good and will wish to hold one share of equity.

At date one, the population consists of the L_0 "old" agents (born at date zero) and gL_0 new agents. To preserve the standard terminology of overlapping generations models, I will refer to the new agents born each period as the "young" during that period. Thus, for instance, the gL_0 agents born at date one are the "young agents" at date one and will be among the "old agents" at all subsequent dates.

At date one, each old agent possesses a share of equity valued at P_1 units of the consumption good and collects d_1 units in dividends. In addition, the economy has a per capita endowment of e_1 units of the consumption good. The endowments of an old and a young agent are $e_1^o = e_1 - \frac{g}{1+g}(p_1 + d_1)$, and $e_1^y = e_1 + \frac{g}{1+g}(p_1 + d_1)$, respectively. A possible interpretation of the difference between e_1^o and e_1^y is that it arises from a head tax of $[g/1 + g]\,(p_1 + d_1)$ units of the consumption good paid by the old (regardless of their decision to hold equity), with the proceeds transferred to the young.

Whatever the interpretation, my assumption that e_1^o and e_1^y depend on the realizations of p_1 and d_1 is admittedly unconventional. But this assumption has the advantage of equalizing the total wealth of a young and old agent, without affecting the incentive to hold equity and without implying that the economy's aggregate endowment depends on share prices. Assuming that old and young agents have the same preferences, the equalization of their wealths facilitates the characterization of equilibria in a stochastic setting by turning this growing economy into a representative-agent economy. A more detailed description of this economy is as follows.

At date t, the population consists of L_{t-1} old and gL_{t-1} young agents. Each old agent possesses $(1 + g)^{1-t}$ shares of equity priced at p_t units of the consumption good per share; each share pays d_t units of the consumption good in dividends. In addition, the economy has a per capita endowment of e_t units of the consumption good, of which

$$e_t^o = e_t - g(1 + g)^{-t}\,(p_t + d_t) \tag{2.1}$$

units (net of taxes) is allocated to each old agent, and

$$e_t^y = e_t + (1 + g)^{-t} (p_t + d_t) \tag{2.2}$$

units to each young agent. These endowments imply that young and old agents have the same budget constraint: each agent chooses consumption c_t and the number of shares s_{t+1} to be carried into next period, subject to

$$c_t + p_t s_{t+1} \leq e_t + (1 + g)^{-t} (p_t + d_t). \tag{2.3}$$

The choice of s_{t+1} will also impinge on the sequence of budget constraints that the agent will face in the future, for $\gamma \leq t + 1$,

$$c_\gamma + p_\gamma s_\gamma + 1 \leq e_\gamma - g(1 + g)^{-\gamma} (p_\gamma + d_\gamma) + s_\gamma(p_\gamma + d_\gamma). \tag{2.4}$$

The agent's objective is to maximize expected utility,

$$U = E_t \sum_{\gamma=t}^{\infty} \beta^{\gamma-t} u(C_\gamma),\ 0 < \beta < 1, \tag{2.5}$$

subject to inequalities 2.3 and 2.4. I will adopt the familiar assumptions (see, for example, Sargent [1987]: 95–100) about the utility function and about the stochastic processes generating d_t and e_t, to ensure the existence of an interior solution to the agent's maximization problem.

The optimization problem posed above is a special case of the one analyzed by Brock [1982], drawing on Benveniste and Scheminkman's [1982] work; the necessary and sufficient conditions for optimality are:

$$p_t u'(c_t) = \beta E_t[(p_{t+1} + d_{t+1})u'(c_{t+1})], \tag{2.6}$$

and

$$\lim_{n \to \infty} E_t[\beta^n u'(c_{t+n}) p_{t+n} s_{t+n}] = 0, \tag{2.7}$$

assuming that the limit in equation 2.7 exists.

The left-hand side of equation 2.6 is the marginal utility from selling a share this period; the right-hand side is the present value of the expected marginal utility from selling a share next period. Equation 2.6, then, ensures that asset holders do not expect to gain utility from a strategy that involves buying (selling) shares at date t and planning to sell (buy) them back at date $t + 1$. More generally, forward iteration of equation 2.6 would reveal that asset holders to not expect to gain utility from a strategy that involves buying (selling) shares at date t and planning to sell (buy) them back at any finite future date.

Free disposal of goods and shares implies that the limit on the left-hand side of equation 2.7 is nonnegative. The optimizing behavior of the agent implies that this limit is not positive. If it were, the expected present value of the agent's shareholdings in terms of foregone utility,

$E_t[\beta^n u'(c_{t+n})p_{t+n}s_{t+n}]$, would be strictly positive beyond some finite future date $t + N$. In which case, an unexploited opportunity for gaining utility—from selling shares to finance extra consumption at date $t + N$ and never buying back the shares—would exist. Equation 2.7, the transversality condition, states that such an opportunity does not exist along the optimal path.

Incorporating the market-clearing conditions in equation 2.6, following Lucas [1978], turns this equation into an equilibrium asset pricing equation. Since all the agents alive at date t have the same objective function and face the same constraints, they will choose the same consumption and shareholding strategies. In equilibrium, each agent will choose to carry $s_{t+1} = (1 + g)^{-t}$ shares into next period and to consume the per capita supply of the perishable good,

$$c_t = e_t + (1 + g)^{-t}d_t \equiv e_t^*.$$

In equilibrium, then, equation 2.6 implies

$$p_t u'(e_t^*) = \beta E_t[p_{t+1}u'(e_{t+n}^*)] + \beta E_t[d_{t+1}u'(e_{t+n}^*)]. \qquad (2.8)$$

Since equation 2.8 is linear in $p_t u'(e_{t+n}^*)$, its general solution potentially involves the stochastic bubbles that arise in DLRE models.

Forward iteration of equation 2.8, using the law of iterated expectations, yields

$$p_t u'(e_t^*) = \beta^n E_t[p_{t+n}u'(e_{t+n}^*)] + \sum_{j=1}^{n} \beta^j E_t[d_{t+j}u'(e_{t+n}^*)]. \qquad (2.9)$$

Assuming the existence of the relevant limits as n tends to infinity, the right-hand side of equation 2.9 converges to the sum of a bubble term B_t and a term F_t representing market fundamentals:

$$\begin{aligned} p_t u'(e_t^*) &= B_t + F_t, \\ B_t &= \lim_{n\to\infty} \beta^n E_t[p_{t+n}u'(e_{t+n}^*)], \qquad (2.10) \\ F_t &= \sum_{j=1}^{\infty} \beta^j E_t[d_{t+j}u'(e_{t+j}^*)]. \end{aligned}$$

Note that if $u'(.)$ is a constant and B_t is set equal to zero, equation 2.10 simplifies to the more familiar specification of market fundamentals, which equates the stock price to the present value of expected future dividends.

The assumption of rational expectations restricts the process generating B_t. In particular, the law of iterated expectations implies:

$$E_t B_{t+1} = \lim_{n\to\infty} \beta^n E_t[p_{t+1+n}u'(e_{t+1+n}^*)]$$

$$= \beta^{-1} \lim_{m\to\infty} \beta^m E_t[p_{t+m}u'(e^*_{t+m})]$$

$$= \beta^{-1}B_t \tag{2.11}$$

Equation 2.11 states that a rational bubble must be expected to grow exponentially at the rate β^{-1}.

Solutions to equation 2.11 conclude with those of the stochastic difference equation

$$B_{t+1} = \beta^{-1}B_t + z_{t+1}, \tag{2.12}$$

where z_{t+1} is any random variable with the property

$$E_t z_{t+1} = 0 \tag{2.13}$$

The innovation of the bubble term z_{t+1} can reflect new information about intrinsically irrelevant variables, or it can be related to truly relevant variables, like d_{t+1}, through parameters that are not present in F_{t+1}.

Would the existence of bubbles violate the transversality condition implied by the optimality of agents' decisions? Substituting the market-clearing conditions, and the expression for B_t from equation 2.10, into equation 2.7 yields

$$\lim_{n\to\infty} E_t[\beta^n u'(c_{t+n})p_{t+n}s_{t+n}] = B_t \lim_{n\to\infty} s^*_{t+n}, \tag{2.14}$$

where s^*_{t+n} is the (nonstochastic) number of shares that the representative agent must hold in equilibrium.

Consider first an economy without population growth. As Tirole [1982] observes, in such an economy agents cannot rationally expect to reduce their shareholdings over time. With s^*_{t+n} bounded above zero, a nonzero value of B_t would contradict the transversality condition according to equation 2.14 and, therefore, could not arise. Consider next the growing economy with $s^*_{t+n} = (1 + g)^{1-t-n}$. For this economy, as in the model of O'Connell and Zeldes [1988], the right-hand side of equation 2.14 tends to zero, for any positive value of g and any finite B_t. Accordingly, the transversality condition has no bearing on the possible existence of bubbles in an economy with population growth.

In the models of Tirole [1985] and of O'Connell and Zeldes, bubbles cannot exist if the economy grows at a slower rate than the rate of interest. The problem is that the aggregate wealth of the young must grow at least as rapidly as the bubble, which grows at the rate of interest; otherwise, the young could not buy the asset from the old beyond some finite date. This problem does not arise in the present setup because my arbitrary allocation scheme ensures that the young will always have the funds to acquire their (equilibrium) share of the asset. An analogous question, however, arises with respect to the endowment of the old.

To see the analogy, suppose that risk free indexed loans were introduced into the present setup. It is straightforward to show that the gross real interest rate R_t on such loans in the present model, as is generally the case in consumption-based asset pricing models (e.g., Sargent [1987]: 102–103), would satisfy $R_t^{-1} = \beta E_t[u'(e_{t+1}^*)/u'(e_t^*)]$. Accordingly, if the interest rate exceeds the growth rate of population, then $u'(e_t^*)$ is of mean exponential order less than $[(1 + g)\beta]^{-1}$. By the definition of B_t in equation 2.10, however, a nonzero bubble term implies that $p_t u'(e_t^*)$ is of mean exponential order β^{-1}. It follows that if a bubble exists while the interest rate exceeds the population growth rate, then p_t must be of mean exponential order greater than $(1 + g)$; that is, $(1 + g)^{-t}p_t$ must be expected to grow over time. But, with a stationary per capita endowment e_t, the (net of tax) endowment of the old, e_t^o in equation 2.1, would eventually become negative if $(1 + g)^{-t}p_t$ grew over time.

Such negative net endowments would not alter the present model's equilibrium in which old agents liquidate some of their assets to pay their taxes and to finance their consumption. Thus, in contrast to the models of Tirole [1985] and of O'Connell and Zeldes, the present model does not preclude the existence of bubbles even if the interest rate exceeds the population growth rate. This feature of the present model, of course, is an artifact of the unconventional tax structure I have assumed.

To summarize my discussion so far: 1) Once we allow for population growth, the transversality condition necessary for the optimality of consumption-saving decisions does not rule out rational bubbles; 2) We can rule out the existence of bubbles if we assume that the wealth of potential new asset holders will at some point be too small to buy the asset on which a bubble has grown.

Allowing for population growth, however, does not circumvent Diba and Grossman's [1987, 1988b] argument for restricting the inception of rational bubbles. This argument is based on the implication of equation 2.11 that if B_t equals zero at some date t, $E_t B_{t+1}$ will also equal zero. Because free disposal implies that B_{t+1} is a nonnegative random variable, the restriction $E_t B_{t+1} = 0$ implies that B_{t+1} equals zero, almost surely.

This result says that if a rational bubbles does not exist at date t, $t \geq 0$, a rational bubble cannot get started at date $t+1$, nor, by extension, at any subsequent date. Therefore, if a rational bubble exists at present, it must have started at date zero, the first date of trading; hence, shares of equity must have been overvalued relative to market fundamentals at every past date. The intuition behind this result is simple: 1) Under the assumption of rational expectations, negative bubbles cannot exist because their existence would imply negative expected share prices at a finite future date; 2) If negative bubbles cannot arise and agents attach a nonzero probability to the inception of a positive bubble next period, then they will be willing to pay more than market fundamentals for shares *this* period.

A simple extension of the preceding argument, presented in Diba and Grossman [1988b], imposes a further restriction on the inception of rational bubbles if we think of date zero, not as the first day agents are born (which is the case in our theoretical models), but rather, as the first day shares of equity are issued by a firm. This further restriction is that a rational bubble cannot start even at date zero unless the issuer of the stock and potential stockholders who anticipated the initial pricing of this stock expected it to be overvalued relative to market fundamentals. And if we assumed that the stock was expected to be overvalued, we would have to explain why its issuer would want to sell only a finite quantity.

In sum, although theoretical reasoning does not preclude the existence of rational bubbles, it casts doubt on the view that such bubbles have significantly contributed to the fluctuations of U.S. aggregate stock prices. To the extent that the existence of rational bubbles seems plausible at all, they seem more likely to be pressent in new issues of equity. Yet, for statistical reasons, empirical tests for the existence of rational bubbles in stock prices (including my own work) have mostly focused on a long time series (going back over a hundred years) of the S&P index.

2.3. Testing or Rational Bubbles

Several of the empirical studies to be discussed below focus on a special case of the model of the preceding section; in this special case $u'(.)$ is a constant and β is set equal to $(1 + r)^{-1}$, where r denotes the constant required rate of return from holding equity. For future reference, it is convenient to present the counterparts of some of the equations of the preceding section for this special case:

$$p_t = (1 + r)^{-1}E_t p_{t+1} + (1 + r)^{-1}E_t(d_{t+1}), \tag{2.8'}$$

$$p_t = (1 + r)^{-n}E_t p_{t+n} + \sum_{j=1}^{n} (1 + r)^{-j}E_t d_{t+j}, \tag{2.9'}$$

$$p_t = B_t + F_t, \tag{2.10'}$$

$$F_t = \sum_{j=1}^{\infty} (1 + r)^{-j}E_t d_{t+j},$$

$$E_t B_{t+1} = (1 + r) B_t, \tag{2.11'}$$

$$B_{t+1} = (1 + r) B_t + z_{t+1}, \tag{2.12'}$$

where z_{t+1} is random variable satisfying equation 2.13.

The basic difficulty involved in testing for the existence of rational bubbles, pointed out by Flood and Garber [1980] and emphasized by Hamilton and Whiteman [1985], is that the contribution of hypothetical rational bubbles to asset prices would not be directly distinguishable from the contribution to market fundamentals of variables that the researcher cannot observe. For example, the empirical finding that stock prices do not conform to the specification of market fundamentals given by equation 2.10′ could arise either because this specification does not model market fundamentals correctly or because rational bubbles exist.

To avoid such problems of interpretation, Hamilton and Whiteman [1985] and Diba and Grossman [1988a] advocate tests based on the stationarity properties of observable time series. The first step in these tests is to note that if the unconditional mean of the bubble term EB_t exists, equation 2.12′ implies

$$EB_{t+1} = (1 + r) EB_t. \tag{2.15}$$

Equation 2.15 implies that a rational bubble has either an explosive mean or a constant mean of zero.

In the existing literature, the only specifications of the process generating B_t that do not have an explosive mean—the specifications of Blanchard [1979], Blanchard and Watson [1982], and Quah [1985]—involve rational bubbles that almost surely woudl burst at a finite future date. Quah demonstrates that such bubbles, despite their explosive conditional expectations, would possess a stationary unconditional mean of zero. (Quah's result is related to the fact that the innovations of such bubbles would have infinite variance.)

Diba and Grossman's [1987, 1988b] arguments, outlined in the preceding section, imply that if an existing rational bubble bursts at some finite date t, it cannot subsequently restart. Accordingly, the only theoretically possible rational bubble with zero mean is one that, as in Blanchard's [1979] specification, starts at date zero, almost surely bursts at a finite date, and does not subsequently restart. Setting aside the possibility of such transient bubbles, then, equation 2.15 implies that a rational bubble would possess an explosive mean. The explosive mean of B_t, in turn, would imply that first differences of a rational bubble do not possess a stationary mean.

Empirical analyses of the stationarity properties of stock prices and dividends (e.g., Kleidon [1986], Campbell and Shiller [1987a], Diba and Grossman [1988a]) do not seem to contradict the hypothesis that prices conform to market fundamentals, as specified in equation 2.10′. In particular, for Shiller's [1981] annual S&P time series going back to the 1870s, both real dividends and real stock prices seem to be first-difference stationary. This finding suggests that any deviations of stock prices from market fundamentals, as specified in equation 2.10′, are first-difference stationary and, therefore, do not involve explosive rational bubbles.

A stronger piece of evidence against the existence of explosive rational bubbles is based on rearranging terms in question 2.10′ to obtain.

$$p_t - r^{-1}d_t = B_t + r^{-1} \sum_{j=1}^{\infty} (1 + r)^{1-j} E_t(d_{t+j} - d_{t+j-1}). \qquad (2.16)$$

Equation 2.16 implies that if rational bubbles do not exist and dividends are first-difference stationary, then $p_t - r^{-1}d_t$ is stationary—that is, to use the terminology of Engle and Granger [1987], P_t and d_t are cointegrated of order (1, 1) with cointegrating vector $(1, -r^{-1})$. In contrast, if explosive rational bubbles exist, equation 2.16 implies that stock prices and dividends are not cointegrated. Overall, the tests reported by Campbell and Shillder [1987a] and Diba and Grossman [1988a] suggest that real stock prices and real dividends are cointegrated. Thus, any deviations of stock prices from market fundamentals, as specified in equation 2.10′, seem attributable to variables that, unlike explosive rational bubbles, possess a stationary mean.

Would stationarity tests have enough power to detect any theoretically possible rational bubble, given the size of available samples? The answer, unfortunately, is that they would not. Consider the following example taken from West [1987]:

$$B_{t+1} = \begin{cases} (1 + r)(B_t - B^*)/\pi & \text{with probability } \pi \\ (1 + r)B^*/(1 - \pi) & \text{with probability } (1 - \pi) \end{cases} \qquad (2.17)$$

with $B^* > 0$ and $0 < \pi < 1$; note that this process satisfies equation 2.11′. In this example, the bubble grows at the rate $(1 + r)/\pi$, with probability π, and crashes to its *positive* lower bound of $(1 + r)B^*/(1 - \pi)$, with probability $(1 - \pi)$. With B^* set equal to zero, equation 2.17 would yield a Blanchard-Watson type bubble—which, as Quah shows, would possess a stationary mean. With $B^* > 0$, equation 2.17 would generate a bubble with explosive mean, whose fluctuations in a finite sample could obviously mimic the behavior of a stationary bubble arbitrarily well, as long as B^* is sufficiently close to zero.

An attractive alternative to stationarity tests for existence of rational bubbles is the empirical strategy of West [1987]. The first step in this strategy is to perform a battery of specification tests of a model's one-period intertemporal equilibrium condition—e.g., equation 2.8′. The second step is to test the cross equation restrictions imposed by the model's market fundamentals solution—e.g., equation 2.10′ with B_t set equal to zero—on the projections of p_t and d_t on lagged variables. If the tests fail to reject the intertemporal equilibrium condition but reject the implied specification of market fundamentals, it follows logically that rational bubbles are present.

West's strategy resolves the basic difficulty (referred to at the beginning of this section) involved in distinguishing bubbles from unobserved fundamentals. The resolution is based on the fact that the existence of *rational* bubbles would not cause rejection of the one-period intertemporal equilibrium condition, while misspecification of market fundamentals most likely would.

Applying his test to Shiller's [1981] annual S&P and (modified) Dow-Jones data sets, West fails to reject equation 2.8′ but strongly rejects the specification of market fundamentals given by equation 2.10′. He also reports similar tests of linearlized models that allow for time variation in expected returns. Although the results of his tests of these models are somewhat mixed, he concludes that overall his tests suggest that rational bubbles are present in real stock prices.

The reliability of West's inference hinges on the power of his specification tests of one-period intertemporal equilibrium conditions such as equation 2.8′. The findings of Flood, Hodrick, and Kaplan [1986] suggest that these tests may in fact have low power in detecting misspecifications of the one-period intertemporal equilibrium condition. An important aspect of these findings is that West's specification tests applied to the same data strongly reject the two-period intertemporal equilibrium condition obtained by setting n equal to two in equation 2.9′. Since equation 2.9′ is an implication of equation 2.8′ and the law of iterated expectations, regardless of whether or not rational bubbles exist, the rejection of equation 2.9′ suggests that equation 2.8′ is in fact misspecified. Flood, Hodrick, and Kaplan also report tests of more general models, including versions of equation 2.6 for standard specifications of the utility function. The two-period intertemporal equilibrium conditions implied by these models are also rejected by the data.

In sum, empirical tests for existence of rational bubbles in stock prices remain inconclusive. The stationarity tests, which are not very sensitive to possible misspecification of market fundamentals, would not detect rational bubbles whose nonstationarity is masked in finite samples. And West's empirical strategy, although in principle attractive, requires a more adequate model of time variation in expected returns than we presently seem to possess. Whatever the verdict on the existence of rational bubbles, however, the results of Flood, Hodrick, and Kaplan point to misspecification of standard models of stock-price fluctuations. The following section discusses some other manifestations of the inadequacy of these standard models.

2.4. Stock Market Volality and Related Issues

A possible manifestation of the empirical failure of the constant required rate of return model of the stock market, described by equation 2.8′, is the apparent excess volatility of stock prices detected by several recent studies. The original volatility tests of LeRoy and Porter [1981] and Shiller [1981] have been criticized on a number of technical grounds (see, for example, Flavin [1983], Kleidon [1986], Marsh and Merton [1986]). But the basic result of these original tests—that stock prices are too volatile to represent the present value of expected future dividends, discounted at a constant rate—has survived in several studies that attempt to deal with the technical criticisms (see, for example, Mankiw, Romer, and Shapiro [1985], West [1988a]).

It would be misleading to claim that the debate over whether or not stock prices exhibit excess volatility is over. In particular, the findings of studies that assume dividends have a logarithmic unit root remain contradictory—Campbell and Shiller's [1987b] tests, for example find excess volatility, while the tests of Kleidon [1986] and LeRoy and Parke [1987] don't. West's [1988b] survey of the literature, however, suggests that the majority of existing studies find excess volatility. The existing literature, especially Campbell and Shiller's [1987b] study, seems also to cast doubt on the view that standard models of time variation in expected returns can account for the volatility of the stock market.

Another manifestation of the empirical failure of the constant required rate of return model of the stock market is recent evidence of predictable variation in stock market returns (Flood, Hodrick, and Kaplan [1986], Poterba and Summers [1987], Campbell and Shiller [1988], Fama and French [1988]). The predictable pattern of excess returns (over their mean) seems consistent with a model of irrational bubbles (fads) that cause prices to overreact to news and subsequently to revert partially to their previous levels.[2] Fama and French estimate that such a mean reverting component of stock prices may account for up to 45% of the variances of three- to five-year returns. Campbell and Shiller find predictable movements in excess returns (both over their constant mean and over real interest rates) even for a ten-year holding period.

Campbell and Shiller also point out that excess volatility of stock prices would imply that long (infinite) horizon excess returns are predictable. Accordingly, excess volatility and predictability of returns may be different manifestations of the same phenomenon. Can the documented predictability of long-horizon returns account for the apparent excess volatility of stock prices? To explore this possibility, I will report a rather crude experiment using the volatility test of Mankiw, Romer, and Shapiro [1985]—henceforth, MR&S.

The basic idea behind the MR&S approach is as follows. 1) Consider equation 2.9′ and define the corresponding perfect foresight stock price as:

$$p_t^* = (1 + r)^{-n} p_{t+n} + \sum_{j=1}^{n} (1 + r)^{-j} d_{t+j}. \tag{2.18}$$

Equation 2.9′ then states:

$$P_t = E_t p_t^* \tag{2.19}$$

2) Estimate the constant α (from the cointegrating regression of p_t on d_t such that $(p_t - \alpha d_t)$ is stationary. Note that equation 2.16, with B_t set equal to zero, implies $\alpha = r^{-1}$. MR&S interpret $r^{-1} d_t$ as the naive forecast of the present value of expected future dividends, based on the arbitrary assumption that dividends take a random walk.[3]

3) Note that equation 2.19 and the fact that p_t and d_t are observable at date t imply

$$E_t(p_t^* - \alpha d_t)^2 = E_t(p_t^* - p_t)^2 + E_t(p_t - \alpha d_t)^2,$$

and, therefore,

$$E(p_t^* - \alpha d_t)^2 = E(p_t^* - p_t)^2 + E(p_t - \alpha d_t)^2. \tag{2.20}$$

MR&S find that estimates of the right-hand side of equation 2.20 are several times larger than the left-hand side. As MR&S observe, and Flood and Hodrick [1986] elaborate, this finding of stock-price volatility cannot be attributed to the existence of rational bubbles, because equation 2.9′ must hold if equation 2.8′ is correctly specified even if rational bubbles exist. It follows that the finding of excess volatility reflects the misspecification of equation 2.8′.

Turning to my crude experiment, I first calculated the two sides of equation 2.20 for Shiller's S&P data set, setting n equal to ten in equation 2.19 and using the value of r implied by the cointegrating regression of p_t on d_t.[4] The results were as follows:

$$\underset{399}{E(p_t^* - \alpha d_t)^2} \stackrel{?}{=} \underset{423}{E(p_t^* - p_t)^2} + \underset{288}{E(p_t - \alpha d_t)^2}. \tag{2.21}$$

Note that according to the point estimates, the naive forecast (αd_t) of p_t^* has a lower mean squarred error (MSE) than the stock market forecast (399 vs. 423). And the sum of the two terms on the right-hand side is 75% large than the left-hand side.

I next repeated the same exercise, this time setting the required rate of return r in equation 2.19 equal to the predicted value of the ex post average return over the following ten-year period from a regression on a constant and a single lag of the dividend-price ratio. (I used the dividend-price ratio as the explanatory variable because Flood, Hodrick, and Kaplan [1986] and Campbell and Shiller [1988] have found that it helps predict returns.) The results were:

$$\underset{620}{E(p_t^* - \alpha d_t)^2} \stackrel{?}{=} \underset{261}{E(p_t^* - p_t)^2} + \underset{288}{E(p_t - \alpha d_t)^2}. \tag{2.22}$$

Comparison of equations 2.21 and 2.22 suggests that the assumption that predictable movements in long-horizon returns reflect changes in the market's required rate of return suffices to eliminate the evidence of excess volatility, by increasing the MSE of the naive forecast of p_t^* (from 399 to 620), and by reducing the MSE of the stock market forecast (from 423 to 261).

This elimination of apparent excess volatility occurs even though in my first-step forecasting equation the dividend-price ratio explains less than 14% variance of the ten-year return, which fluctuates much less than the one-year return. This finding suggests that to explain the apparent excess volatility of stock prices, future research should address the question of why the fluctuations of *long-horizon* returns are predictable.

2.5. Conclusions

Although the discussion of the theoretical literature in section 2.2 does not preclude the existence of rational bubbles in stock prices, it suggests that the proposition that such bubbles are present in long time series of U.S. aggregate stock prices is tenuous. If rational bubbles exist, they seem more likely to be present in new issues of equity. Since the empirical tests discussed in section 2.3 also fail to provide convincing evidence that rational bubbles are present in aggregate stock prices, it seems reasonable to assume that the apparent empirical failure of standard stock market models reflects either departures from rational behavior or misspecification of market fundamentals.

The discussion of section 2.4 suggests that the apparent excess volatility of stock prices, relative to what standard models can account for, may be due to predictable movements in long-horizon returns. If we assume that bubbles (rational or irrational) are likely to be transient phenomena (not lasting ten years), it follows that they cannot fully account for the observed volatility of stock prices.

Notes

1. Some early contributions to the literature, including Taylor [1977], do not use the term *bubble* in their discussions of multiple equilibria in DLRE models. Burmeister, Flood, and Garber [1983] show that the existence of multiple equilibria in these linear models is formally equivalent to the possibility of rational bubbles.

2. It is, of course, also conceivable that market fundamentals lead to such a mean reverting component.

3. This interpretation is not central to the logic of the test. The critical step is to transform p_t into a stationary time series.

4. The cointegrating regression yields an estimate of 0.03 for r, which may seem implausibly low. For higher values of r (up to its sample mean of 0.08), MR&S report even more pronounced excess volatility.

References

Benveniste, L. M., and Scheinkman, J. A. 1982. "Duality Theory for Dynamic Optimization Models of Economics: The Continuous Time Case." *Journal of Economic Theory* 27 (June):1–19.

Blanchard, O. J. 1979. "Speculative Bubbles, Crashes, and Rational Expectations." *Economics Letters* 3:387–389.

Blanchard, O. J., and Watson, M. W. 1982. "Bubbles, Rational Expectations, and Financial Markets." *Crises in the Economic and Financial Structure*. Lexington, MA: Lexington Book.

Burmeister, E.; Flood, R. P.; and Garber, P. M. 1983. "On the Equivalence of Solutions in Rational Expectations Models." *Journal of Economic Dynamics and Control* 5 (August):311–321.

Campbell, J. Y., and Shiller, R. J. 1987a. "Cointegration and Tests of Present

Value Models." *Journal of Political Economy* 95 (October):1062–1088.
Campbell, J. Y., and Shiller, R. J. 1987b. "The Dividend-Price Ratio and Expectations of Future Dividends and Discount Factors," unpublished.
Campbell, J. Y., and Shiller, R. J., 1988. "Stock Prices, Earnings, and Expected Dividends." *Journal of Finance* 43 (July):661–676.
Diba, B. T., and Grossman, H. I. 1987. "On the Inception of Rational Bubbles." *Quarterly Journal of Economics* 8:697–700.
Diba, B. T., and Grossman, H. I. 1988a. "Explosive Rational Bubbles in Stock Prices?" *American Economic Review* 78 (June):520–530.
Diba, B. T., and Grossman, H. I. 1988b. "The Theory of Rational Bubbles in Stock Prices." *Economic Journal* 98 (September):746–754.
Fama, E. F., and French, K. R. 1988. "Permanent and Temporary Components of Stock Prices." *Journal of Political Economy* 96 (April):246–273.
Flavin, M. A. 1983. "Excess Volatility in the Financial Markets: A Reassessment of the Empirical Evidence." *Journal of Political Economy* 91 (December): 929–956.
Flood, R. P., and Garber, P. M. 1980. "Market Fundamentals Versus Price Level Bubbles: The First Tests." *Journal of Political Economy* 88 (August):745–770.
Flood, R. P., and Hodrick R. J. 1986. "Asset Price Volatility, Bubbles and Process Switching." *Journal of Finance* 41 (September):831–842.
Flood, R. P., and Hodrick R. J.; and Kaplan, P. 1986. "An Evaluation of Recent Evidence on Stock Market Bubbles," unpublished.
Hamilton, J., and Whiteman, C. 1985. "The Observable Implications of Self-fulfilling Expectations." *Journal of Monetary Economics* 16 (November):353–373.
Kleidon, A. W. 1986. "Variance Bounds Tests and Stock Price Valuation Models." *Journal of Political Economy* 94 (October):953–1001.
LeRoy, S. F., and Porter R. 1981. "The Present Value Relation: Tests Based on Variance Bounds." *Econometrica* 49 (May):555–74.
LeRoy, S. F., and Parke, W. R. 1987. "Stock Price Volatility: A Test Based on the Geometric Random Walks," unpublished.
Lucas, R. E. 1978. "Asset Prices in an Exchange Economy." *Econometrica* 46 (November):1429–1445.
Mankiw, N. G.; Romer, D.; and Shapiro, M. D. 1985. "An Unbiased Reexamination of Stock Market Volatility." *Journal of Finance* 40 (July):677–687.
Marsh, T. A., and Merton, R. C. 1986. "Dividend Variability and Variance Bounds Tests for the Rationality of Stock Market Prices." *American Economic Review* 76 (June):483–498.
O'Connell, S. A., and Zeldes, S. P. 1988. "Rational Ponzi Games." *International Economic Review* forthcoming.
Poterba, J. M., and Summers, L. H. 1987. "Mean Reversion in Stock Prices: Evidence and Implications," unpublished.
Quah, D. 1985. "Estimation of a Nonfundamentals Model for Stock Price and Dividend Dynamics," unpublished.

Sargent, T. J. 1987. *Dynamic Macreconomic Theory*. Cambridge, MA: Harvard University Press.

Shiller, R. J. 1978. "Rational Expectations and the Dynamic Structure of Macroeconomic Models: A Critical Review." *Journal of Monetary Economics* 4 (January):1–44.

Shiller, R. J. 1981. "Do Stock Prices Move Too Much to Be Justified by Subsequent Movements in Dividends?" *American Economic Review* 71 (June):421–436.

Shiller, R. J. 1984. "Stock Prices and Social Dynamics." *Brookings Papers on Economic Activity* 475–498.

Tirole, J. 1982. "On the Possibility of Speculation Under Rational Expectations." *Econometrica* 50 (September):1163–1181.

Tirole, J. 1985. "Asset Bubbles and Overlapping Generations." *Econometrica* 53 (September):1071–1100.

Taylor, J. 1977. "Conditions for Unique Solutions in Stochastic Macroeconomic Models with Rational Expectations." *Econometrica* 45 (September):1377–1385.

West, K. D. 1987. "A Specification Test for Speculative Bubbles." *Quarterly Journal of Economics* 8:553–580.

West, K. D. 1988a. "Dividend Innovation and Stock Price Volatility." *Econometrica* 56 (January):37–61.

West, K. D. 1988b. "Bubbles, Fads and Stock Price Volatility Tests: A Partial Evaluation." *Journal of Finance* 43 (July):639–656.

COMMENTARY

by Robert P. Flood, Jr.

What Is the Problem?

Stock prices have behaved differently than our prior beliefs led us to think that they would behave. How differently? Not very if looked at in a fairly long horizon. But quite differently if we focus on the events of mid-October 1987. These events have led us to question our ways of thinking about the pricing of equity shares specifically and all assets in general. Stated baldly—*we have no idea what is going on.*

What Do We Have?

We have representative-agent and heterogenous-agent models of the consumption-saving decision that yield, as fallout, prices of assets in equilibrium. Often we use market observations of these prices to gain information about the usefulness of the model environment. Unfortunately, the model environment is not very specific about the kind of behavior implied for asset prices.

For example, consider the following equation derived from an optimizing consumption-saving model:

$$\pi_t = \beta E_t[\pi_{t+1} + \delta_{t+1}] \qquad (2C.1)$$

where π is the agent's marginal utility of a unit of the asset, and δ is the agent's marginal utility attached to a unit of the asset's dividend.

In order to make this equation useful empirically for explaining asset prices, we need to take some additional steps to relate the theory to data. Let's consider some of those steps:

1. We must choose an asset to price;
2. We must identify the agent making the asset pricing decision;
3. We must specify how the agent translates asset price in a currency unit into π, the marginal utility to the agent of the asset;
4. We must specify how the agent today (at t) forms beliefs about next period's π and the dividend payout;
5. We must make arbitrary statistical assumptions about (for example) sample size and data stationarity;
6. We must make assumptions about which of many of possible solutions to the equation is chosen by the market.

I have listed six assumptions about the treatment of equation 2C.1 required in order to check its usefulness in helping to understand asset prices. All of the assumptions, except 1, are extremely contentious. Consider them in order.

1. Since all assets must be priced, it really makes little difference which one or which group of them is chosen to be priced. There is, however, good reason to think that beliefs may be quite diffuse concerning assets that are relatively new.
2. Often it is assumed that the agent is a "representative" one. It is quite possible that heterogeneity in information sets, access to markets, tastes, period of life, or tax treatment may play an important role in the market pricing of assets.
3. Since the marginal utility of an asset to an individual is not observable, we need to make additional assumptions about marginal utility in order to put this in terms of observables. Further, and in the same vein, it may not be that individuals discount the future at a constant rate.
4. Often we assume rational expectations plus some possibly incorrect

aspects of the agent information sets and the way agents use the information they have.

5. It may be that our assumptions concerning the nature of the data are not correct and our inferences from the data therefore possibly faulty.
6. Conditional on making that the right choices for all of the above, we can begin to think about what kinds of solutions the market would choose to equation 2.6. Remember that equation 2.6 is an example with one equation and at least two unknowns: price today and expected price next period. As is well understood, it requires exceptional circumstances to solve a single equation for two unknowns and this is what the transversality conditions are about. For some models the transversality conditions provide an additional useful condition. For other models transversality is not such a help.

If the model has a useful transversality condition and conditions 1–5 are maintained as correct, then a bubbles test is a test of the transversality condition. Since the transversality condition is implied by the model, a finding of bubbles is a *reason to reject the model*. If the model does not have a useful transversality condition, as is true with all models not derived from a maximizing problem and is even true of some models of real assets derived from optimizing behavior and is true of many models of nominal assets (money) derived from maximization, then a finding of bubbles is not a reason to reject the model.

A finding of bubbles cannot, however, be distinguished from misspecification of the model. Remember that we had to maintain that we had correctly identified agent's information sets, when in fact we have very little idea what information is known by some of the agents who are pricing the assets. We also have very little idea of a sensible utility function to use for asset pricing. All of the utility functions I have tried have failed miserably—and not in a way that could be due to bubbles.

Conclusions

What do we conclude when we see asset pricing that is not in accord with our prior beliefs? One simple thing that we can conclude is that we don't really understand the asset markets very well. An alternative is to act as if we really to understand some aspects of asset pricing very well and would be able to explain asset prices if only bubbles didn't get in the way. There is, however, little evidence that we understand asset markets well enough to make a convincing case for or against bubbles in the data.

3 DO FUNDAMENTALS, BUBBLES, OR NEITHER DETERMINE STOCK PRICES? SOME INTERNATIONAL EVIDENCE*

Gerald P. Dwyer, Jr., and R. W. Hafer

3.1. Introduction

It has been one year since the global decline in stock prices and the principal cause remains a mystery. For some observers, the decline was a natural conclusion to an unfounded run-up in prices that occured especially during 1987, both in the United States and abroad. For example, the Brady Commission noted that "[A]s in the U.S., stock valuation in these [foreign] markets in 1987 began to rise above levels apparently justified by historical precedent or economic factors." (Brady Commission [1988], p. 9) Indeed, in its study of stock price behavior in other markets, the section exploring the events of October 1987 is titled "Bursting the Bubble."[1]

The notion that stock price behavior can be explained by bubbles suggests that stock prices deviate from the level implied by their underlying fundamental value. The idea that stock prices may deviate from their fundamentals is not unique to commissions appointed after a market crash,

---

* This paper was written while the authors were, respectively, Visiting Scholar and Research Officer at the Federal Reserve Bank of St. Louis. The conclusions are the authors' and may not represent views of the Federal Reserve Bank of St. Louis or the Federal Reserve System.

however. For example, a recent study by Hardouvelis [1988] concludes that, based on an analysis of stock prices for Japan, the United Kingdom, and the United States, the hypothesis of a bubble is not inconsistent with stock price behavior leading up to October 1987. Previous investigation of the role of "fundamentals" has been given content by associating the fundamentals with dividends. There is a relatively large literature that finds much of the variance in stock prices is not explained by dividends (Shiller [1981] and Campbell and Shiller [1987]).

At the same time, other studies present evidence that bubbles do not play an important role in explaining the movement in stock prices. Diba and Grossman [1988] recently have provided evidence that supports the fundamentals hypothesis. Using U.S. annual stock price data from 1871 to 1986, their evidence does not support the bubble hypothesis. Using daily data for the periods before the 1929 and 1987 crashes, Dwyer and Santoni [1988] also find no support for the hypothesis that rational bubbles are consistent with the time-series characterization of stock prices during these two episodes.

Most previous tests of the fundamentals versus bubble models of stock prices focus on the behavior of U.S. stock prices, use data of long periodicity, or both. Because the crash of 1987 offers an almost-laboratory setting in which to test these alternative hypotheses, we set out first to see whether the behavior of stock prices during the final stages of the recent run-up is consistent with the implications of a rational bubble model. We do this using daily stock price data for Australia, Canada, France, Germany, Japan, the United Kingdom, and the United States.

We also investigate the importance of fundamentals as determinants of stock prices. Because daily data are not well suited to this task, we use monthly stock price data for the past 15 years. Our analysis extends beyond the United States and includes stock markets in Canada, Germany, Japan, and the United Kingdom. The analysis using monthly data allows us to examine the generality of the fundamentals model across different markets.

The format of our study is as follows: To provide some perspective, the second section presents a descriptive analysis of daily stock prices for the year preceding the October 1987 crash. In the third section we present a theoretical analysis of a model of stock prices with a rational bubble. We also present empirical tests of this model's implications for the behavior of daily stock prices for our sample of seven countries. We examine the fundamentals model in the fourth section, deriving some implications of this model under the alternative assumptions of constant and varying expected real interest rates. Empirical tests derived from the theoretical discussion also are presented. Conclusions close the article.

3.2. Descriptive Analysis of Daily Data

The daily stock price data used in this study are taken from Morgan Stanley's Capital International Perspective.[2] We use the index values for Australia, Canada, France, Germany, Japan, the United Kingdom, and the United States. The daily stock price indexes used are available since July 29, 1986. Our analysis uses the data from this point through December 31, 1987, a period that encompasses the worldwide decline in equity values in October 1987.

To summarize the relative behavior of the seven indexes, percentage changes in the indexes over various periods are presented in table 3–1. These periods are: 1) from the beginning of the data sample to each index's peak, 2) from the peak to October 12, 1987, and 3) from October 26, 1987, through December 31, 1987. We end the second sample period on the Monday prior to the crash of the U.S. market because the dating of the crash is not the same in all markets, thus making uniform timing impossible.[3] Also, the notion that stock prices around the world ratcheted up in some kind of global bull market is best examined using data prior to the declines that occured around October 19. These periods allow us to compare the relative magnitudes of the price increases, to assess the movements of the indexes prior to the crash, and to compare their recovery. The percentage changes for these periods are presented in the upper half of table 3–1.

The statistics reported in the first column indicate that the increase in equity values was quite disparate. The best performer in own currency terms was Australia, with an increase of 114.46%. In contrast, the German index only gained 10.68% from July 1986 to its peak, and France 19.32%. The average gain during this period was 51.32%.

The second column shows that most stock price indexes had lost ground even before the crash.[4] From the respective peak dates to October 12, the decline in stock prices ranged from 4.28% for the United Kingdom to 14.46% for France. Indeed, in Germany and France, the declines from their respective peaks to October 12 essentially wiped out the gains realized since July 1986. All of the entries indicate that market values fell prior to the crash and, in some instances, had been declining for some time.

The period after the crash, here measured from October 26 through December 31, 1987, also reveals disparate behavior in the different stock indexes. After the crash, stock prices continued to fall in Australia, France, Germany, and Japan, with the German index registering an 18.52% decline. In Canada, the United Kingdom, and the United States, stock prices increased from 1.92% in the United Kingdom to 10.88% in Canada.

Table 3–1. Summary Statistics—Percentage Changes in Indexes

Country	*7/29/86–Peak*[1]	*Peak–10/12/87*	*10/26/87–12/31/87*
		Own Currency	
Australia	114.46%	−5.66%	−0.91%
Canada	47.99	−8.66	10.88
France	19.32	−14.46	−9.58
Germany	10.68	−7.92	−18.52
Japan	65.46	−5.95	−4.35
United Kingdom	59.73	−4.28	1.92
United States	41.59	−8.09	7.55
		U.S. Dollars	
Australia	159.84%	−7.01%	1.22%
Canada	54.50	−6.97	11.87
France	34.87	−14.09	0.37
Germany	27.37	−6.21	−8.57
Japan	81.31	−6.40	11.76
United Kingdom	75.93	−3.02	12.73
United States	41.59	−8.09	7.55

[1] The dates of the peaks are: Australia—9/21/87; Canada—8/13/87; France—3/26/87; Germany—8/17/87; Japan—6/11/87; United Kingdom—7/16/87; and United States—8/25/87.

It is also instructive to compare the behavior of the different stock price indexes when measured in some common currency. This is done in the lower half of table 3–1, where the indexes are denominated in dollars. The largest percentage increase again is for Australia, with a 159.84% increase. The smallest is Germany, showing a 27.37% increase. The average increase in dollar terms is 67.92%, compared with 51.31% when the indexes are denominated in local currencies.

The most striking difference between the dollar-denominated and own-currency measures of the stock indexes comes after the crash. Again using October 26 as the beginning of the post-crash period, the data presented in the lower panel of table 3–1 show that only the German index continues to decline after the crash, falling 8.57% further by the end of 1987. In contrast to the own-currency measures, the dollar-denominated indexes for Australia, France, and Japan now show increases during the post-crash period.

3.3. Tests for Rational Bubbles in Stock Prices

Depending on the time-series properties of the fundamentals, any time-series process can be used to charactrize stock prices and can be consistent with the fundamentals. That said, we show in the first part of this section that a particular class of rational bubbles adds certain patterns to the time-series behavior of stock prices. We then examine daily stock price indexes for evidence of these patterns and test the notion suggested in the Brady Report [1988] that stock markets around the world ratcheted up together.

3.3.1. Implication of Bubbles and Fundamentals

Assume that investors equate the expected holding period return on a stock to a constant expected real interest rate, r. With the price measured at the start of the period just after the divided is paid, the expected holding period return in period t then is

$$r = \frac{E_t p_{t+1} + E_t d_{t+1} - p_t}{p_t}, \tag{3.1}$$

where $E_t(\cdot)_{t+1}$ is the expected value of $(\cdot)$ in period $t{+}1$ conditional on all information available in period t including the price in period t, p_t, and the dividend in period t, d_t. Equation 3.1 can be rewritten as

$$p_t = \beta(E_t p_{t+1} + E_t d_{t+1}), \tag{3.2}$$

where $\beta = (1 + r)^{-1}$. Equation 3.2 is the basis for both the model of the fundamentals and the model for bubbles.

3.3.1.1. The Fundamentals. The fundamental price in period t, p_t^f, is the discounted present value of the expected future stream of dividends,[5]

$$p_t^f = \sum_{i=1}^{\infty} \beta^i \, E_t d_{t+i} \tag{3.3}$$

given the transversality condition that

$$\lim_{i \to \infty} \beta^i E_t p_{t+i} = 0.$$

The implications of the fundamentals model can be shown using a particularly simple time-series process for expected dividends. If the expected growth rate of dividends is constant, the fundamental model implies that proportional changes in the stock price are unpredictable except for a constant growth rate. If dividends grow at a constant rate g^d and deviations of dividends from this constant rate are unpredictable, then

$$d_{t+1} = (1 + g^d)d_t + \eta_{t+1}, \tag{3.4}$$

where η_{t+1} is the unexpected part of dividend growth in period $t + 1$, and $E_t\eta_{t+1} = 0$. Substitution of equation 3.4 into 3.3 and calculation of the proportional change in the fundamental price yields:

$$\frac{\Delta p^f_{t+1}}{p^f_t} = g^d + \frac{\eta_{t+1}}{p^f_t} \sum_{i=1}^{\infty} \beta^i (1 + g^d)^i. \tag{3.5}$$

Letting g^f denote the growth rate of the fundamental price, equations 3.4 and 3.5 then imply that

$$E_t g^f_t = g^d. \tag{3.6}$$

An immediate result of equation 3.6 is that the proportional changes in the price of the stock are unpredictable except for a constant.

3.3.1.2. Rational Bubbles. Suppose that a bubble is superimposed on this simple structure. Assume that the actual stock price in period t deviates from the fundamental price by an amount b_t with a positive probability $\pi > 0$ of continuing each period. This specification of a bubble follows Blanchard and Watson [1982], although a deterministic specification yields similar conclusions (Diba and Grossman [1988]). A solution for the price that includes the bubble, p^b_t, and is consistent with equation 3.2 is

$$p^b_t = p^f_t + b_t, \tag{3.7a}$$

where

$$b_t = \begin{cases} (1 + r)\pi^{-1} b_{t-1} & \text{with probability } \pi \\ 0 & \text{with probability } 1 - \pi. \end{cases} \tag{3.7b}$$

The term π^{-1} appears in the bubble part of the price because purchasers of the stock must be compensated for the possibility that the bubble will burst: A lower probability of the bubble continuing is associated with a higher rate of increase of the bubble part of the stock price if the bubble continues. As long as the bubble continues, the bubble part of the price grows at the rate

$$g^b = r + (1 + r)\frac{(1 - \pi)}{\pi}. \tag{3.8}$$

Because $1 - \pi$ and π are greater than zero, the bubble part of the price grows at a rate greater than the real interest rate. When the bubble bursts, the expected growth rate of this part of the price is zero, and the stock price is determined by the fundamentals.

If there is a bubble, however, proportional changes in the stock price are predictable for any finite period. If the expected dividend grows at a constant rate, from equation 3.7a the proportional change in price including the bubble is

$$\frac{\Delta p_{t+1}^b}{p_t^b} = g_t^f \frac{p_t^f}{p_t^b} + \frac{\Delta b_{t+1}}{p_t^b}. \quad (3.9)$$

From this definition and using equation 3.7a to rearrange it,

$$\frac{\Delta p_{t+1}^b}{p_t^b} = g_t^f - g_t^f \frac{b_t}{p_t^b} + \frac{\Delta b_{t+1}}{p_t^b}. \quad (3.10)$$

The result of using equations 3.7b and 3.8 to replace Δb_{t+1} and rearrangement is

$$\frac{\Delta p_{t+1}^b}{p_t^b} = g_t^f + (g^b - g_t^f) \frac{b_t}{p_t^b}. \quad (3.11)$$

Using equation 3.7a, we find that

$$\frac{\Delta p_{t+1}^b}{p_t^b} = g_t^f + (g^b - g_t^f) \frac{1}{1 + p_t^f/b_t}. \quad (3.12)$$

The proportional change in the stock price equals the proportional change in the fundamental price plus a term due to the bubble. The first part of the term due to the bubble is $g^b - g_t^f$, which has a strictly positive expected value because $g^b > r$, and the expected value of g_t^f is $g^d < r$. The second part of the term due to the bubble is not stationary in finite time. To see this, let period 0 be any period when the bubble is on. The ratio of the fundamental price to the bubble part of the price in later periods when the bubble is on is

$$\frac{p_t^f}{b_t} = \frac{(1 + g_t^f)^t p_0^f}{(1 + g^b)^t b_0}, \quad (3.13)$$

where p_0^f/b_0 is constant for all $t > 0$. Because g_d is less than g^b, this ratio is a decreasing function of time. This means that, for any finite period when a bubble is on, the proportional change in price is an increasing function of time. Consequently, the proportional change in observed stock prices is predictable from its own past value. As time goes to infinity, the ratio in equation 3.13 goes to zero, because the bubble part of the price eventually dominates the fundamental component in the stock price.[6]

3.3.2. Tests for Unit Roots

Before we actually test for the presence of bubbles in the different stock indexes, it is useful to determine whether the data can be characterized in a manner that is consistent with the simple model presented above. An implication of the model is that stock prices should be difference stationary. This property of the data can easily be tested using the procedures of Dickey and Fuller [1979] to determine whether there is a unit root in the levels and first difference of the stock prices for the countries in our sample.

To test for unit roots in the levels of the stock price indexes, changes in stock prices are regressed on a constant, the lagged level of the index, and

Table 3–2. Unit Root Tests on Stock Price Indexes[1]—Daily Data (in own currency)

		T-Ratio on Lag Variable		*Durbin-Watson*	
Country	*Sample*[2]	*Levels*	*Changes*	*Levels*	*Changes*
Australia	8/4/86–9/21/87	1.162	−9.190	2.00	2.01
	1/2/87–9/21/87	0.887	−7.899	2.00	2.00
Canada	8/4/86–8/13/87	−0.094	−8.275	1.97	2.00
	1/2/87–8/13/87	−2.081	−6.473	1.95	2.00
France	8/4/86–3/26/87	−0.350	−7.264	2.02	1.99
	1/2/87–3/26/87	−0.439	−5.569	1.89	1.90
Germany	8/4/86–8/17/87	−1.486	−8.725	1.98	2.00
	1/2/87–8/17/87	−2.032	−6.561	1.97	1.99
Japan	8/4/86–6/11/87	0.208	−7.952	2.02	1.99
	1/2/87–6/11/87	−0.637	−6.258	2.01	1.98
United Kingdom	8/4/86–7/16/87	1.706	−8.843	1.98	1.99
	1/2/87–7/16/87	−0.091	−7.540	1.98	1.98
United States	8/4/86–8/25/87	0.010	−10.122	1.99	1.99
	1/2/87–8/25/87	−1.656	−7.337	1.97	1.97

[1] All regressions include a constant term and lagged dependent variable.
[2] Sample period endpoints represent peaks in stock price indexes.

one lagged value of the change. The test statistic is the reported t-ratio. If the calculated t-ratio is greater than the critical value, one cannot reject the hypothesis that the series contains a unit root. If the t-ratio is smaller than or equal to the critical value, however, then the notion of a unit root is rejected. For example, with a sample size of 250 observations, the critical value is -2.88 at the 5% level of significance.[7] Calculated t-ratios smaller than this are inconsistent with the hypothesis of a unit root in the series at this significance level.

The Dickey-Fuller test is conducted on the levels and the first-differences of the stock prices for each country. Moreover, two periods are used for each country: One period uses data from the beginning of the data set in July 1986; the other uses data from the beginning of 1987. In both instances, the endpoint is the peak in each country's index. In this way, we can determine whether stock prices behave differently during the final stages of the bull market.[8] The results of the Dickey-Fuller test for unit roots in the stock prices are presented in table 3–2.[9]

The test statistics reported for the levels of stock prices, regardless of country or sample period, indicate that one cannot reject the hypothesis of a unit root in the series. Not only are the reported t-ratios far above the relevant critical values, but some even are incorrectly signed. The evidence for the first-differences, however, uniformly rejects the hypothesis of a second unit root. The calculated test statistics are much less than the critical value (approximately -2.88).

3.3.3. Time Trend Regressions

Equation 3.13 indicates that if a bubble is on, the proportional increase in the stock price is an increasing function of time. This is because a portion of the observed price rise is due to the fact that the bubble component increasingly dominates the stock price. In addition to being a positive function of time, the observed proportional change of the stock price should increase at a decreasing rate. This characterization of the data can be tested by regressing the proportional change in stock prices on time.

Table 3–3 provides the results of regressions of the proportional changes in stock prices on time for the period from the beginning of the sample to each country's peak. Two regression results are reported: one in which time enters only as a linear term and another that adds a quadratic term. In every instance, the regressions with time entered only linearly indicate that the proportional change in stock prices has no statistically significant trend (5% level). Moreover, adding the quadratic term does not alter this

Table 3–3. Time Regression Results (own currency, percentage changes) July 30, 1986–Peak[1]

Country	*Constant*	*Time*	*(Time)*^{2}	R^2	*DW*	$\chi^2(MSL)$
Australia	0.002	2.696×10^{-6}		0.001	1.79	0.217
	(2.32)	(0.46)				(0.642)
	0.004	-2.353×10^{-5}	8.861×10^{-8}	0.004	1.80	1.710
	(2.66)	(−1.09)	(1.24)			(0.425)
Canada	0.001	3.223×10^{-6}		0.001	1.42	0.373
	(1.20)	(0.61)				(0.541)
	0.001	5.729×10^{-6}	-9.285×10^{-9}	0.001	1.42	0.382
	(0.66)	(0.25)	(−0.12)			(0.826)
France	−0.0001	1.448×10^{-5}		0.006	1.82	1.106
	(−0.11)	(1.05)				(0.293)
	0.002	-4.351×10^{-5}	3.391×10^{-7}	0.012	1.83	2.754
	(0.80)	(−0.91)	(1.27)			(0.252)
Germany	9.222×10^{-5}	2.642×10^{-6}		0.0003	1.78	0.097
	(0.07)	(0.31)				(0.755)

	0.005	-9.936×10^{-5}	3.750×10^{-7}	0.028	1.84	8.337
	(2.16)	(−2.50)*	(2.74)*			(0.015)
Japan	0.001	1.176×10^{-5}		0.003	1.82	0.635
	(0.52)	(0.80)				(0.426)
	0.001	9.648×10^{-6}	9.406×10^{-9}	0.003	1.82	0.636
	(0.40)	(0.19)	(0.04)			(0.728)
United Kingdom	0.0003	1.260×10^{-3}		0.011	2.07	2.873
	(0.33)	(1.70)				(0.090)
	0.0004	1.007×10^{-5}	1.010×10^{-8}	0.011	2.07	2.984
	(0.28)	(0.35)	(0.10)			(0.225)
United States	0.001	5.205×10^{-6}		0.002	1.84	0.591
	(0.51)	(0.77)				(0.442)
	0.001	-2.357×10^{-6}	2.720×10^{-8}	0.002	1.84	0.795
	(0.53)	(−0.08)	(0.29)			(0.672)

[1] The dates of the peaks are: Australia—9/21/87; Canada—8/13/87; France—3/26/87; Germany—8/17/87; Japan—6/11/87; United Kingdom—7/16/87; and United States—8/25/87. Asterisks(*) indicate significance at 5 percent level.

finding except in the case of Germany. For Germany, both the linear and quadratic terms are highly significant. Even so, the signs of the coefficients are counter to the theory: They indicate negative and then increasing rates of increase of stock prices up to the peak.

To determine if the data are consistent with a bubble at work in the latter stages of the bull market, the time regressions are re-estimated for the period from January 1987 to the respective peak of each stock market. These results, reported in table 3–4, yield many more significant estimated coefficients than those from the longer sample. This is true for Canada and the United States. Even so, the coefficients are incorrectly signed to support the bubble hypothesis. Only for Germany is there evidence that supports the bubble hypothesis: These results indicate a positive and significant trend term for 1987.[10]

3.3.4. Autoregressions

We also can test for the presence of bubbles by examining autoregressions of the proportional change in stock prices. If bubbles are present, observed changes in stock prices should exhibit significant serial correlation. To test this, the proportional change in the stock price index from each country is regressed on a constant and 25 lagged values of the change. The bubble hypothesis is rejected if the lag terms are not positive and significant.

The relevant statistics for this test are reported in table 3–5. Again results are presented for two periods as in previous tests. To test the hypothesis that the autoregressive parameters are significant as a group, χ^2-statistics are calculated. For the longer period, the estimated χ^2 is significant for Canada and Germany. Only for Canada, however, do we also find that the sum of the lagged coefficients is significant at some reasonable level. This evidence is therfore consistent with the hypothesis that a bubble was present in Canadian stock prices during 1986–1987.

At first glance, the results for 1987 only seem to provide even stronger evidence of bubbles in stock prices. During this period of the bull market, the χ^2 statistics are significant for Canada, France, Germany, Japan, and the United States, thus supporting the bubble hypothesis. Note, however, that for France, Japan, and the United States we find that the coefficients' sum is negative, contrary to the bubble hypothesis being tested. Moreover, the summed terms for Canada and Germany are not significantly different from zero. Thus, except for some evidence of bubbles at work in Canadian stock prices, the data are largely inconsistent with the presence of bubbles in the different stock price indexes.

3.3.5. Contagious Bubbles

The rise of stock prices since the early 1980s in markets around the world and their subsequent crash in October 1987 have led some observers to argue that this coincident behavior cannot be explained by chance alone. The Brady Commission, for example, argues that "investors made comparisons of valuations in different countries often using higher valuations in other countries as justification for investing in lower valued markets. Consequently, a process of ratcheting up among worldwide stock markets began to develop." (Brady Report [1988], p. 10) This view suggests that higher prices in one market begat higher prices in another, a hypothesis that might be called one of a "contagious bubble."

We can investigate this claim by examining the behavior of relative stock prices during 1986 and 1987. To do this, consider the following. Assume that transaction costs to buy and sell stock anywhere in the world are zero. If investors are risk-neutral, the expected return from holding stock in any common currency must be the same anywhere. This implies that

$$Eh_t^i = Eh_t^j + E\Delta e_t, \tag{3.14}$$

where Eh_t^i is the expected rate of return from holding stock in country i in terms of i's currency in period t, Eh_t^j is the expected return from holding stock in country j in terms of j's currency and $E\Delta e_t$ is the expected rate of change in the price of country j's currency in terms of country i's.[11] If the condition in euqation 3.14 holds, the expected return from holding stock in country i is the same as the expected return from holding a foreign stock, a condition that might be called "stock-return parity" by analogy with "interest-rate parity."

Equation 3.14 can be written in ex post terms as

$$h_t^i = h_t^j + \Delta e_t + \varepsilon_t^i - \varepsilon_t^j - \varepsilon_t^e, \tag{3.15}$$

where ε^i and ε^j terms are the unexpected part of the holding period returns for stocks i and j, and ε^e is the unexpected part of the rate of change of the exchange rate. If expectations are rational, the ε's are independent of the expected portions of the holding period returns and the unexpected part of the change in the exchange rate. If dividends are zero, equation 3.15 can be written in terms of the levels of stock prices as

$$p_t^i - p_{t-1}^i = p_t^j - p_{t-1}^j + e_t - e_{t-1} + \varepsilon_t^i - \varepsilon_t^j - \varepsilon_t^e, \tag{3.16}$$

where p is the logarithm of the stock's price, and e is the logarithm of the exchange rate. If we define a stock price relative as

Table 3–4. Time Regression Results (own currency, percentage changes) January 2, 1987–Peak[1]

Country	*Constant*	*Time*	*(Time)*^{2}	R^2	*DW*	$\chi^2(MSL)$
Australia	0.001	8.939×10^{-6}		0.003	1.83	0.582
	(1.47)	(0.76)				(0.446)
	0.012	-4.268×10^{-5}	2.775×10^{-7}	0.008	1.84	1.697
	(1.76)	(−0.81)	(1.01)			(0.428)
Canada	0.003	-1.722×10^{-5}		0.012	1.17	2.350
	(2.85)	(−1.53)				(0.125)
	0.007	−0.0002	8.337×10^{-7}	0.057	1.23	11.194
	(4.39)	(−3.30)*	(3.09)*			(0.004)
France	0.001	3.385×10^{-5}		0.004	1.77	0.206
	(0.44)	(0.45)				(0.650)
	0.004	-2.789×10^{-4}	5.126×10^{-6}	0.027	1.82	1.920
	(0.87)	(−0.79)	(0.99)			(0.383)
Germany	−0.005	5.635×10^{-5}		0.037	1.86	5.644
	(−1.76)	(2.38)*				(0.018)

	−0.007	1.291×10^{-4}	-4.491×10^{-7}	0.041	1.86	5.731
	(−1.63)	(1.34)	(−0.87)			(0.057)
Japan	0.004	-7.800×10^{-6}		0.0004	1.89	0.051
	(1.80)	(−0.22)				(0.822)
	0.004	-5.014×10^{-6}	-2.423×10^{-8}	0.0004	1.89	0.052
	(1.14)	(−0.04)	(−0.02)			(0.974)
United Kingdom	0.003	-2.074×10^{-6}		0.000	2.13	0.014
	(2.02)	(−0.12)				(0.905)
	0.030	-1.226×10^{-4}	8.612×10^{-7}	0.019	2.16	3.577
	(2.84)	(−1.80)	(1.89)			(0.167)
United States	0.003	-1.038×10^{-5}		0.003	1.88	0.578
	(1.94)	(−0.76)				(0.447)
	0.007	-1.584×10^{-4}	8.809×10^{-7}	0.040	1.96	6.433
	(3.38)	(−2.52)*	(−2.40)*			(0.040)

[1] The dates of the peaks are: Australia—9/21/87; Canada—8/13/87; France—3/26/87; Germany—8/17/87; Japan—6/11/87; United Kingdom—7/16/87; and United States—8/25/87. Asterisks(*) indicate significance at 5 percent level.

Table 3–5. Autoregression Test Results[1]

	9/3/86–Peak		*1/2/87–Peak*	
Country	$\chi^2(MSL)$	$\Sigma\beta_i(MSL)$	$\chi^2(MSL)$	$\Sigma\beta_i(MSL)$
Australia	28.961	−0.098	31.874	0.069
	(0.27)	(0.75)	(0.16)	(0.85)
Canada	81.098	0.419	67.471	0.451
	(0.00)	(0.09)	(0.00)	(0.12)
France	28.182	−0.181	90.337	−1.187
	(0.30)	(0.64)	(0.00)	(0.20)
Germany	44.686	0.112	50.891	0.301
	(0.01)	(0.75)	(0.00)	(0.43)
Japan	24.001	−0.140	41.819	−1.108
	(0.52)	(0.72)	(0.02)	(0.08)
United Kingdom	30.946	0.112	29.848	−0.104
	(0.19)	(1.00)	(0.23)	(1.00)
United States	32.645	−0.190	39.070	−0.348
	(0.14)	(0.52)	(0.04)	(0.43)

[1] The dates of the peaks are: Australia—9/21/87; Canada—8/13/87; France—3/26/87; Germany—8/17/87; Japan—6/11/87; United Kingdom—7/16/87; and United States—8/25/87. Marginal significance levels in parentheses.

$$x = p^i - p^j - e, \tag{3.17}$$

equation 3.16 can be rewritten as

$$x_t = x_{t-1} + \varepsilon_t^i - \varepsilon_t^j + \varepsilon_t^e. \tag{3.18}$$

Equation 3.18 is useful because it shows that relative stock prices this period equal their value last period plus the difference between the unexpected parts of the holding period returns (the ε^i's and ε^j's) and the unexpected part of the change in the exchange rate (ε^e). What equation 3.18 says is: Even if expected rates of return among different stocks are the same, relative stock prices are a random walk. This conclusion is specific to the assumption of stock-return parity but, in general, relative stock prices will be characterized as having a unit root.[12]

To test whether stock prices ratcheted up worldwide in a contagious bubble, we examine the levels of the relative stock prices for unit roots over the period from the beginning of the sample through October 12, 1987, and from January 1987 through October 12. The results of the

Dickey-Fuller tests on the levels of the stock price relatives are presented in table 3–6.[13] The top half of the table reports the results for the longer period. There we find no test statistics that are smaller than the relevant 5% critical value of about −2.88. These results are inconsistent with the notion that stock prices ratchet up or down with each other. When the sample period is shortened to only data from 1987, this outcome does not always hold. As shown in the bottom half of table 3–6, the hypothesis of a single unit root in the level of the stock price relatives is rejected for Canada and Germany, Germany and the United Kingdom, and Germany and the United States. The statistical evidence using data only from 1987 suggests that German stock prices increased in unison with those in other markets.

The test statistics for Germany are the most consistent with the Brady Commissions' notion of prices rising only because others did. How much weight should be attached to this result for Germany? It is interesting that the result exists only if one deletes data from the second half of 1986. This suggests that finding or rejecting unit root processes in these stock price relatives is sensitive to the sample period tested.

3.4. Stock Prices, Dividends, and Bond Yields: Tests for Fundamentals

We now develop, in this section, implications for the joint time-series properties of stock prices, dividends and interest rates, focusing on the relationships between the levels of the series. Because the results in the second part of this section provide little support to the fundamentals model, we then estimate some simple regressions to examine how much of the variance of stock prices is explained by some readily available factors suggested by the fundamentals model.

3.4.1. Stock Prices and the Fundamentals

We develop the implications for the joint behavior of stock prices and dividends first with the maintained hypothesis that the expected real interest rate is constant. We then develop the implications for stock price behavior when the expected real interest rate is allowed to vary.

3.4.1.1. A Constant Expected Real Interest Rate. If stock prices are governed by the fundamentals as defined in equation 3.3 with a constant

Table 3–6. Unit Root Tests on Relative Stock Prices: Levels (daily data in U.S. dollars)

Country	Australia	Canada	France	Germany	Japan	United Kingdom
			8/4/86–10/12/87 (N = 307)			
Canada	−1.205					
France	−0.392	−0.869				
Germany	−0.724	−1.011	−1.260			
Japan	−1.620	−1.906	−0.693	−0.802		
United Kingdom	−2.216	−0.918	0.334	−0.411	−1.917	
United States	−1.252	−1.546	−1.173	−1.096	−1.494	−0.678

Country	Australia	Canada	France	Germany	Japan	United Kingdom
			1/2/87–10/12/87 (N = 200)			
Canada	−0.284					
France	−0.010	−1.395				
Germany	−1.801	−3.508*	−2.033			
Japan	−1.099	−1.618	−1.264	−2.845		
United Kingdom	−1.368	−1.208	−0.709	−2.937*	−1.406	
United States	−0.609	−1.916	−1.187	−4.163*	−1.499	−1.515

* Denotes significance at 5% level.

expected real interest rate, there are testable implications concerning the relationship between stock prices, dividends, and bond yields. Equation 3.3 for the fundamental price (p^f) can be written as

$$p_t^f = d_t \sum_{i=1}^{\infty} \beta^i + \sum_{i=1}^{\infty} \beta^i (E_t d_{t+i} - d_t). \tag{3.19}$$

Suppose that the actual price p_t equals the fundamental price. If the price and dividends each have one unit root (as is consistent with the data), then equation 3.19 implies that the price and dividends are cointegrated.[14] That is, a regression of stock prices on dividends of the form

$$p_t = \gamma_0 + \gamma_1 d_t + \varepsilon_t \tag{3.20}$$

will yield a residual that does not have a unit root. To see this, note that

$$E_t d_{t+i} - d_t = \sum_{j=1}^{i} (E_t d_{t+j} - E_t d_{t+j-1}), \tag{3.21}$$

which implies that, after simplification, equation 3.14 can be rewritten as

$$p_t^f = r^{-1} d_t + r^{-1} \sum_{i=1}^{\infty} \beta^i (E_t d_{t+i+1} - E_t d_{t+1}). \tag{3.22}$$

By the hypothesis that the dividend has one unit root, $E_t d_{t+i+1} - E_t d_{t+i}$ does not have a unit root. In addition, the discount factors form a set of geometrically declining coefficients on these stationary values. This implies that the second term in equation 3.22 does not have a unit root.[15]

In addition to assuming that changes in dividends do not have a unit root, assume that expected changes in dividends are strictly stationary. If the expected real interest rate is constant and the fundamentals determine stock prices, the cointegrating regression is the projection of equation 3.22 and d_t, which will have stationary residuals if d_t has one unit root.[16]

This implication for a projection of the stock price on dividends does not hold when a rational bubble is added to the stock price, however. If bubbles are an important component of the observed stock price, then the stock price will not be cointegrated with dividends.[17] This is because, as discussed above, when a bubble is on, the bubble part of the price increases with time. Since the bubble part of the price is independent of the dividend by assumption, it therefore appears in the residual of equation 3.22. Hence, the estimated residuals in equation 3.22 increase with time, reflecting the bubble part of the price, and have a root greater than one.[18]

3.4.1.2. A Variable Expected Real Interest Rate. What are the implications for the relationship between stock prices and dividends if the expected real interest rate is not constant? The basis of the relationship is the arbitrage condition, equation 3.2, which can be written as:

$$p_t^f = \beta_t[E_t d_{t+1} + E_t p_{t+1}], \tag{3.23}$$

where $\beta_t = (1 + r_t)^{-1}$. The discount factor now has a time subscript to reflect its nonconstancy. To simplify the notation, we suppress the superscript "f" for the fundamental price. The solution for the fundamental price is based on iteration and successive substitution using equation 3.23. Iterating equation 3.23, we find that:

$$E_t p_{t+1} = E_t[\beta_{t+1}[E_{t+1}d_{t+2} + E_{t+1}p_{t+2}]], \tag{3.24}$$

and so forth. By repeated substitution into equation 3.23 with transversality conditions imposed,

$$\begin{aligned} p_t = {} & \beta_t E_t d_{t+1} + \beta_t E_t[\beta_{t+1}E_{t+1}d_{t+2}] + \beta_t E_t[\beta_{t+1}E_{t+1}[\beta_{t+2}E_{t+2}d_{t+3}]] \\ & + \beta_t E_t[\beta_{t+1}E_{t+1}[\beta_{t+2}E_{t+1}[\beta_{t+3}E_{t+3}d_{t+4}]] + \ldots . \end{aligned} \tag{3.25}$$

This equation is the analogue with a variable interest rate of the fundamental equation 3.3.

This rather complicated fundamental equation for the stock price can be rewritten in terms of contemporaneous conditional expectations and covariance terms. Because β_t is known, the first term on the right in equation 3.25 is simply the known discount factor times the expected divided next period. The remaining terms are the conditional expectations of products of random variables.[19] These terms are more complicated but actually have a simple structure.

It is useful to have a general characterization of the joint distribution of the interest rate and dividend series. While it may be somewhat stronger than necessary, we assume that the joint distribution of changes in dividends and changes in the discount factors is stationary. By Wold's decomposition theorem [Hannan, 1970, pp. 136–137; Sargent, 1979, pp. 256–260], there exists a joint moving-average representation of the form

$$\begin{aligned} \Delta\beta_t &= \alpha^\beta + \sum_{j=0}^{\infty} w_j^1 \varepsilon_{t-j}^\beta + \sum_{j=0}^{\infty} w_j^2 \varepsilon_{t-j}^d \\ \Delta d_t &= \alpha^d + \sum_{j=1}^{\infty} w_j^3 \varepsilon_{t-j}^\beta + \sum_{j=0}^{\infty} w_j^4 \varepsilon_{t-j}^d, \end{aligned} \tag{3.26}$$

where α^β and α^d are deterministic,

$$w_0^1 = w_0^4 = 1,$$
$$E\varepsilon_t^\beta = E\varepsilon_t^d = 0,$$

$$E\varepsilon_t^\beta \varepsilon_t^\beta = \sigma_\beta^2,\ E\varepsilon_t^d \varepsilon_t^d = \sigma_d^2, \text{ and } E\varepsilon_t^\beta \varepsilon_s^d = 0 \text{ for all } s, t.$$[20]

For notational simplicity, we suppress the deterministic part of this moving-average representation.

Consider the second term on the right-hand side of equation 3.25. With the multiplier β_t suppressed, rearrangement using the law of iterative expectations reduces this term to

$$E_t[\beta_{t+1}E_{t+1}d_{t+2}] = E_t\beta_{t+1}E_td_{t+2} + E_t[\beta_{t+1} - E_t\beta_{t+1}][E_{t+1}d_{t+2} - E_td_{t+2}] \quad (3.27)$$

where $E_t\ [x][y]$ denotes the conditional covariance of x and y.[21] By definition and from equation 3.26,

$$\beta_{t+1} - E_t\beta_{t+1} = \beta_{t+1} - \beta_t - E_t\Delta\beta_{t+1} = \varepsilon_{t+1}^\beta + w_0^2\varepsilon_{t+1}^d. \quad (3.28)$$

And similarily,

$$E_{t+1}d_{t+2} - E_td_{t+2} = \varepsilon_{t+1}^d. \quad (3.29)$$

Because the conditional and unconditional expectation of the covariance of these innovations is the same, the second term in equation 3.25 reduces to

$$\beta_tE_t[\beta_{t+1}E_{t+1}d_{t+2}] = \beta_tE_t\beta_{t+1}E_td_{t+2} + \beta_t(w_0^2)^2\sigma_d^2. \quad (3.30)$$

The remaining terms are more complex, but the end result is the same, with the terms reducing to expectations conditional on information available at t and variance terms.[22]

For example, consider the third term in equation 3.25, namely

$$\beta_tE_t[\beta_{t+1}E_{t+1}[\beta_{t+2}E_{t+2}d_{t+3}]]. \quad (3.31)$$

For compactness of representation, define

$$x_{t+3} = \beta_{t+2}E_{t+2}d_{t+3}. \quad (3.32)$$

Then

$$E_t[\beta_{t+1}E_{t+1}x_{t+3}] = E_t\beta_{t+1}E_tx_{t+3} + E_t[\beta_{t+1} - E_t\beta_{t+1}][E_{t+1}x_{t+3} - E_tx_{t+3}]. \quad (3.33)$$

The first term in this expression is the product of conditional expectations at t, and the second term is a conditional covariance term. Evaluating the covariance terms is tedious but reasonably straightforward. Equation 3.28 provides $\beta_{t+1} - E_t\beta_{t+1}$. By the definition of first differences,

$$\beta_{t+2} = \beta_t + \Delta\beta_{t+1} + \Delta\beta_{t+2} \tag{3.34}$$

and

$$E_{t+2}d_{t+3} = d_t + \Delta d_{t+1} + \Delta d_{t+2} + E_{t+2}\Delta d_{t+3}.$$

This implies that

$$\begin{aligned} x_{t+3} = {} & \beta_t d_t + \beta_t(\Delta d_{t+1} + \Delta d_{t+2} + E_{t+2}\Delta d_{t+3}) \\ & + d_t(\Delta\beta_{t+1} + \Delta\beta_{t+2}) + \Delta\beta_{t+1}(\Delta d_{t+1} + \Delta d_{t+2} + E_{t+2}\Delta d_{t+3}) \\ & + \Delta\beta_{t+2}(\Delta d_{t+1} + \Delta d_{t+2} + E_{t+2}\Delta d_{t+3}). \end{aligned} \tag{3.35}$$

Despite the messiness of this equation, $E_{t+1}x_{t+3} - E_t d_{t+3}$ in equation 3.33 reduces to a manageable function of the parameters in the moving-average representation, as does the expression $E_t[\beta_{t+1} - E_t\beta_{t+1}][E_{t+1}x_{t+3} - E_t x_{t+3}]$.

From this analysis, the third term on the right-hand side of equation 3.25 can be written

$$\beta_t E_t[\beta_{t+1} E_{t+1}[\beta_{t+2} E_{t+2} d_{t+3}]] = \beta_t E_t \beta_{t+1} E_t \beta_{t+2} E_t d_{t+3} + X_3, \tag{3.36}$$

where X_3 is a linear function of the variances. By induction, it is not hard to show that similar algebra goes through for further terms in equation 3.25.

The final result is that

$$p_t = \sum_{j=1}^{\infty} \delta_{t+j} E_t d_{t+j} + X, \tag{3.37}$$

where

$$\delta_{t+j} = \prod_{i=1}^{j} E_t \beta_{t-1+j}$$

where $E_t\beta_t = \beta_t$ and X is a linear function of the variances.

It we suppress the constant term due to the covariance terms, equation 3.37 can be rewritten as

$$p_t = d_t \sum_{j=1}^{\infty} \delta_{t+j} + \sum_{j=1}^{\infty} \delta_{t+j}(E_t d_{t+j} - d_t). \tag{3.38}$$

To make this equation manageable, we add one further assumption, namely, that the expected real interest rate is constant over the relevant horizon. If the term structure is flat, then

$$\delta_{t+j} = \beta_t^j,$$

where $\delta_t = (1 + r_t)^{-1}$. This simplifies equation 3.38 to

$$p_t = \frac{d_t}{r_t} + \sum_{j=1}^{\infty} \beta_t^j(E_t d_{t+j} - d_t). \tag{3.39}$$

After further simplification, equation 3.39 can be written in the form

$$p_t = \frac{d_t}{r_t} + \frac{1}{r_t}\sum_{i=1}^{\infty} \beta_t^i(E_t d_{t+i+1} - E_t d_{t+1}). \tag{3.40}$$

where β_t is defined analogously to above.

At least under some assumptions, equation 3.40 is the basis for a cointegrating regression. Suppose that the expected one-period change in dividends is a constant, c, over the horizon. Then equation 3.40 becomes

$$p_t = \frac{d_t}{r_t} + \frac{c}{r_t^2}. \tag{3.41}$$

This particular assumption suggests regressing the stock price on the dividend divided by the interest rate and on the inverse of the square of the interest rate. Different assumptions about the dividend process would yield different cointegrating regressions.[23]

This analysis suggests possible cointegrating regressions. Perhaps the simplest is the one suggested by equation 3.41. In the next section, we implement a first-order approximation of this equation by regressing the stock price on the dividend relative to the interest rate and on the inverse of the interest rate.[24]

3.4.1.3. Interpretation in Terms of Nominal Interest Rates. Measuring an expected long-term real interest rate on a monthly basis is a daunting task. It is fortunate that all of the analysis of a variable real interest rate can be interpreted in terms of the nominal interest rate instead. If equation 3.23 is interpreted as an equation in nominal terms for all variables and equation 3.26 is assumed to hold in nominal terms, then all of the analysis goes through in terms of nominal variables and the nominal interest rate. In the final estimating equation, the price of stock and other variables measured in terms of current currency values can be placed in real terms by dividing by the price level. The major assumption that is different than in the previous section is an assumption of the existence of a stationary representation of the joint process of changes in nominal dividends and changes in the nominal interest rate. This is not the same as assuming that there is a stationary representation of changes in real dividends and changes in the real interest rate. Given the tenuousness of any estimate of the expected real interest rate on a monthly basis, we use nominal interest rates in the empirical analysis.

3.4.2. Tests for Cointegration

The analyses in the last section leading to cointegrating equations differ in terms of assumptions about the interest rate. In both analyses, it is assumed that real stock prices and real dividends have unit roots. This set up the testable implication that stock prices and dividends are cointegrated. In the theoretical analysis, two different assumptions about the interest rate are used. The first is that the expected real interest rate is constant. This is the assumption used by Campbell and Shiller [1987], Diba and Grossman [1988], and Santoni and Dwyer [1989]. If the expected real interest rate is constant, a regression of the real stock price on the real dividend per share is a cointegrating regression relating the two: The residuals of this regression do not have a unit root. The second assumption about the interest rate loosens the restriction by allowing the real interest rate to vary over time, but the expected interest rate over the horizon is constant at any point in time. This suggests that a regression of the real stock price on the ratio of the real dividend to the interest rate and on the inverse of the interest rate yields residuals that do not have a unit root. These implications can be tested.

3.4.2.1. Empirical Results with International Data. We examine these hypotheses with monthly data for Canada, Germany, Japan, the United Kingdom, and the United States for April 1973 through December 1987.[25] The underlying data on stock prices are indexes from Capital International Perspectives with and without dividends reinvested.[26] These indexes are measured at the end of the period. We calculate dividends from the relationship between the indexes with and without dividends reinvested.[27]

The first issue is to test for the existence of unit roots in the stock·price indexes and dividends per share. The test statistics for unit roots are presented in table 3–7. The table contains unit root tests for real stock prices, real dividends per share, the current yield (dividends per share over the stock price) and the long-term interest rate. The results for the current yield are presented for later reference. The table reports the estimated deviation of the first-order coefficient from 1 and the estimated *t*-ratio of this deviation from 1.[28] Given the number of observations in the regressions, the *t*-ratios for rejecting the hypothesis of a unit root and their marginal significance levels are about −2.58 at the 10% significance level and −3.5 at the 1% marginal significance level (Fuller [1976], p. 373). At the 5% marginal significance level, one reported test statistic is inconsistent with the null hypothesis of a unit root. Under the null hypothesis of a unit root, the test statistic for real dividends per share for Japan are

Table 3–7. Unit Root Tests: Levels[1] (April 1973 to December 1987)

Country	*Real Stock Price*	*Real Dividend Per Share*	*Current Yield*	*Long-term Interest Rate*
Canada	−.056	−.025	−.063	−.030
	(−2.51)	(−1.09)	(−2.40)	(−1.86)
Germany	−.020	−.097	−.039	−.019
	(−1.34)	(−2.28)	(−1.41)	(−1.75)
Japan	.009	−.082	−.002	−.016
	(0.98)	(−3.76)	(−0.15)	(−1.01)
United Kingdom	−.026	−.066	−0.082	−.036
	(−1.55)	(−2.81)	(−2.85)	(−1.99)
United States	−.049	−.071	−.043	−.022
	(−2.69)	(−1.80)	(−2.15)	(−1.62)

[1] Estimated *t*-ratios are in parentheses.

smaller than would be expected. The finding of a unit root for stock prices and not for dividends per share in Japan is inconsistent with the hypothesis of cointegration of real stock prices and real dividends. If the real stock price has a unit root and real dividend per share does not, then the real dividend per share cannot possibly be related to the unit-root component of real stock prices.[29]

The results of estimating cointegrating regressions for stock prices and dividends as well as the unit root tests on the residuals of these regressions are presented in table 3–8. For each country we present the slope coefficient from a regression of real stock prices on real dividends per share, this coefficient's ordinary least squares "*t*-statistic" and the regressions' R^2 and Durbin-Watson test statistics. Because there is no reason for the regressions to have serially uncorrelated residuals, the "*t*-statistics" produced by the regression program are not distributed as student's *t*. With some assistance from the Durbin-Watson statistics though, these *t*-ratios provide some guidance as to whether there is any relationship between real stock prices and real dividends per share. If the *t*-ratio is small and substantial positive serial correlation is present in the residuals, then the evidence is clear that there is little relationship between real stock prices and real dividends per share.

The test statistic in the last column of table 3–8 is the estimated *t*-ratio from the Dickey-Fuller test for a unit root in the regression residuals. The maintained hypothesis in this test is that real stock prices and real dividends per share have unit roots. The null hypothesis tested is that real

Table 3–8. Tests of Cointegration—Real Stock Prices and Real Dividends Per Share (April 1973 to December 1987)

	Cointegrating Regression			*Dickey-Fuller Tests*
Country	*Estimated Coefficient*[1]	R^2	*D–W*	*Estimated Coefficient*
Canada	158.02 (4.35)	.098	.114	−.063 (−2.46)
Germany	172.15 (2.88)	.047	.054	−.014 (−0.76)
Japan	−348.20 (−1.39)	.011	.016	.008 (0.87)
United Kingdom	363.43 (7.20)	.230	.100	−.044 (−1.81)
United States	45.49 (0.61)	.002	.061	−.045 (−2.43)

[1] Estimated *t*-ratios are in parentheses.

stock prices and real dividends per share are not cointegrated. Under the maintained hypotheses and this null hypothesis, the *t*-ratio in the unit root test of the residuals is zero. With the number of observations in the regressions in table 3–8, the null hypothesis that a *t*-ratio is zero is inconsistent with the data at the 5% marginal significance level if the *t*-ratio is less than or equal to −3.37 (Engle and Yoo [1987]). If the *t*-ratio is zero, then the joint hypothesis that the fundamentals model is correct and the expected real interest rate is constant is inconsistent with the data. A small *t*-ratio (negative and large in magnitude) is consistent with this joint hypothesis.

There is hardly any evidence in table 3–8 that supports the hypothesis that real stock prices and real dividends per share are related. The relationships between real stock prices and real dividends per share in the cointegrating regressions are weak at best for Japan and the United States. From the theoretical analysis above, the estimated coefficients in the cointegrating regression should be positive and equal to one over the real interest rate.[30] A negative coefficient estimate implies a negative expected real interest rate, which implies that real stock prices or dividends should be negative. There are unappealing implications of the estimated negative coefficient for Japan. Even ignoring the serial correlation of the residuals, it is clear that the hypothesis that real stock prices are unrelated to real dividends per share cannot be rejected for Japan and the United States. The evidence from the Dickey-Fullar tests for unit roots also is unambiguous. Not a single t-ratio in the last column of table 3–8 approaches −3.37. There is no evidence in this table that lends any support to the fundamentals model of stock prices.

Perhaps this result should not be surprising however. The tests for unit roots in table 3–7 indicate that the current yields of stocks have unit roots. The algebra that leads to the cointegrating regressions in table 3–8, however, suggests that current yields do not have a unit root. Indeed, this can be a different way of testing the same hypothesis. Note that equation 3.22 can be rewritten as

$$\frac{d_t}{p_t} = r - \sum_{i=1}^{\infty} \beta^i (E_t d_{t+i+1} - E_t d_{t+1})/p_t. \tag{3.42}$$

In this equation, if expected changes in future dividends relative to the current price are a stationary process, then the current yield does not have a unit root. Such a specification goes through for certain types of processes on the dividends and prices. For example, if the growth rate of dividends is a stationary process and the expected real interest rate is constant, then the right-hand side of equation 3.42 is stationary. It is clear in table 3–7 that current yields have a unit root. A unit root in current yields basically is inconsistent with the hypothesis that the dividend and the price are cointegrated.

Allowing for variable discount rates provides little help. Table 3–9 presents the results of the cointegrating regressions for real stock prices, real dividends per share, and the long-term nominal interest rates. In general, these regressions appear to be more satisfactory than those in table 3–8. The R^2 of the regressions generally are nontrivial, a marked improvement over table 3–8. Even so, none of the coefficients indicate that the variables are cointegrated at the 5% significance level. The number of observations in these equations requires a t-ratio of about −3.85 to reject the hypothesis of a unit root in the residuals and, therefore, the hypothesis that stock prices are not cointegrated with dividends and bond yields. The tests for unit roots in the residuals provide no support for the hypothesis of cointegration.

The cointegration tests provide no support for the hypothesis that stock prices are determined by the fundamentals.[31] These results may reflect many things, including the length of the sample or the loose relationship between the yields on long-term government bonds and the discount rate on stock. In this regard, it is worth noting that the test results with interest

Table 3–9. Tests of Cointegration—Real Stock Prices, Real Dividends Per Share and Interest Rates (April 1973 to December 1987)

	Cointegrating regression				*Dickey-Fuller Tests*
	Estimated Coefficients[1]				*Estimated Coefficient*
Country	*d/r*	*1/r*	R^2	*D–W*	
Canada	17.03 (4.48)	−9.83 (−3.46)	.105	.116	−.062 (−2.43)
Germany	6.80 (1.88)	6.26 (4.23)	.408	.076	−.032 (−1.47)
Japan	10.98 (1.26)	40.40 (10.12)	.542	.114	−.017 (−0.64)
United Kingdom	10.46 (2.89)	34.61 (7.17)	.731	.246	−.115 (−3.07)
United States	−5.81 (−1.20)	11.32 (4.30)	.457	.119	−.065 (−2.53)

[1] Estimated *t*-ratios are in parentheses.

rates will be negative if the discount rate on stock is not cointegrated with the yield on government bounds. Put in other terms, risk premia on stocks with unit roots are consistent with the fundamentals models and with our results. It also could be that stock prices are just determined by whim and fancy. Before abandoning ourselves to this conclusion, however, we examine some simples regressions suggested by the fundamentals.

3.4.3. Atheoretic Estimates of the Fundamentals Relationship

Tests for cointegration are one approach to analyzing the fundamentals model. Another way of examining the importance of the fundamentals is in terms of the importance of likely fundamental factors affecting changes in stock prices. To do this, we estimate straightforward regressions of changes in the logarithm of real stock prices on changes in the logarithm of the long-term interest rate and on a proxy for unexpected changes in real dividends. We assume that changes in the logarithms for real stock prices and changes in the logarithm of the long-term interest rates are approximately the same thing as the unexpected changes in each. We estimate the unexpected part of the change in dividends from a 12th-order autoregression for the change in the logarithm of real dividends.

The results of these regressions, reported in table 3–10, suggest some generalizations. Unexpected changes in the long-term interest rate do appear to be negatively related to changes in stock prices. This provides some modicum of support for the fundamental model. Dividends, on the other hand, appear to be quite unimportant in the regressions. This may reflect problems with the way dividends are measured. The most obvious problem is our complete ignorance of the timing of dividend announcements. There is evidence that suggests that announcements of dividends do affect share prices.[32] The nonexistence of a statistically significant relationship between dividends and stock prices may reflect the poor measurement of unexpected dividends. In the last analysis, though, we are inclined to think that dividends are relatively unimportant in explaining monthly changes in stock prices.[33]

The R^2 of these regressions also are not overwhelming. The lowest R^2 is .068 for Canada, and the highest is only .127 for the United Kingdom. While each is statistically significant, there is little doubt that much of the variance of stock prices is not directly related to our measures of long-term interest rates and dividends.

As a further examination of the importance of the fundamentals, changes in the logarithm of real stock prices are regressed on a set of macroeconomic variables that are available monthly and are likely to be important for stock prices if the fundamentals model is correct. In addition to the long-term interest rate in each country, proxies for the unexpected change in the logarithm of industrial production are included. For the non-U.S. estimates, possible influences of foreign developments are incorporated by including a proxy for the unexpected change in the logarithm of industrial production in the United States, the change in logarithm of the long-term interest rate in the United States, and the change in the real exchange rate relative to the United States. The unexpected part of the change of industrial production is estimated by the residual from a 12th-order autoregression. We do not explore possible international links beyond these between the United States and each of these countries, nor do we explore links between the United States and the other countries. Such an exploration is beyond the limited scope of our analysis.

The results of these regressions are reported in table 3–11. These additional variables do not explain much of the variation of real stock prices. Because industrial production in the United States does little, the regression for the United States looks little different from its counterpart in table 3–10. The regressions for Germany, Japan, and the United Kingdom

Table 3–10. Regressions of Changes in Real Stock Prices on Real Dividends Per Share and Interest Rates (April 1973 to December 1987)

	Estimated Coefficients[1]					
Country	*Constant*	*Unexpected Change in Real Dividends*	*Change in Interest Rate*	R^2 / s_e	*F*	*D–W*
Canada	−.0001	−.0270	−.3864	.068	5.985	1.864
	(−0.030)	(−0.202)	(−3.441)	.0574		
Germany	.0014	.0942	−.3499	.071	5.057	1.822
	(0.353)	(1.401)	(−2.848)	.0475		
Japan	.0042	.1406	−.2545	.071	5.453	2.057
	(1.280)	(0.901)	(−3.183)	.0394		
United Kingdom	−.0012	−.2168	−.6568	.127	10.740	1.895
	(−0.204)	(−1.219)	(−4.473)	.0728		
United States	.0002	.0553	−.3561	.087	7.715	1.987
	(0.004)	(0.335)	(−3.862)	.0491		

Note: All variables are changes in the logarithms of the variables.
[1] Estimated *t*-ratios are in parentheses.

Table 3–11. Regressions of Changes in Real Stock Prices on Interest Rates, Industrial Production and Exchange Rates (April 1973 to December 1987)

	Estimated Coefficients[1]								
		Change in Interest Rate		Unexpected Change in Industrial Production					
Country	*Constant*	*Domestic*	*United States*	*Domestic*	*United States*	*Change in real exchange rate*	R^2 / s_e	*F*	*D–W*
Canada	.0016	−.0247	−.0068	.2975	−.0068	−1.0801	.186	7.590	1.874
	(0.414)	(−2.165)	(−0.550)	(1.010)	(−0.550)	(−3.427)	.051		
Germany	−.0005	−.0451	.1647	.0613	−.3285	.1647	.089	3.348	1.852
	(−0.130)	(−2.742)	(1.480)	(1.480)	(−0.655)	(1.480)	.051		
Japan	.0042	−0.457	.0032	.2355	−.0553	−.0651	.096	3.518	1.926
	(1.204)	(−3.589)	(0.369)	(0.806)	(−0.125)	(−0.575)	.045		
United Kingdom	−.0008	−.0586	.0002	−.0852	0.232	−0.1127	.158	6.416	2.031
	(−0.162)	(−5.471)	(0.019)	(−0.258)	(0.336)	(−0.678)	.068		
United States	−.0012	−.0326		0.1301			.078	7.378	2.003
	(−0.332)	(−3.827)		(0.273)			.049		

[1] Estimated *t*-ratios are in parentheses.

also show little change from their counterparts in table 3–10. The regression for Canada shows the largest increase in its R^2, increasing from .068 to .186. This increase appears to be mostly related to the inclusion of changes in the real exchange rate, although industrial production does contribute some to the explanation of changes in real Canadian stock prices. That said, there appears to be some relationship between changes in stock prices and interest rates, but the fraction of variation in these indexes explained is hardly overwhelming.

3.5. Conclusions

The results of our analysis can be stated succinctly. The implications of the hypothesis of rational bubbles in stock prices find little support in the data. Our tests of this model are based on daily data taken for the year preceding the October 1987 crash across several countries. Although there are some individual results consistent with the notion of bubbles in stock prices, the weight of the evidence is against this theory. We also find little support for a hypothesis of a contagious bubble driving up stock prices worldwide. An alternative model, a version of the fundamentals, also is examined in a variety of ways using monthly observations that span the past 15 years for several countries. This model also has sparse support in the data.

Our finding that neither a rational-bubble nor the fundamentals model adequately characterizes the behavior of stock prices in several countries raises some interesting questions, all of which form a direction for further research efforts. Have we adequately modeled both processes? While arguing that a model is found wanting because it is not properly specified can lead to vacuous circularity, the proper specification in testing the fundamentals model is crucial. After all, the econometrician is forced to use some measure of interest rates that may not be that used by the market in forming its valuation. Similarly, our test procedures may be unable to disentangle a rational bubble in the variance found in daily stock prices.

Our finding of no cointegration of stock prices and dividends is at odds with previous work by Campbell and Shiller [1987], Diba and Grossman [1988], and others. A natural question that arises concerns the robustness of test results to the time period. Their examinations rely on annual data spanning the past 100 years of U.S. financial history. Our analysis is based on only the past 15 years. Moreover, the periodicity of our data is monthly, not annual. It may be that stock prices and dividends are closely related, but only across a broad enough span of time. If this is so, an important issue is what this implies about the joint process of stock prices, dividends, and interest rates.

Notes

1. The conclusions of the Brady Commission are the subject of several studies, all of which find little support for the conclusion or recommendations of the Commission. See Roll [1988] and Santoni [1988].

2. See the data appendix for more detail on these data.

3. Roll [1988] discusses the timing of the crashes.

4. The peak dates used are Australia—9/21/87; Canada—8/13/87; France—3/26/87; Germany—8/17/87; Japan—6/11/87; United Kingdom—7/16/87; and United States—8/25/87.

5. If the limit of the present value of the expected price sufficiently far into the future were not zero, there would be no forward solution to equation 3.2 such as 3.3.

6. An idea of the order of magnitude of a bubble's effect on the serial correlation of the price can be gained from Diba and Grossman's simulations [1988, pp. 527–28]. Their simulations suggest that a rational bubble adds a component to the stock price that is highly positively serially correlated with a first-order serial correlation coefficient that is typically 0.8 or above and that has a slowly damped autocorrelation function.

7. The critical values are taken from Fuller [1976, p. 373].

8. Note that the models suggest that passing the peak value, not the date of a large downward adjustment some time later, is the correct date for the end of a rational bubble.

9. All regression results reported are based on White's [1980] heteroskedasticity-consistent estimates. For the most part, ordinary least squares regressions yielded the same qualitative conclusions.

10. It should be noted that the true peak of the German index in 1987 was in January. That is, from January 6 to the peak used in the regression analysis (August 17), the market actually fell the recovered slightly, although never regaining the highest 1987 value.

11. We ignore the second-order term $h\Delta e$ in this discussion.

12. Another interpretation of the test for unit roots in the relative stock prices is in terms of the cointegration of the stock price indexes with an imposed coefficient of unity in the cointegrating equation (Granger [1986]; Engle and Granger [1987]).

13. Tests also were run for changes in the relatives. The existence of second unit roots is inconsistent with the data.

14. A variable does not have a unit root if none of the roots of the stochastic difference equation characterizing the variable equals one. Two variables are cointegrated (of order one) if each variable has a unit root and the residuals of the simple linear equation characterizing the relationship of the two variables does not have a unit root. Engle and Granger [1987] provide a more general definition and some explanatory discussion.

This implication for stock prices and dividends has been derived in somewhat different fashions by Campbell and Shiller [1987] and Diba and Grossman [1988].

15. Under certain assumptions, the two terms on the right-hand side of equation 3.22 are not independent. Nonetheless, the part orthogonal to d_t does not have a unit root. For example, suppose that d_t has a constant expected growth rate. Then the constant expected growth rate is impounded into the first term in the cointegrating regression.

16. The projection of $r^{-1}d_t$ yields a coefficient of r^{-1}. Suppress any deterministic component of expected changes in dividends. Then the projection on d_t of the remainder of the equation, which does not have a unit root, yields a coefficient of zero. Because d_t has a unit root and therefore is nonstationary and since $E_t d_{t+i+1} - E_t d_{t+1}$ is stationary, the projection of $E_t d_{t+i+1} - E_t d_{t+1}$ on d_t must be zero. Any constant coefficient in the projection other than zero would imply that either both variables are stationary or both are nonstationary.

17. Diba and Grossman [1988] present a related analysis.

18. The root is not a unit root, because the root is $1 + r\pi^{-1}$. As a practical matter, the ability to discern this root in a finite sample depends on the proportion of periods with bubbles on, without bubbles, and with crashes.

19. The conditional expectations at $t + j$, $j > 0$, are random variables from the standpoint of a conditional expectation at t.

20. The contemporaneous orthogonality of the ε's is a result of including ε_t^d in the equation for $\Delta\beta_t$. This representation imposes no restrictions on the data not imposed in the assumptions above. This simply is *a* representation, not *the* representation of the relationships. This particular one is convenient.

21. The law of iterative expectations says that $E_t[E_{t+1}[d_{t+2}]] = E_t[d_{t+2}]$, because the information set at t is a subset of the information set at $t + 1$. By the assumptions we have made, namely that β_{t+1} and d_{t+1} are known at $t + 1$ but not t, the expectation at $t + 1$ is conditional on a proper superset of the information available at t.

22. On another level, the variance term is a covariance term because it reflects the covariance of $\Delta\beta$ and Δd.

23. For example, suppose that the expected growth rate of dividends is constant. This assumption is inconsistent with the hypothesis that changes in the level of dividends are strictly stationary. This assumption implies that the price of stock is a nonlinear function of the real interest rate and the dividend of the form:

$$p_t = \frac{1+g^d}{r_t-g^d} d_t .$$

This equation is nonlinear in the interest rate and the dividend and cannot be written as a linear function of a simple term such as the ratio of the two.

24. We included the dividend in addition to these two variables in a set of regressions. This has no effect on the conclusion.

25. In addition to these countries, we also collected data for France. In the process of constructing the data on dividends, we found substantial oddities in the behavior of dividends leading us to drop that country. Data availability also forced us to remove Australia from the sample.

26. Capital International Perspectives has two series with dividends reinvested. The one that we use has gross dividends reinvested. The other, which we do not use, has dividends net of tax reinvested.

27. Define $x1$ as the ratio of the index with dividends reinvested to its value last period and $x2$ as the ratio of the index without dividends reinvested to its value last period. The yield is $x1/x2 - 1$. We recover the dividend per share from this yield by multiplying by the level of the index without dividends reinvested.

In a few periods, the calculated yield and dividend are negative or are relatively large followed by a relatively small value (or vice versa) compared to surrounding values. Negative values make no sense, and large inverse changes in consecutive periods also suggest errors. As a result of these likely problems, a few observations are not used. We do not use yields for West Germany, January and February 1974, May through August 1946; Japan, November and December 1985; and United Kingdom, November and December 1982. Capital International Perspectives is investigating these apparent problems with the data.

28. For each variable for each country, each equation is estimated with from 0 to 2 lagged changes in the variable. If a t-ratio exceeds 1.95 in absolute value, the lag distribution includes that lag and any lesser lags. For real stock prices, all of the estimated equations

include no lag except for the world index, which includes one lag. For real dividends per share, all of the estimated equations include two lags except for the United Kingdom, which includes one lag. For the yield on stocks, all of the equations include no lag except for Germany and the United Kingdom, which include one lag. For the long-term interest rates, the equation for the Canadian rate includes no lag, the equations for Germany and Japan include one lag, and the equations for the United Kingdom and the United States include two lags.

29. The estimates indicate that the real stock price index for Japan has a unit root with an estimated first-order autoregressive coefficient of 1.009, and the coefficient for real dividends per share is .918. Arguably, these are best interpreted as a preliminary indicator of a lack of cointegration of real stock prices and real dividends per share.

30. As the analysis in Santoni and Dwyer [1989] indicates, even though this coefficient can be affected by the expected real growth rate of dividends per share, it still should be positive.

31. It is obvious that a "souped-up" version of the model of the fundamentals above always can explain any observation. The same holds true for the rational bubbles model in the last section. This is the same as saying that, in the same sense that utility maximization is vacuous, both the fundamental theory and the bubble theory are vacuous. With an emphasis on the impossibility of refuting the fundamentals model, Hamilton and Whiteman [1985] discuss these points.

32. Among other, see Litzenberger and Ranaswamy [1982].

33. Indeed, recall that support for the fundamentals model often comes from tests based on long time series of annual data. See, for example, Diba and Grossman [1988].

References

Blanchard, Olivier, and Watson, Mark. 1982. "Bubbles, Rational Expectations, and Financial Markets." *Crises in the Economic and Financial Structure*. Lexington, MA: Lexington Books.

Brady Commission. 1988. *Report of the Presidential Task Force on Market Mechanisms*.

Campbell, John, and Shiller, Robert. 1987. "Cointegration and Tests of Present Value Models." *Journal of Political Economy* 95 (October):1062–1088.

Diba, Behzad T., and Grossman, Herschel I. 1988. "Explosive Rational Bubbles in Stock Prices?" *American Economic Review* 78 (June):520–529.

Dickey, David A., and Fuller, Wayne A. 1979. "Distribution of the Estimators for Autoregressive Time Series with a Unit Root." *Journal of the American Statistical Association* 6:427–431.

Dwyer, Gerald P., Jr., and Hafer, R.W. 1988. "Are National Stock Markets Linked?" *Federal Reserve Bank of St. Louis Review* (November/December): 3–14.

———, and Santoni, G.J. 1988. "Tests for Rational Bubbles in the 1920s and 1980s Bull Markets." Unpublished paper, Federal Reserve Bank of St. Louis. September.

Engle, Robert F., and Granger, C.W.J. 1987. "Co-integration and Error Correction: Representation, Estimation, and Testing." *Econometrica* 55 (March): 251–276.

Flood, Robert P., and Garber, Peter M. 1980. "Market Fundamentals Versus Price-Level Bubbles: The First Tests." *Journal of Political Economy* 88 (August):745–770.

Fuller, Wayne A. 1976. *Introduction to Statistical Time Series*. New York: John Wiley & Sons.

Granger, C. W. J. 1986. "Developments in the Study of Cointegrated Economic Variables." *Oxford Bulletin of Economics and Statistics* 48 (August):213–228.

Hamilton, James D., and Whiteman, Charles H. 1985. "The Observable Implications of Self-Fulfilling Expectations." *Journal of Monetary Economics*. 16 (November):353–373.

Hannan, E. J. *Multiple Time Series*. 1970. New York: John Wiley & Sons.

Hardouvelis, Gikas A. 1988. "Stock Market Bubbles Before the Crash of 1987: Japan, United States and Great Britain." unpublished paper, Federal Reserve Bank of New York, April.

Litzenberger, Robert H., and Ramaswamy, Krishna 1982. "The Effects of Dividends on Common Stock: Tax Effects or Information Effects?" *Journal of Finance* 37 (May):429–443.

Roll, Richard W. 1988. "The International Crash of October 1987." In *Black Monday and the Future of Financial Markets*, ed. Robert Kamphuis, Roger Kormendi, and J. W. Henry Watson, Chicago: Mid America Institute.

Santoni, G. J., and Dwyer, Gerald P., Jr. 1989. "Bubbles or Fundamentals: Some Evidence from the Great Bull Markets of 1924–29 and 1982–87." In *The 1987 Stock Market Crash in Historical Perspective*, ed. Eugene White, Homewood, Illinois: Richard D. Irwin, Inc.

Sargent, Thomas. 1979. *Macroeconomic Theory* New York: Academic Press.

White, Halbert. 1980. "A Heteroskedasticity-Consistent Covariance Matrix Estimator and a Direct Test for Heteroskedasticity." *Econometrica* 48 (May): 817–838.

Data Appendix

Stock Prices

The stock price indexes used are generated from "Morgan Stanley Capital International Perspective," edited by Capital International Perspective S. A. in Geneva, Switzerland, and published by Morgan Stanley & Co., Inc. in New York. For each index, the sample of companies included represents an attempt to match the industry profile of the country. Each index is a market weighted concept. Indexes measured in terms of U.S. dollars adjust for fluctuations in the local currency relative to the dollar. The indexes with dividends, available only on a monthly basis, consist of the price index with dividends reinvested. Daily index values are available beginning July 29, 1986; monthly values begin December 1969.

Prices

The price data are series 64 in *International Financial Statistics*.

Canada: Data for all cities with a population of over 30,000. Weights correspond to family expenditure patterns of 1982, base 1981.

Germany: Cost of living index for all households, base 1980. Index covers 753 items in 118 municipalities with 1980 weights.

Japan: Index covers whole country excluding one-person households and those engaged mainly in agriculture, forestry, and fishing. Base is 1985.

United Kingdom: General index of retail prices, all items, base January 1987. The weights are revised annually on the basis of a continuing family expenditure survey.

United States: Index covers all urban consumers representing about 80% of the noninstitutional population. Beginning January 1983, cost of shelter to homeowners is measured by a rental equivalence. From January 1987, an enhanced housing survey represents more adequately both owners and renters in estimating cost of shelter. Weights based on Consumer Expenditure Survey, carried out from 1982 through 1984.

Long-term Interest Rates

These data are series 61 in *International Financial Statistics*.

Canada: Average yield to maturity of issues with original maturity of 10 years or more.

Germany: Calculated as the weighted average of all bonds with an average remaining life to maturity of more than three years, or four years for bonds included before January 1977. Monthly figures are calculated as averages of four bank week return dates including the end-of-month yield of the preceding month.

Japan: Arithmetic average yield to maturity of all government bonds with seven years to maturity. Monthly series are compiled from end-of-month prices quoted on the Tokyo stock exchange.

United Kingdom: Issue at par with 20 years to maturity. Data for 1972 onwards are averages of Wednesday yields.

United States: Data based on 10-year constant maturities.

Industrial Production

These data are series 66 in *International Financial Statistics*.

Canada: Beginning 1984, data refer to industrial production in constant prices, base year 1981. Industrial production includes services related to mineral extraction as part of the mining sector.

Germany: Index including construction, base 1980.

Japan: Series covers 9 mining and 523 manufacturing industries weighted by 1980 value-added data.

United Kingdom: Base 1980, series covers manufacturing industries, energy and water.

United States: Data are an index produced with value-added weights.

Exchange Rates

Series used is ag (end-of-period) in *International Financial Statistics*.

Canada: Midpoint rate quoted by the Bank of Canada at noon in the Montreal-Toronto interbank exchange market.

Germany: Midpoint rate determined officially during the official session of the Frankfurt foreign exchange market.

Japan: Midpoint rate in the interbank foreign exchange market in Tokyo.

United Kingdom: Midpoint rate at noon in the London market.

COMMENTARY

by George M. von Furstenberg and Bang Nam Jeon

Following Gerald P. Dwyer and R.W. Hafer's article, we will go from bubbles to suds, and then ask why such litttle substance has been found in either for explaining daily (July 29, 1986, or January 2, 1987, to peak later in 1987) or monthly (April 1973 to December 1987) movements in stock prices in seven countries.

Bubbles

Self-fulfilling beliefs that diverge from outcomes consistent with fundamentals are quite as offensive to rational man as extraneous intervention by unidentified flying objects such as angels or messengers from Mercury. While Stanley Jevons [1878, 1879] seriously tried to hold sunspots responsible for commercial crises, no famous economist has yet rested his claim on *bubbles*. For this reason we should be relieved that the authors have found that whatever crashed in October 1987 was not a bubble or something similarly abhorrent to right-thinking persons.

Nevertheless, we feel that the authors' confirmation of our professional skepticism about bubbles has little force because they require any bubbles of interest to follow a particular dynamic. In their view, like that of most economists, bubbles, to be respectable, must be rational and inflate at an increasing rate. This leads to the refutable implication that for any finite period when a bubble is on, the proportional change in price is an increasing function of time.

Jeffrey Frankel's work can be used to shed further light on where such advance restrictions come from and why they leave little prospect of ever confirming bubbles. Frankel [1985] asked whether the dollar was on a bubble path before it reached a peak of appreciation in March 1985. If there is such a thing as a long-run equilibrium level of the dollar in terms of foreign currency, $\bar{s}$, at time t, but the spot price of the dollar has gone higher to s_t because the dollar has appreciated further, then $\ln(s_t/\bar{s}_t)$ is positive as $s_t/\bar{s}_t > 1$. Here *ln* denotes the operation of taking natural logarithms. If the foreign-currency price of the dollar is expected to go even higher, by a_t percent, with probability $(1 - \pi_t)$, there remains the probability π_t that the bubble will burst and return s_t to fundamentals, i.e., to $\bar{s}_t$, through a sudden depreciation of the dollar by a percentage amount equivalent to $\ln(s_t/\bar{s}_t)$. Hence a risk-neutral investor, say in Japan, would be indifferent towards two alternative courses of action if they are expected to yield the same return: One involves investing at home and earning the domestic interest rate r_t^*; the other riding the bubble in the United States with the same amount of principal converted to dollars, earning a dollar rate of r_t in interest on it and then taking chances on the foreign exchange rate to get back into yen at maturity. Suspending the cross-national aspect for a moment in order to keep sight of the stock market, the same equality of expected yields could be attributed to domestic rates of return by reinterpreting some of the symbols on the right of equation 3C.1 below. Thus having a risk-neutral investor earn, for example, the Treasury bill rate would have to be expected to yield the same as riding the stock market bubble ($s_t' > \bar{s}_t'$) in his country, earning a dividend rate of r_t' and taking his chances on stock price index (s_t') appreciation at the rate a_t' over the same period.

Continuing with the foreign exchange analogy, equivalence of expected returns is expressed as:

$$r_t^* = r_t - \pi_t \, ln(s_t/\bar{s}_t) + (1 - \pi_t)a_t. \qquad (3C.1)$$

If $r_t > r_t^*$, so that there is a forward discount on the dollar, and the bubble continues, the Japanese investor in interest-bearing dollar denominated assets would get a higher interest rate than at home on that investment and more yen per dollar at maturity than at the start of the contract. He would gain on both counts. On the other hand, if the bubble bursts, he would lose

$\ln(s_t/\bar{s}_t) - (r_t - r_t^*)$ on each yen's worth originally invested abroad rather than at home. If risk-neutral investors dominate international price relations, something (most likely s_t) will have to give way until equation 3C.1 is satisfied precisely ex ante.

Of course over time, several things can change without causing the bubble necessarily to burst. Using the time difference operator d, and writing the rate of dollar appreciation (a_t) as $d\ln s_t > 0$ when the foreign price of the dollar goes up, the derivative of equation 3C.1 is:

$$dr_t^* = dr_t - d\pi_t \ln(s_t/\bar{s}_t) - (\pi_t + d\pi_t)d\ln s_t + \pi_t d\ln\bar{s}_t + (1 - \pi_t)d^2\ln s_t. \qquad (3C.2)$$

Now clearly if, as in Dwyer and Hafer (this volume), nothing but s_t is allowed to change, equation 3C.2 reduces to

$$\pi_t d\ln s_t = (1 - \pi_t)d^2\ln s_t. \qquad (3C.3)$$

Hence as long as the bubble is growing ($d\ln s_t > 0$) rationally under these advance restrictions, s_t must be growing at an increasing rate ($d^2\ln s_t > 0$).

In reality, however, equation 3C.2 could just as well be satisfied by having s_t increase at a constant rate ($d^2\ln s_t = 0$) while π_t (the probability that the bubble will burst) declines to keep the bubble growing. Assuming that bubblemania builds while stock prices change at a constant rate is no more arbitrary, but possibly more typical of a "rational" bubble (if there is one), than assuming that the market estimate of the probability of the bubble bursting is constant, but that stock prices must increase at an increasing rate as the bubble grows. In the former case one gets the result implied by Frankel's [1985, pp. 205–206] procedure:

$$d\pi_t/(\pi_t + d\pi_t) = -d\ln s_t/[\ln(s_t/\bar{s}_t)]. \qquad (3C.4)$$

Unless survey evidence is available on beliefs about π_t, process 3C.4, no matter how plausible, is untestable. If bubbles, small and large, had already been identified in the past, one might find that the probability of a bubble bursting actually declined over some range with its size. It could do so without violating global stability conditions for a reason analogous to that causing the remaining life expectancy of humans to rise from immediately after birth to early infancy before declining. All the same, recourse to frequentism is not likely to be of much help in aging the probability, π_t, that the bubble will burst.

Other possibilities raised by equation 3C.2 for $d\ln s_t$ to be constant may be more interesting. The interest rate differential could change ($dr^* \neq dr$) progressively in an immediately ascertainable manner to support a rational bubble. So could the equilibrium level, $\bar{s}_t$, thought to correspond to the fundamental conditions prevailing at time t, if a theory of fundamental determinants, and what causes them to change, had been provided. For instance, if estimates of $\bar{s}_t$ begin to be raised as the current actual value, s_t, rises above it, as would be common in rational learning processes if bubbles are hard to believe, then s_t need not be expected to rise at an increasing rate even if π_t falls very little. Indeed, it is paradoxical to specify that agents cling to a fixed estimate of the rate that represents fundamental equilibrium, thereby providing a metric for the size of the bubble, $s_t/\bar{s}_t$, even if a bubble is not what is ultimately found. Instead, prior beliefs about $\bar{s}_t$ should be allowed to be sufficiently diffuse (or "imprecise" in the language of information theory) for agents to be able to learn from data developments.

The point appears worth elaborating. Like the elusive fundamental equilibrium of exchange rats, a stock price index equilibrium can hardly be depicted as a point estimate that anyone could strongly believe in. Absolute purchasing power parity (ppp) and a value of Tobin's average "q" equal to unity are thin markers of equilibrium in view of all the exceptions that have been taken to interpreting these constructs in this way (for appraisals see Alan Shapiro, 1983; Frankel and Richard Meese, 1987; Dean Corbae and Sam Ouliaris, 1988; Mark Precious, 1987). However, if one could use the concept of an equilibrium stock index whose value rises predictably over time (with as little justification as the authors have provided by way of their fundamentals model that failed to test out), then, any rate of change in a stock index that persistently exceeds the equilibrium rate of change would lead to the formation of a bubble. It would be perfectly sufficient for the systematic part of that ultimately unsustainable rate of change to be constant and uncorrelated with past rates of change in the presence of noise. Hence, the outcome of tests of autoregression with a constant, conducted for potential bubbles and reported in the authors' table 3–5, cannot prove very much. Rather, if anomalies can give rise to a number of possible symptoms that may be encountered jointly or in isolation, deducing the absence of just one symptom may do little to lower the likelihood that anomalies are in fact present.

International Comovements

Just as the absence of a rare or unusual symptom of a disease does little to increase confidence that the patient being tested does not, in fact, have that disease, the authors' negative test results on international contagion effects between stock markets have very little power. These tests require stock price ratios to be stationary because innovations in one stock price index must eventually be communicated to the stock price index of another country, if stock prices are to ratchet up and down together internationally. Thus, the unit root test should be rejected if the contagion hypothesis is to remain viable in the authors' view. The outcome of such tests is likely to be time-dependent and not robust and may not show at all what is intended. We will develop these points one by one.

First, consider the following: If news arises just after the close of the New York Stock Exchange, it can start to be processed in the Tokyo market only the next day, with any possible ripples relayed to New York via the major intermediate stock exchanges such as London or Frankfurt. If the news is of common import around the globe and all markets react to it equally (equiproportionately) as soon as they can, one would therefore expect perfect comovement in stock prices to be registered on the date after the news broke. Any other tendency being absent, the stock price ratio would repeat, presumably near its stationary equilibrium, without helping to reject the unit root hypothesis.

Now consider what happens if the news breaks and is fully reflected while the New York market is still open. Stock prices in Tokyo, London, and Frankfurt follow the next day, but the wave of this news tide stops at the European edge of the Atlantic because New York already had time to adjust. There is then zero correlation between price movements in the New York market and price movements in all other markets on the same date (whether the date the news broke or the day after). While economically nothing would be different from the previous example, the data sequence would contribute to failing the unit root test: International stock price ratios on the same date would be disturbed and then return to their original levels.

In the real world news can break at any time, although expected news intensity will vary. Hence, even if the economic effect of a news event on stock prices were perfectly global, the test results for unit roots would depend on the timing of the release of news. Anyone who might then follow the authors in accepting the alternative hypothesis, that there have been no contagion effects between international stock markets, is invited to take a look at the numbers in table 3C–1. They show what very much appears to be comovement of first and second moments at a low frequency to the naked eye.

Of course, the naked eye has been torn out by economists long ago, since it has given our profession almost as much offense as bubbles. For this reason more technical considerations need to be raised about what correlations between national stock markets one might expect under

Table 3C–1. Indexes of Foreign Currency and Stock Prices, Quarterly Averages and Standard Deviation (1986:1–1988:1)

A. Indexes of the Foreign Currency Price of U.S. Dollar[1]

	1986				*1987*				*1988*
Quarter	*1*	*2*	*3*	*4*	*1*	*2*	*3*	*4*	*1*
JP Yen	100	90.4	83.0	85.4	81.5	76.0	78.3	72.2	68.1
DE Mark	100	95.6	88.8	85.4	78.4	76.9	78.3	72.7	71.4
GB Pound	100	95.5	96.9	100.7	93.5	87.8	89.1	82.2	80.2

B. Stock Price Index and Its Standard Deviation(s)[2]

	1986				*1987*				*1988*
Quarter	*1*	*2*	*3*	*4*	*1*	*2*	*3*	*4*	*1*
U.S. [585]	92.47	100.85	100.81	101.16	115.09	120.11	130.20	104.23	105.36
(s)	(4.70)	(2.04)	(3.19)	(2.23)	(5.58)	(3.40)	(3.77)	(11.91)	(3.24)
Japan [457]	67.24	79.59	92.36	94.14	112.04	136.95	130.25	119.69	124.20
(s)	(4.15)	(2.61)	(5.09)	(4.81)	(6.37)	(5.46)	(4.14)	(8.24)	(8.38)
Germany [94]	98.52	100.08	96.05	98.87	87.75	87.73	96.17	72.88	65.04
(s)	(3.11)	(5.34)	(5.17)	(1.71)	(5.19)	(2.19)	(2.41)	(11.95)	(3.61)
Britain [327]	88.51	97.11	96.00	97.14	113.02	127.44	140.04	109.98	108.74
(s)	(6.19)	(1.95)	(2.48)	(1.75)	(6.68)	(7.67)	(3.66)	(16.96)	(2.29)

[1] Quarterly averages of daily (noon) buying rates in New York prepared by U.S. Department of Commerce, Bureau of Economic Analysis in index form (1977 = 100) from data provided by the Federal Reserve Board, here rebased to 1986:1 = 100.

[2] Quarterly averages of daily (close) values of the FT (Financial Times)–Actuaries World Indices in local currency based on December 31, 1986 = 100. Figures in brackets show number of stocks included in the index for each country toward the end of the period shown.

various circumstances. How are these stock price movements to be measured? If exchange rates follow a random walk, as much research has been unable to refute (see Meese and Kenneth Rogoff [1988] for a recent appraisal), perfect capital mobility and risk neutrality would require that expected returns are equal in the respective *home* currencies of the different national indexes. Rebasing these indexes to dollars, as the authors have done, would add noise to the rates of return in all indexes outside the United States. Indeed, daily holding period returns on foreign stocks so defined would then likely be dominated by random exchange rate movements. As a result, inability to reject the unit root hypothesis for most countries would provide indirect confirmation of the random walk hypothesis of exchange rate movements and not amount to a definitive refutation of the proposition that stock prices ratchet up and down together internationally.

Obviously Dwyer and Hafer do not view exchange rate change as noise or as something that is not to be added to foreign rates of return and hence to the movement of their dollar-based stock prices from day to day. Instead, in order for the "Fisher-open" condition in their article to be supported, the real exchange rate must be expected to change to compensate for any difference in holding-period real rates of return between home and abroad. This, of course, was the reason why the authors placed all foreign stock indexes on a dollar basis before dividing them by the U.S. index, or each other's index, to construct the bilateral stock price ratios examined for unit roots. Their equation 3.14 requires that as long as any expected differences in real national rates of return exist, the real exchange rate must keep on changing. If real exchange rates are to approach fundamental equilibrium ($\bar{s}_t$) under this condition, then the total depreciation of the dollar from its elevated level $s_t > \bar{s}_t$, which coincides with a positive initial real rate of return differential for the United States, $r_t > r_t^*$ (as assumed before), must compensate all future real interest rate differentials expected. Assuming changes in $\bar{s}_t$ are not forecastable, the level of the foreign-currency price of the dollar k periods from now, s_{t+k}, must be expected (operator E) to be such that

$$E[(s_t/\bar{s}_t)/(s_{t+k}/\bar{s}_t)] = E \prod_{i=0}^{k-1} [(1 + r_{t+i})/(1 + r_{t+i}^*)]. \qquad (3C.5)$$

This equation can equally be expressed in logarithms (with periodic but continuously compounding rates of interest) as

$$E[\ln s_{t+k} - \ln \bar{s}_t] = \ln s_t - \ln \bar{s}_t - E\left[\sum_{i=0}^{k-1} (r_{t+i} - r_{t+i}^*)\right]. \qquad (3C.6)$$

Now, if the expected value of s_{t+k} is required ultimately to reach $\bar{s}_t$ as time distance from the present becomes large (as k goes to "infinity"), the real rate of return differntial, $r_{t+k} - r^*_{t+k}$, must decline to zero from its initial level of $r_t - r^*_t > 0$. It can then be shown that perceived changes in fundamentals may well be an important source of unequal percentage movements in the stock price indexes of different countries even after those indexes have been converted into dollars. For once s_{t+k} has approached $\bar{s}_t$, there must be the equality:

$$\ln s_t - \ln \bar{s}_t = E\left[\sum_{i=0}^{k-1} (r_{t+i} - r^*_{t+i})\right]. \tag{3C.7}$$

This implies that any systematic change in $\bar{s}_t$, due, for instance, to a perceived loss in U.S. international competitiveness ($d\ln\bar{s}_t < 0$) would have to be accompanied by unequal movements in expected national real rates of return. This would happen, for instance, if the authorities tried to defend the exchange rate ($d\ln s_t = 0$) when $\bar{s}_t$ falls. When pressure on exchange rates is countered by changes in international yield differentials, brought about by nonsterilized intervention, unequal movements in stock price indexes are likely to occur that would not be reversed as long as the pressure persists. They would thereby contribute to failure to reject the unit root test.

In the example just given, real interest rates could well rise and stock prices decline in the United States, causing initial holding period returns to be negative and raising *future* expected returns. There would be a lasting change in stock price ratios. Similarly, if there were no intervention and no change in yield differentials, the spot exchange rate, s_t, would fall as much as $\bar{s}_t$ right away, and dollar rates of return on foreign stock holdings would still be much greater than on U.S. dollar stocks during the process of adjustment. Since exchange rate considerations appear to have loomed large in the conduct of monetary policy in 1987, the complete absence of such considerations from the authors' article raises questions about their procedure of leaving this analysis largely uninformed by the economic background of their data period.

Another technical reason for unequal percentage changes in national stock price indexes, in the face of common factors that could easily leave stock price index ratios changed for many months, is that these indexes (from Morgan Stanley) are subject to composition effects. The authors inform us that they are constructed in such a way as to "match the industry profile of the country." Needless to say, there can be persistent differences in stock price developments by industry. There are marked differences between the industry profiles of, say, Australia and Germany due to the large weight of extractive industries, particularly metal mining and agricultural and animal products in the former. Differences between Japan and the United Kingdom appear, most notably, with regard to crude oil production. Hence, even if the stock market valuations of all companies within the same industries would fare identically around the globe, the national stock price indexes would normally move at different rates on account of composition effects. Under these conditions there could be a high degree of persistence in stock price ratio changes. This would work in favor of finding unit roots and rejecting international contagion when international stock market integration is, in fact, so complete in this example that industry effects are all that exist.

Thus we can come up with several reasons why the data should pass the unit root test conducted on ratios of dollar-based national stock price indexes by the authors, even if globalization of some important stock market impulses is complete. Other impulses, namely those that alter the relative position or prospects of national economies, would not produce identical rate of return experiences during adjustment under any conditions nor is there any reason to suppose that such impulses average out in the span of a few months. Thus, the outcome of unit root tests cannot be taken in any simple way to discriminate between country-specific and global processing or to say very much about their relative importance: There are too many reasons why such tests could falsely reject the hypothesis of contagion to make such failure as yet very informative. Nevertheless, what the tests lack in generality and sometimes in power of discrimination, they make up in rigor of specification. As a result, they lay foundation stones and provide points of orientation for future work, and this is a durable and conspicuous achievement.

Fundamentals

Having dismissed international contagion effects and commonalities as a result of tests with daily data, the authors turn to the first 15 years of monthly data under managed floating to study the effects of unexpected changes in fundamentals on real stock price index values in five countries. They are the G-5 countries minus France and plus Canada. The surprises in fundamentals generated as explanatory variables for real monthly stock price changes in the United States contain no reference to foreign developments at all. Instead they are limited to univariate forecasts of the U.S. monthly index of industrial production and to apparently unforecastable changes in long-term real interest rates. The equations estimated for the four other countries include these U.S. variables in addition to their own. They also contain the change in the bilateral real exchange rate of the U.S. dollar with the entire change treated as unexpected.

This rigorous U.S.-centric construction of the exchange rates that matter for the national stock price indexes of different countries is rather more apt for Canada than it is for Japan, Germany, or the United Kingdom. It yields results of significance only for Canada. Apparently, when the U.S. dollar price of the Canadian dollar goes up, so that the latter appreciates, stock prices in Canada tend to fall. A rise in Canadian interest rates would appear to have the same effect, but a rise in U.S. interest rates would also depress Canadian stocks insignificantly. Relations between long-term real interest differentials and real exchange rate changes remain unexplored, and the findings of Meese and Rogoff [1988] would lead us to expect little from any such investigation. Unexpected changes in dividends generated as the residual from a 12th-order (seasonally adjusting) autoregression (for the change in the logarithm of real dividends paid in any month on the stocks in each index) do not help explain real stock price changes either for Canada or (significantly) for any other country, including the United States.

How such findings may be explained and what they do, or do not, prove has been well explained by Allan Kleidon [1986]. Having already tackled at least two other important issues and derived an important theoretical result on stock valuation, Dwyer and Hafer have not been able to add much more to the discussion or how changing perceptions of fundamentals, and their influence on stock prices, should be modeled empirically. An interesting question that arises once again—one that could almost lead us back to sunspots and multiple equilibria with which this comment started—is whether major stock price movements of themselves can alter fundamentals. We end by marking this question with a quote from Hayne Leland and Mark Rubinstein [1988, p. 49] from after the crash of October 19, 1987:

> The U.S. market did not rebound because there may be only a few truly "value-based" investors who are willing to put their money down. Most investors are on the sidelines, implicitly confessing incompetence when it comes to security valuation, themselves confused about whether the crash could reflect a fundamental weakness in the economy. To the extent stocks take value from their perceived liquidity and to the extent the events of the week of October 19th revealed that the market was not as liquid as people believed, stocks are not worth as much today as they were prior to the crash. With thinner markets and with heightened uncertainty stemming from concern over rational expectations and the viability of market mechanisms, price volatility and bid-ask spreads have remained much higher than prior to the crash.

References

Corbae, Dean, and Ouliaris, Sam. 1985. "Cointegration and Tests of Purchasing Power Parity." *Review of Economics and Statistics* 70(3):508–511.

Frankel, Jeffrey A. 1985. "The Dazzling Dollar." *Brookings Papers on Economic Activity* 1:199–217.

———, and Meese, Richard. 1987. "Are Exchange Rates Excessively Variable?" Working Paper No. 2249. Cambridge, MA: National Bureau of Economic Research, May.

Jevons, W. Stanley. 1878. "Commercial Crises and Sunspots." *Nature* 19:33–37.

———. 1879. "Sunspots and Commercial Crises." *Nature* 19:588–590.

Kleidon, Allan W. 1986. "Variance Bounds Tests and Stock Price Valuation Models." *Journal of Political Economy* 94(5):953–1001.

Leland, Hayne, and Rubinstein, Mark. 1988. "Comments on the Market Crash: Six Months After." *Journal of Economic Perspectives* 2(3):45–50.

Meese, Richard, and Rogoff, Kenneth. 1988. "Was It Real? The Exchange Rate-Interest Differential Relation Over the Modern Floating-Rate Period." *Journal of Finance* 43(4):933–948.

Precious, Mark. 1987. *Rational Expectations, Non-Market Clearing, and Investment Theory* Oxford: Clarendon Press.

Shapiro, Alan C. 1983. "What Does Purchasing Power Parity Mean?" *Journal of International Money and Finance* 2(3):295–318.

4 ECONOMIC AND FINANCIAL DATA AS NONLINEAR PROCESSES*

James B. Ramsey

4.1. Introduction

The last decade has witnessed a resurgence of interest in nonlinearity as applied to a wide variety of disciplines including economics. This renewed interest has been occasioned by the development of new research tools and the growing disenchantment, in economics at least, with the forecasts that our linear models have produced. We have now come to the realization that models of money demand and supply of the stock market, of national aggregates, such as GNP, investment in plant and equipment, consumption, and savings, provide reasonable forecasts only in those cases where the models are not really needed, that is, where the next period is simply last period plus an approximately constant growth factor, or plus a random change with zero mean.

Efforts to forecast the effects of significant changes in the institutions of

* The support and technical services of the C. V. Starr Center for Applied Economics is gratefully acknowledged. I am pleased to thank Connie Dorfschmidt, Gerald Dwyer, and Charles de Bartolome for constructive comments.

an economy, such as the creation of a futures market, the development of new financial instruments, or a change in tax policy, or efforts to forecast the response to a substantial shift in industrial organization, such as the effective creation of OPEC, have all failed to meet reasonable requirements of forecasting usefulness. Notwithstanding our elaborate econometric sophistication and clever modeling, our predictions, even when right in qualitative terms, are seldom more informative than intuition guided by "first principles."

What is even more embarrassing is the discovery that many economic variables are easily transformed into "uncorrelated noise" by such simple procedures as taking log first differences. Alternatively and nearly as damaging, is the fact that log first differences may produce a simple low order autoregressive (AR) or moving average (MA) model, but seemingly with no further structure, except for some evidence of time varying variances.

Apparently this result indicates that the only information in economic time series is contained in the first two moments and those have been milked to little effect. A major question is whether or not analysis directed to non-linear relationships can detect anything that is not revealed by the current procedures. A related question is whether the discovery of non-linearity will yield innovations that are stationary; that is, whether any observed nonstationarity might be due to the presence of a nonlinear model.

The situation on the face of it is depressing. Economic forces do not seem to be much in evidence in economic or financial time series. Market fundamentals do not seem to matter, confirming the assumptions of the Black-Scholes model. Once common drift has been eliminated from economic or financial time series, the only possibility seemingly left for economic interaction is in the time variation of the variances of the series. Noise dominates.

As I will discuss in the body of this article, economic data are different from the data that are analyzed in biology, chemistry, physics, or pure statistical time series generated by simulation with linear models. We may not yet know what they are, but we can say what they are not. Economic data are not simple autoregressive-integrated-moving average (ARIMA) processes; they are not describable by simple linear structural models; they are not simple white noise; they are not random walks. Finally there is no evidence that there are any low-dimensional attractors, that is, there is no evidence of a deterministic nonlinear dynamical system with highly complicated behavior.

The time has come to reevaluate the analysis of economic data and more importantly to reconsider our basic modeling procedures. A key question is what type of modeling is most relevant and productive for economic data. For some of us the search is on to discover how economic data might be modeled in generic terms.

The next section of this article introduces some concepts of nonlinearity and tries to indicate what the potential advantages of a nonlinear approach might be. In this section it is claimed that, while there may be no evidence of chaos in real economic data, the ideas and concepts in the new literature on qualitative dynamics is nonetheless useful in providing insights. As a part of this discussion, system modeling is contrasted to the analysis of isolated time series in the following section.

The next short section identifies the economic and financial data series that have been examined as examples of the general conclusions to be drawn from this article.

The following section discusses some of the statistical tools that can be used to address some issues of nonlinearity and their possible occurrence in economic and financial data. Some empirical examples are worked up as illustrative exercises.

The final section is important in that it contains the conclusions and speculations about the empirical results. Particular attention is paid to the problem of forecasting, and some ideas are presented about what can be expected for forecast improvement from the use of nonlinear analysis. The key implication in this context is that the main benefits from a nonlinear analysis is in the timing of reactions to an intervention, as well as the ability to detect subtle possibilities for instabilities.

4.2. Why Nonlinear Dynamic Analysis?

Nonlinear dynamic models have a long and venerable history in economic analysis, both theoretical and empirical. The empirical literature began with the early work on cycles with which endeavor the name of Wesley C. Mitchell [1913] is justifiably linked, even if not the first. The theoretical literature began with the early articles of Frisch [1933], Samuelson [1939], Kalecki [1943], Hicks [1950], Goodwin [1951], Phillips [1954], and finally Goodwin [1972] to mention just a few of the classic works in the field of those that were interested in more than equilibrium or balanced growth. An amusing, iconoclastic, yet insightful, review of this literature is contained in Blatt [1983]. An item of interest in this connection is Baumol and Benhabib [1988].

Nonetheless, the analysis of nonlinear dynamic models cannot be said to have dominated center stage; they have remained exceptions to the mainstream of the literature, albeit often brilliant exceptions. This is surprising because the effectiveness of policy in a possibly nonlinear world depends so heavily upon getting the timing of policy decisions correct, as well as the important issue of the stability of even profitable speculation (see for example, Baumol [1957, 1961]).

Perhaps the best way to illustrate the role of nonlinear dynamics is to consider some examples. I will develop a simple model of market reaction to excess demand that is made more realistic step by step. None of the models is meant to be a serious candidate for the dynamical description of actual markets, but the discussion should be enlightening as to the potential role to be played by nonlinear systems.

The objective at this time is not to present models of immediate applicability, but to stress the inherent properties of a dynamical system. Some form of oscillatory behavior is at the root of all but the most trivial of dynamical systems. Thus, the equations that we will discuss below should be regarded as fundamental prototypes that have provided, not only useful insights, but practical predictions in an incredible array of disciplines. As simple prototypes, the equations to follow should be taken seriously; they are not just another economist's idea of a micro-relation.

We do know that excess demand creates economic forces that usually offset that excess demand. If that is so, then the initialization of that reaction must be through the acceleration of the change in excess demand. This is the basic key to understanding the main idea underlying the discussion to follow. The concept goes back at least to Samuelson, Goodwin, Kalecki, and Phillips.

4.2.1. Some Simple Alternative Dynamical Models of Market Ajustment

The first simple model will do some violence to the known strong interdependencies between markets and will not stress the role played by prices as equilibrating market forces. However, its very simplicity will enhance the ideas to be illustrated.

The symbol X designates for some market the amount of excess demand for a given commodity at a given point in time t. The commodity could as easily be shares of some stock as a specific real commodity such as wheat or cookies. X is assumed to be a continuously differentiable function of time t. At this stage of the analysis there is no random error component.

$\dot{X}$ designates the time derivative of X, it is the rate of flow of excess demand.

The total stock, or size of the market, is designated by S; S is assumed fixed for the purposes of this analysis as it determines the scale within which the effect of excess demand, denoted by X, operates.

$\ddot{X}$ is the acceleration in the change in excess demand; $\ddot{X}$ is a continuously differentiable function of time t. This idea is not only intuitively plausible; it is fundamental to the notion of oscillatory dynamics as both Samuelson and Goodwin realized so many years ago.

If economic forces are to react to an exogenous shock in excess demand in order to restore equilibrium, then to go from a zero velocity of excess demand to some nonzero velocity, the acceleration must first be nonnegative to achieve this result. What changes "first" is the acceleration in the excess demand and if the local linear system has a first necessary condition for stability, then the direction of the accelerated reaction is to oppose the displacement.

Price is an indicator function that translates demand and supply relationships into an excess demand function. Price is implicit in the formulation of this model. We can conclude from this formulation that

$$\dot{P} = k\dot{X}; \tag{4.1}$$

and therefore that

$$P = k_0 + kX, \tag{4.2}$$

where k and k_0 are constants that are determined by economic conditions and the units of measurement, k_0 is the equilibrium price. A more realistic model would recognize the lags that will exist between the occurrence of a nonnegative excess demand and a change in P and between the change in P and the acceleration of the 'restoring force'. This added complexity can be ignored for now as its effects are unessential for our current purposes.

If there has been a displacement in equilibrium by an amount X, the restoring force is assumed to be $-\sigma X$, where σ is the "coefficient of stiffness" in the restoring force; the greater the value of σ, the greater the economic force to restore the original equilibrium. We can now write our first "equation of motion" for our economic market,

$$\ddot{X} = -\sigma(X/S), \tag{4.3}$$

or,

$$S\ddot{X} + \sigma X = 0,$$

which can in turn be rewritten as

$$\ddot{X} + (\varkappa\eta)^2 X = 0. \tag{4.4}$$

The idea of equation 4.3 is that the restoring force accelerates the total stock against the displacement. Alternatively stated, the equation shows that the direction and magnitude of change is proportional to the relative size of the excess demand relative, that is, to the size of the total market.

Equation 4.4 anticipates results later in the article and indicates that σ/S can be reexpressed in terms of η, the frequency of oscillation of the response; that is,

$$\eta = 1/(2\pi)\ (\sigma/S)^{1/2}. \tag{4.5}$$

The constant $\varkappa$ in this simple case is 2π. Equation 4.5 shows that the frequency of response decreases in S, but increases in σ. This is as would be expected. The larger S, the larger the inertia of the system to a given size of displacement X. The larger the value of σ, the larger the restoring force, and so the greater the impact on the acceleration of change. As X approaches the value of zero, the acceleration slows as shown by equation 4.3.

It is easy to show that one expression for the general solution of the differential equation 4.3 is

$$X = a\sin(\omega t + \phi);\ \omega = (\varkappa\eta); \tag{4.6}$$

where a is the amplitude of the oscillation, ω is the natural frequency of oscillation, and ϕ is the phase; a and ϕ are determined by the initial conditions.

That equation 4.6 is a solution to equation 4.3 is easy to demonstrate by taking its derivative with respect to time twice:

$$\dot{X} = a\omega\cos(\omega t + \phi) \tag{4.7}$$

$$\ddot{X} = -a\omega^2\sin(\omega t + \phi) = -\omega^2 X. \tag{4.8}$$

These last two equations are interesting, notwithstanding the extreme simplicity of our defining differential equation. We see immediately that the first time derivative of excess demand, that is, the flow of excess demand, "leads" the state of excess demand, X, and the acceleration, $\ddot{X}$, by $\pi/2$ radians or 90°; lack of phase matching between the derivatives of a flow is not generally given much attention by economists. While the amplitude of the excess demand oscillation is a, that of the velocity is $a\omega$, where ω is defined in terms of radians modulo 2π; more precisely, the velocity has an amplitude of $a(\sigma/S)^{1/2}$ and the amplitude of oscillation of the acceleration is $a(\sigma/S)$. Thus, for a given amount of excess demand, the larger the size of the total market, the smaller the amplitude of the velocity of change. This is not surprising.

The current model is too simple even for physical applications, much less economic ones. As our first step towards approaching reality, let us modify equation 4.3 to allow for friction in, or damping of, the system; that is, let us assume that the acceleration in response to the restoring force is reduced in proportion to the velocity of change. We now have

$$S\ddot{X} = -\sigma X - \beta\dot{X}; \tag{4.9}$$

where $-\beta\dot{X}$ represents the effect of friction in the system.

Before continuing, it is useful to note that an alternative expression for the general solution to equation 4.3 is

$$aEXP\{i(\omega t + \phi)\},\ i = \sqrt{-1}, \tag{4.10}$$

where the constants have the same interpretation as before.

The general solution of equation 4.9 is of the type $X = CEXP\{\alpha t\}$, where C is a constant to be determined by initial conditions and α may be complex. If we substitute this suggestion into equation 4.9 we obtain:

$$CEXP\{\alpha t\}\ (S\alpha^2 + \beta\alpha + \sigma) = 0, \tag{4.11}$$

and solving this equation yields the result

$$\alpha = -\beta/(2S) \pm \{\beta^2/4S^2 - \sigma/S\}^{1/2}. \tag{4.12}$$

There are, as is well known, three types of results depending on the sign of the term in curly brackets in equation 4.12. If the term in { } is positive, that is the damping effect outweighs the restoring effect, it can be shown that the general solution is expressible in terms of hyperbolic sines and cosines. The solution path of excess demand, X, increases at first, then decreases to produce a single humped curve as a function of time; there are no oscillations.

The case where the term in { } is zero is not of great interest in this case, being merely a boundary situation between the one just discussed and that to follow.

The last situation is one in which there are complex conjugate roots for the solution of α. The solution can be written

$$X = AEXP\{\ (-\beta/2S)t\}\sin(\omega' t + \phi), \tag{4.13}$$

where ω' is given by

$$\omega' = (\sigma/S - \beta^2/4S^2)^{1/2}. \tag{4.14}$$

Clearly, this solution path is a damped oscillatory one where the damping effect depends on the damping coefficient and the size of the total market or the total volume of the stock of the commodity being traded. The rate at which the oscillations decay to zero is given by $\beta/2S$. It is also useful to note that the natural frequency of oscillation of this damped system differs from the undamped system. From equation 4.14, it is clear that the frequency of the damped system is less by $\beta^2/4S^2$ and that the larger the market, the lower the frequency of oscillation. The undamped system's frequency decreases according to $\sqrt{S}$. But, while the damped system's frequency also decreases according to $\sqrt{S}$, the difference between the two frequencies itself decreases for larger S; that is, for very large markets. The difference in frequency of oscillation between damped and undamped systems is small.

So far we have concentrated on linear versions of the market reaction to a single impulse shock. We might consider the effect of a series of random shocks on the solution path, but a more informative alternative to begin with is to consider a sinusoidal path of shocks to the market system. We can define the effect of the "forcing function" by:

$$S\ddot{X} + \beta\dot{X} + \sigma X = \delta\cos(\psi t), \tag{4.15}$$

where ψ is the frequency of the "forcing equation" and δ is an appropriate constant. The idea is that excess demand in our market of interest is stimulated by activities elsewhere, for example, excess demand in some other competitive or complementary market, or an oscillation in the exogenous factors determining demand or supply that are not included in the formulation of our basic differential equation 4.3.

There are two components to the solution, the first is the solution to the homogeneous portion of equation 4.15, but that solution is the same as the solution to equation 4.9. This part of the solution is the transient part of the solution. Our more important concern is for the long-term dynamics, and that solution is given by a solution to the nonhomogeneous equation.

The real part of that solution is

$$X = (\delta/(\psi Z))\sin(\psi t - \phi), \tag{4.16}$$

$$\dot{X} = (\delta/Z)\cos(\psi t - \phi), \tag{4.17}$$

where

$$Z = [\beta^2 + (\psi S - \sigma/\psi)^2]^{1/2}.$$

The quantity of excess demand and its velocity differ in phase by $\pi/2$ as before, but more importantly velocity and the forcing term also differ in phase by ϕ, where

$$\mathrm{Tan}(\phi) = (\psi S - \sigma/\psi)/\beta. \tag{4.18}$$

The importance of this result is that if ϕ is zero then, but only then, are the forcing term and the velocity in phase; that is, only when ψ satisfies the equation $\psi S - \sigma/\psi = 0$.

Otherwise, we see that for low frequencies $\dot{X}$ leads the forcing term and for high frequencies $\dot{X}$ lags the forcing term. This seemingly innocuous statement is potentially important for empirical research because it points up clearly that the timing relationship between exogenous shocks and the response in velocity may vary from leading to lagging and only in rare circumstances will the two be in phase. Parenthetically, we might note that economists do not often, if ever, consider the possibility that $\dot{X}$ will lead the forcing term.

Before leaving these simple linear models, we should consider one last possibility, that of the damping factor being close to zero. In this case, if the natural frequency of the harmonic oscillation, ω, in equation 4.6 is incommensurate with ψ, the frequency of the forcing term (that is, ω/ψ is not a rational), then the oscillations of the forced system are said to be quasi-periodic. A quasi-periodic oscillation is one that returns to any neighborhood of a given point infinitely often, but never repeats its path exactly. At least in one respect we have at last achieved a result that is a characteristic of economic data.

The introduction of nonlinearity into these models can be achieved in either of two nonexclusive ways. We can allow the stiffness coefficient to be a nonlinear function of X, the quantity of excess demand, or we can recognize the importance of modifying the damping factor.

A very simple model to illustrate anharmonic oscillators is to return to the undamped model with a forcing term. The main change in the model is that now we allow the stiffness coefficient to be a function of X and not a constant. Let us retain the symmetry of the reaction in terms of the sign of X by setting

$$\sigma(X) = -(\sigma_1 X + \sigma_3 X^3), \tag{4.19}$$

where the basic equation of motion is

$$S\ddot{X} + \sigma(X) = \delta\cos(\psi t). \tag{4.20}$$

As in the previous equations, the first-order response might naturally be thought to be positive, i.e., $\sigma_1 > 0$. But now we have a choice for the sign of σ_3. If σ_3 is positive, the nonlinear term reinforces the linear part, or the reaction to a displacement is even greater than in the linear case. If σ_3 is negative, then the restoring force is less.

The other way in which we can obtain a nonlinear model is to modify the damping term. Our basic linear differential equation that described damped harmonic motion in equation 4.9 is only an approximation for small amplitudes. The equation indicates that if β is negative, there is anti-damping, and the energy of the system would increase indefinitely. This result is not at all plausible, even if it might be for very small displacements. A simple and well-known procedure to overcome this problem is to make β, the friction coefficient, a nonlinear function of X, the displacement. Let us allow for the friction coefficient to be negative for very small displacements, X, and to be positive for large displacements; that is, the system generates energy for small values of X and dissipates it for large values. Let $\beta(X)$ be defined by

$$\beta(X) = -\beta_0[1-(X/X_0)^2],\ \beta_0 > 0; \tag{4.21}$$

so that for small X, $\beta(X)$ is negative and for large X, $\beta(X)$ is positive; X_0 is a parameter of the system that determines what constitutes large or small. If this definition for β is substituted into equation 4.9, the resulting expression is called the Van der Pol equation. Our full equation is

$$S\ddot{X} + \beta(X)X + \sigma X = 0. \tag{4.22}$$

The economic interpretation is that for relatively small amounts of excess demand the restoring force is offset by the velocity term, but that if the excess demand gets to be too large, then the usual process applies. Intuitive examples might be the demand for the equity stock of some firm or the demand for a popular restaurant, where *popular* is defined by positive excess demand. In this formulation, the equation holds even when the excess demand is negative (that is, there is excess supply) in which case the intuition may be less appealing. In both cases, small changes from equilibrium have destabilizing components.

The solution of this equation is a limit cycle; small deviations from the unstable equilibrium, called the *center*, diverge out to the limit cycle, but large displacements converge to the limit cycle. By choosing the unit of time to be one period, i.e., $1/(\sigma/S)^{1/2}$, and by a suitable choice of units for the amplitude, we can simplify equation 4.22 to read:

$$\ddot{X} -(\varepsilon - X^2)\dot{X} + X = 0, \tag{4.22'}$$

where ε is β_0/ω, $\omega^2 = \sigma/S$. For small values of ε, the limit cycle is nearly sinusoidal and the oscillations are nearly symmetric, but as ε gets bigger, the limit cycle ceases to be symmetric and the amplitude has a "saw tooth" shape.

This is the first time that we have had a need for a phase diagram. A phase diagram is a diagram of the phase space. Phase space is the space of all possible states of the system as described by a suitable choice of coordinates, or variables. The phase space summarizes the long-term dynamics of the system, when the points that are due to transients created by specific initial conditions, are deleted. The set of points in phase space towards which the actual dynamical path is converging is called the (forward) limit set. The limit set might be a fixed point, a limit cycle, or a chaotic attractor, or a strange attractor; the attractor is simply the "attracting set" of the dynamical path.

Consider a very simple example. The frictionless pendulum when once started by some force will keep oscillating at a constant frequency and a fixed amplitude. The phase space for this example can be expressed either in terms of the angle of deviation of the pendulum from the vertical, θ_t, and the velocity, v_t; or in terms of θ_t and its first derivative, θ_t'; or in terms of v_t and its first derivative, v_t'. The phase plot produced in any one of the three cases is qualitatively the same. As will be justified later, we can also obtain the same qualitative phase plot by plotting either v_t or θ_t on suitably lagged values of itself. The choice of lag is to produce pairs $(v_t, v_{t-\tau})$, $(\theta_t, \theta_{t-\tau})$ such that the autocorrelations of lag τ are approximately zero.

An example of a phase diagram is shown in figure 4–1 in which $\dot{\theta}_t$ is plotted against θ_t for angles measured from the vertical that is normalized to zero. The rate of change of θ is minimal, zero in fact, when θ has reached its maximum value either side of the vertical. Correspondingly, when θ_t is 0, $\dot{\theta}_t$ is maximal; the lower side of the nearly circular plot represents the pendulum swinging from right to left and the upper side of the plot represents the pendulum swinging from left to right. It is a

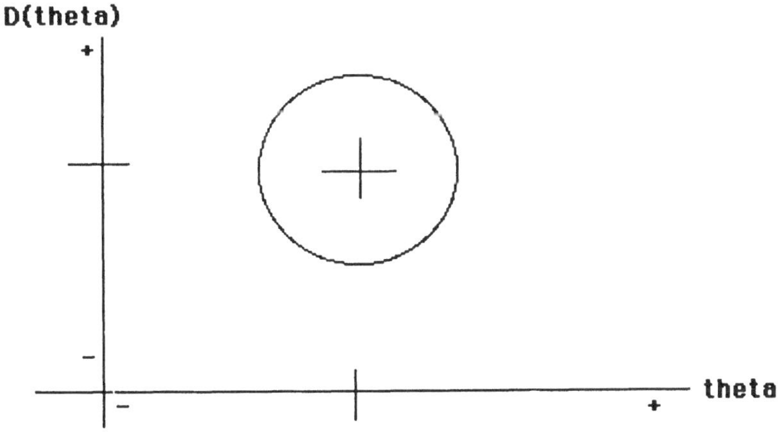

Figure 4–1. Illustration of Phase Plots

remarkable fact that the same shape of plot can be obtained by any one of the combinations of variables chosen to represent the dynamical system.

In our examples above, the phase space could be represented by the pairs $(X, \dot{X})$ that were consistent with the flow, or solution, to the differential equations defining the dynamic system. For the damped oscillator when ε is small, the phase diagram for equation 4.22 is nearly a circle as in figure 4–1, but when ε is large, the phase diagram is approximately the shape of a tilted rectangle. In any case, the phase space diagram usually demonstrates the long-term dynamics of the system. The dynamics are called long term because the idea is to examine the path of the dynamical system long after the transient behavior has died out, that is, after the dependence of the path on the initial conditions has been reduced to near zero.

The points in the long-term solution set that are represented by the phase space diagram is known as an attractor, an obvious choice of terms because it *attracts* the solution paths of all dynamical orbits that start at least sufficiently close to the attracting set, or *attractor*.

As an aside, the class of models defined by equation 4.22 can be used to illustrate the concepts of both supercritical and subcritical bifurcations, that is, qualitative shifts in behavior as one of the parameters passes a critical value. See for example, Bergé, Pomeau, and Vidal [1984], or Guckenheimer and Holmes [1983].

In addition, this model can also illustrate the idea of hysteresis [Bergé, Pomeau, and Vidal, 1984, p. 42] that will be discussed later. Hysteresis can be intuitively defined in terms of a nonuniqueness in a response function so that when the unstable portion of the response function is reached the response *jumps* across the unstable portion; the point at which this occurs differs depending on the direction from which the unstable portion is reached. The idea is illustrated in figure 4–2. If inputs are being increased, the output function is continuous up to the point t_1, at which point the output continues on the lower (stable) branch of the output response function. However, if the input level is being reduced from above the point t_1, then the path is continuous along the curve down to t_0, at which point the response jumps to the upper (stable) portion of the function and as the input continues to decline the output declines continuously thereafter.

While these possibilities are interesting, a more specific example would be instructive. We can combine our previous experiments into one general, but still very simple, statement. The following equation is known as Duffing's equation; by now its constituent parts are familiar:

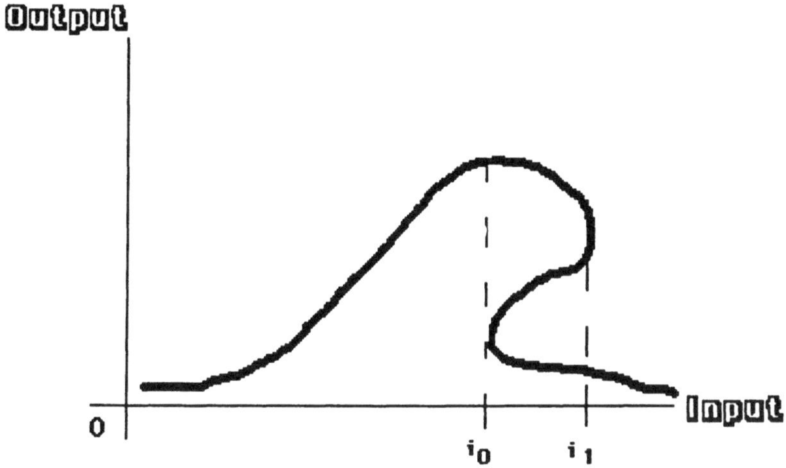

Figure 4–2. Illustration of Hysteresis Effects

$$\ddot{X} + \delta\dot{X} - \beta X + X^3 = \gamma\cos(\omega t). \tag{4.23}$$

Equation 4.23 has been expressed in the simplest possible manner, instead of in terms of economically meaningful coefficients in order to shorten an already lengthy discussion.

$\gamma\cos(\omega t)$ is the forcing term. $\delta\dot{X}$ is the damping factor, assumed once again to be linear, but positive. The term $-\beta X + X^3$ is the nonlinear version of the stiffness coefficient first defined in equation 4.19. But in this version there is an important difference. The sign of the coefficient for the X term is negative in equation 4.23, while that of X^3 is positive; contrast the situation shown in equation 4.19. The dynamical effect is that for small changes in excess demand the market reacts in an unstable manner in that the excess demand is reinforced by the reactive force, but as the excess demand builds, the final effect is strongly in the opposite (stabilizing) direction.

Simple though this equation is, the potentially observable results are dramatically different. So far all our models have generated recognizably deterministic solution paths, even if the time paths of the solutions apparently involve discontinuous jumps. Our solution paths have all involved fixed points, periodic solutions, or the discontinuous hysteresis effects alluded to just above. The Duffing model in contrast can produce time paths of solutions that appear to be the realizations of random variables, certainly the paths are not periodic, see, for example, Kawakami [1984]. Here at last is our first example of a chaotic attractor as opposed to our earlier examples of attractors that were fixed points or simple cycles.

The first of the two keys to this dramatic shift in the properties of the solution path is that one requires solution paths that are characterized by exponential divergence of nearby paths, the so-called sensitivity to initial conditions. The second key is that the limit set of the long-term solution path, that is, the ultimate path of the long-term dynamics, must be compact. The mathematically inevitable result is that while the time paths are recurrent, the exact same path is never followed twice.

These verbal comments are illustrated in figures 4–3 to 4–7. In figure 4–3 we see the time path of the solution of equation 4.23 and figure 4–4 shows the corresponding phase diagram. The parameter values chosen for this solution were $\delta = .3$, $\beta = -1$, $\gamma = .3$, and $\omega = 1$. By changing δ to .05, setting β to 0, and raising γ to 7.5, the more chaotic data shown in figures 4–5 to 4–7 were produced. The choice of a lag of 40 for the phase plots was dictated by the necessity to plot points at a nearly zero auto-correlation lag in order to emphasize the shape of the attractor.

The generation of statistical complexity that we have observed in this last version of our excess demand model can easily be supplemented by adding to the model specification the presence of lags, or delays, in the reaction mechanism. As is now well known to dynamicists, the addition of delays in a differential equation essentially introduces an infinite number of degrees of freedom into the system, so that even more complex solutions are possible. See, for example, the analysis of the Mackey-Glass [1977] equation. Delays are an obvious extension to economic models as has already been mentioned. One would expect a delay between the occurrence of excess demand and the onset of the reaction, in part because the reaction must usually work through prices, and one would expect a delay between the occurrence of excess demand and a consequent change in price.

So as not to elaborate endlessly, let me merely indicate some further behavioral alternatives that nonlinear relationships can generate without necessarily tying them to the models discussed above. Some of the concepts that should be mentioned are amplitude-frequency dependence, frequency entrainment, and time reversibility.

Amplitude-frequency dependence is characterized by time series in which two or more frequency components occur with their own characteristic amplitudes and the series oscillates between the two components. Amplitude-frequency dependence is ostensibly quite a common observation in economic data. U.S. foreign exchange data certainly has the appearance

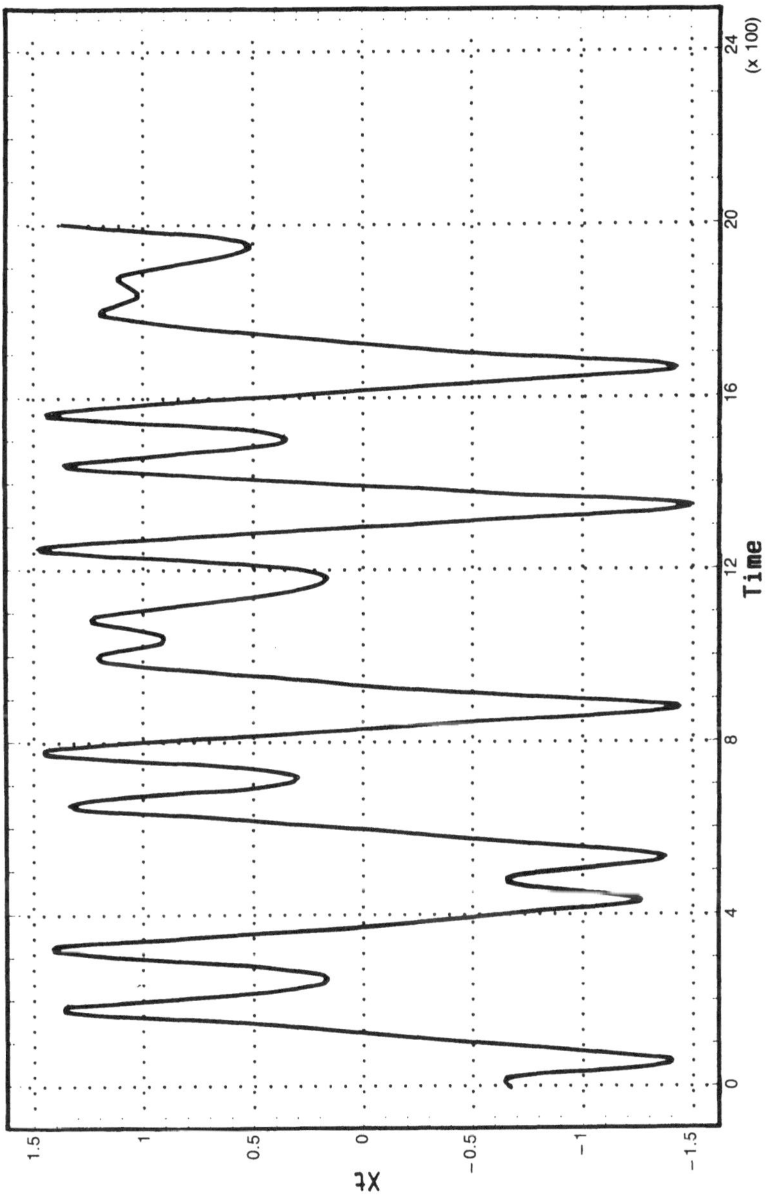

Figure 4–3. Time Sequence Plot: Duffing's Equation near Periodic Solution Path

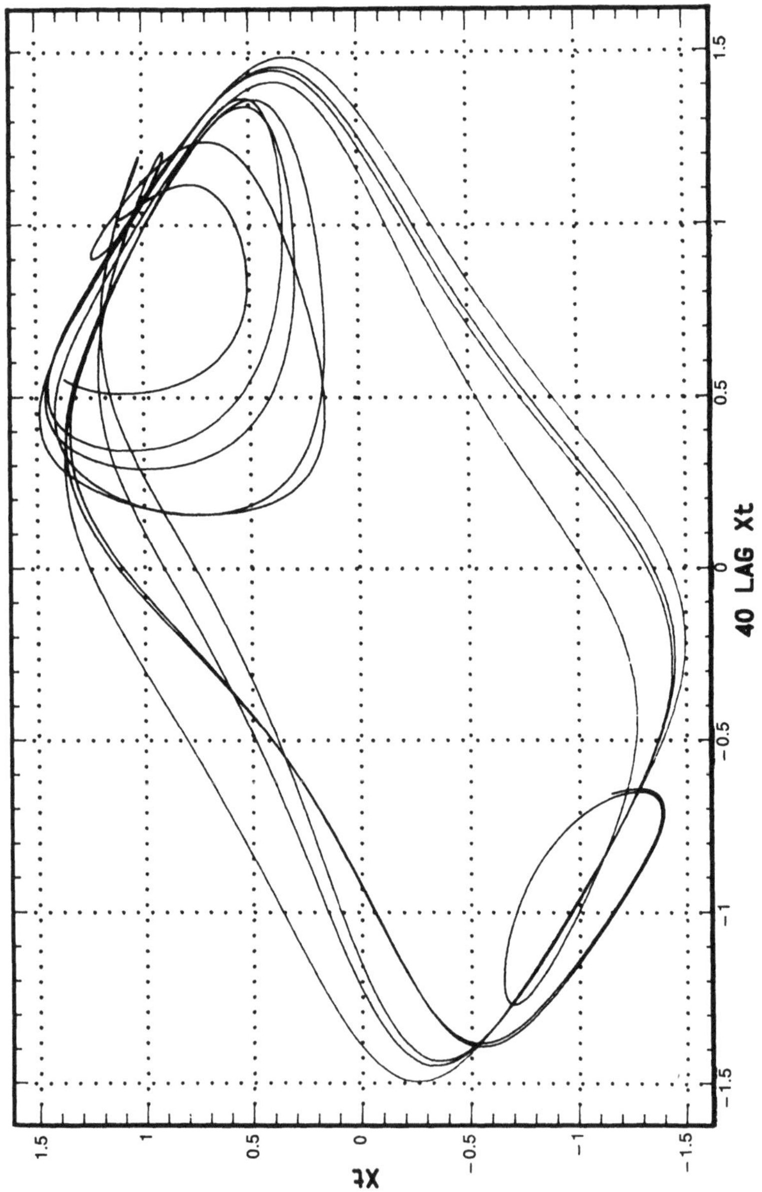

Figure 4–4. Phase Diagram for the Duffing's Equation near Periodic Solution Path

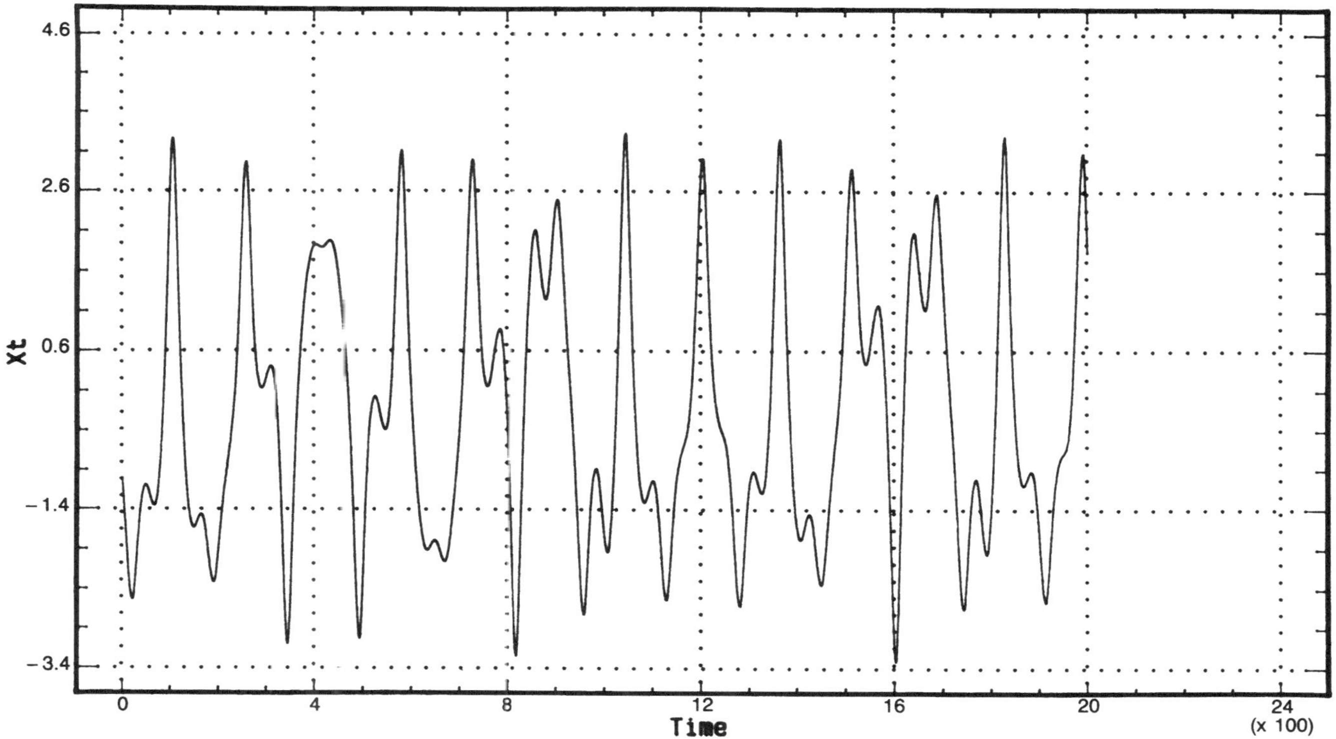

Figure 4−5. Time Sequence Plot: Duffing's Equation (Chaotic Path)

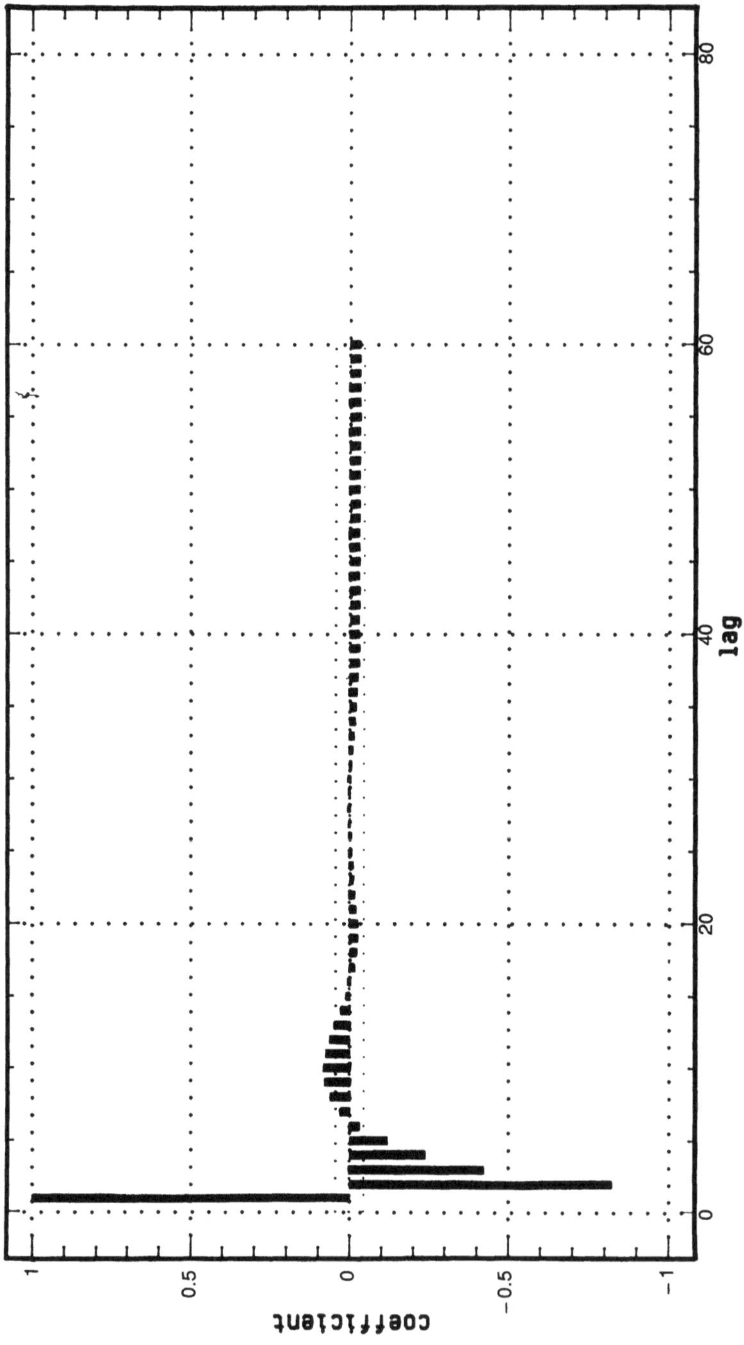

Figure 4–6. Estimated Partial Autocorrelations for Duffing's Equation (Chaotic Path)

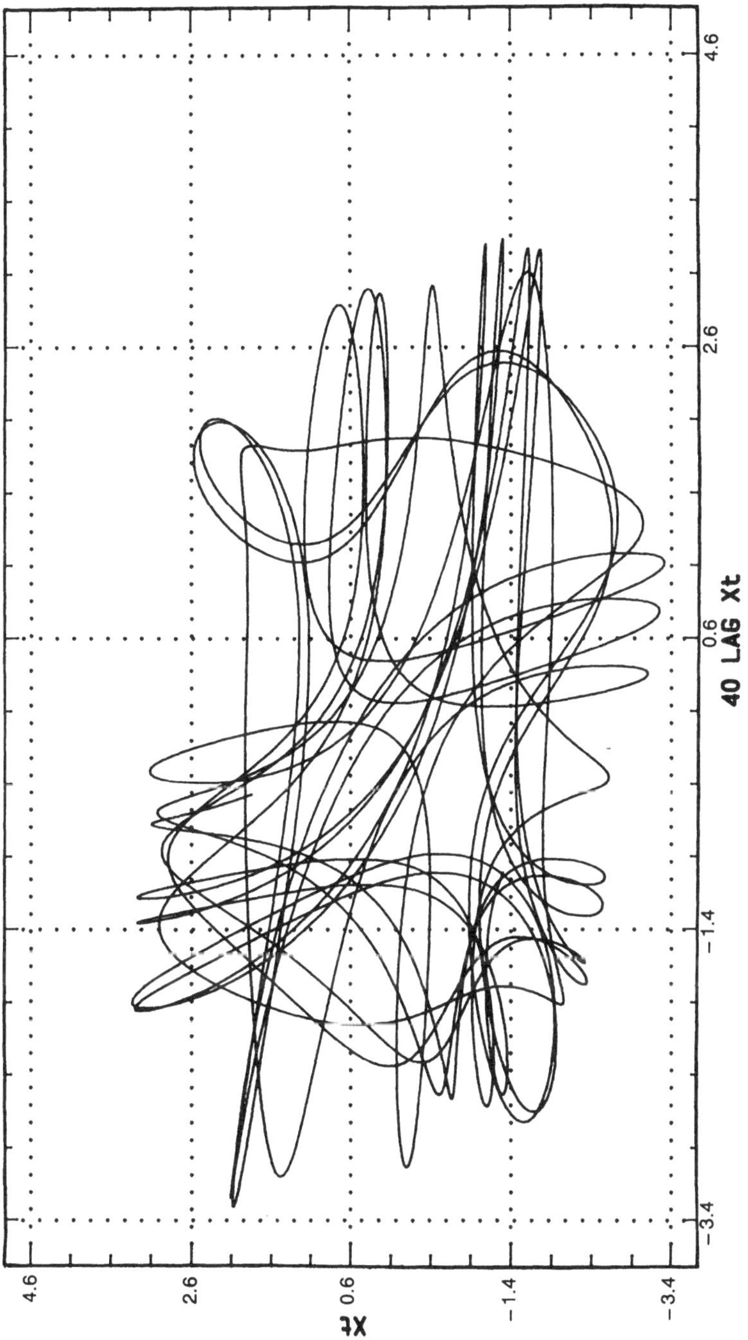

Figure 4–7. Phase Diagram for Duffing's Equation (Chaotic Example)

of this in that the exchange rate with respect to most major currencies has the characteristic of high-frequency, low-amplitude oscillations interspersed with low-frequency, high-amplitude oscillations. Stock market data have a similar appearance, but not as pronounced.

Frequency entrainment, or frequency locking, is a very common phenomenon in the physical sciences; the phenomenon occurs when two or more nearby frequencies are attracted to a common frequency. It is plausible that the idea may also have relevance in economics insofar as there exist economic phenomena that exhibit sinusoidal behavior, even if buried in noise. Imagine a nonlinear market system oscillating with a frequency ω_0. Now consider the effect of a complementary market that has an oscillation with a frequency of ω_1. The frequency of the combined market has a frequency of $\omega_0 - \omega_1$ called the "beat frequency," which will decrease linearly as ω_1 increases towards ω_0. However, as ω_1 approaches ω_0 the beat frequency suddenly drops to zero until the frequency ω_1 has risen substantially above the frequency ω_0, at which point the beat frequency reappears and then will increase linearly as ω_1 diverges from ω_0. The same phenomenon occurs for ω_1 approaching ω_0 from above. One interesting speculation is that if related economic markets differ in frequency by small amounts, then the frequency of the resultant joint market will not be perceptible, whereas disaggregation and separation of the markets would eventually reveal the nature of the oscillation.

The last example is the concept of "time reversibility". Time reversibility can be defined statistically:

$$F(x_{t1}, X_{t2}, x_{t3}, \ldots, x_{tn}) = F(x_{-t1}, x_{-t2}, x_{-t3}, \ldots, x_{-tn}); \quad (4.24)$$

that is, if the joint probability distribution function is characterized by equation 4.24, the time series $\{x_{ti}\}$ is said to be "time reversible" and if not, then the series is said to be "time irreversible;" the essential idea is that the "picture show does not run backwards." Both stationary and nonstationary processes may be time irreversible and reversible, but any ARMA process with Gaussian distribution, including noninvertible processes, is time reversible.

This idea would be unremarkable if it were not the case that virtually all economic models implicitly assume that economic time series are time reversible. One hint that one is dealing with a time irreversible process is that the time series exhibits asymmetries in the "slopes" of the upward portion of the series as compared to the downward portion of the series. By this criterion one should immediately suspect that GNP statistics may be time irreversible. Further discussion of this important topic is contained in Tong [1983] and in Ramsey and Rothman [1988].

4.3. System Modeling or the Analysis of an Isolated Time Series

The traditional approach to economic modeling for some considerable time now has been one of analyzing a complete market, if not an entire economy that is described by a set of simultaneous behavioral equations. The known strong interdependencies between markets (the problem of identification of a singly specified equation) seemed to necessitate the use of multiple equations and many variables. Let me label this approach the *system modeling approach*. It is the basis for almost all of the literature since the beginning of the 1950s until the introduction of the vector autoregressive models and what might be labeled the *Sims' methodology*. One advantage of the chaos literature is to add a third alternative.

The key to the modeling approach in the new qualitative dynamics literature is the "reconstruction of phase space," a concept that was introduced above. For an excellent introduction to the language of dynamical systems, see Arnold [1985], or for some very brief intuitive comments on phase space reconstruction see the appendix.

In practice, phase spaces are reconstructed by the following procedure. The graph of the flow is related to the phase space by tracing in that phase space the time dependent path created by linking time successive points from the flow of the dynamical system. As we saw, the qualitative properties of the phase space can be obtained by plotting either the actual variables in the system, one of the variables in the system together with enough of its time derivatives, or most easily by plotting lagged values of one of the variables in the system. The lag length must be chosen to emphasize the shape of the attractor, and that is done approximately by choosing the lag such that the auto-correlation is approximately zero. Essentially this procedure of choosing the zero auto-correlation lags provides a nearly orthogonal basis for representing the attractor.

An analysis of phase space and its changes to variations in the parameters of the dynamical system can reveal a wealth of qualitative information about the system: the presence of fixed points, of cycles, the stability of fixed points or of cycles, the existence of singularities in the system, and so on. This is why physicists pay so much attention to phase space, especially when the phase space can be portrayed graphically.

The natural coordinates to use are often those of the state of the system: its position, its velocity, and so on. The phase space of a dynamical system can also be represented in terms of the dynamical path of just one of the natural coordinates of the system, or even in terms of some monotonic but nonconstant transformation of a natural coordinate. If the dimension, that is, "the number of essential variables, or coordinates, of the system", is $\varkappa$, then the vector representation of the system in terms of one of the original coordinates must be in terms of a $\varkappa$ dimensional vector. For example, one might consider a sequence of $\varkappa$ dimensional points $\{x, D(x), D^2(x), D^3(x), \ldots, D^{\varkappa}(x)\}_t$, t indicating a sequence of observations through time in order to represent the phase space of the original system. An alternative and often equally useful, but simpler procedure is to use $\{x_t, x_{t+r}, x_{t+2r}, \ldots, X_{t+\varkappa r}\}$ for some suitable choice of r. This last procedure has become the standard procedure in most of the chaotic dynamics literature.

The formal justification for this approach to representing phase space is due to Ruelle and Takens [1971], but the mathematical antecedents are due to Whitney's Embedding theorem [Whitney, 1944]. While the theorem was proven only when the limit set of the dynamical system is a smooth manifold, it is a remarkable fact that in very many actual examples phase space reconstruction has worked for a wide variety of nonsmooth, fragmented limit sets.

Why phase space reconstruction works is perhaps intuitively clear. The flow, or solution path, of the differential equation system is unique, so that the parametric equations of the flow, $\{x_t, y_t, z_t, w_t\}$ say, can, under suitable regularity conditions, be mapped bijectively onto the parametric equations $\{x_t, D(x_t), D^2(x_t), D^3(x_t)\}$, which in turn can be mapped bijectively onto $\{x_t, x_{t+r}, x_{t+2r}, x_{t+3r}\}$. A bijective mapping is one that is both one to one and onto.

This is the justification for examining, at least to begin with, a single time series in the chaotic literature. The phase space reconstruction from observations on a single variable can provide the same qualitative information as observations on the path of the complete set of natural coordinates.

Of course, this approach to modeling implies that if one were to do two reconstructions of phase space from two coordinates of a dynamical system, say x_t and w_t, then up to scale transformations and inessential rotations of axes, the reconstructions should be the same; although there is a difficulty that we are skirting for now in the appropriate choice of the delay r to be chosen in each case. In terms of our previous examples, it will not matter whether we use excess demand, X, or price, P, to reconstruct the phase diagram, and both reconstructions should be qualitatively the same.

This approach provides a strong test for the presence of underlying systematic variation in economic or financial data: Make two phase space reconstructions and compare them. The difficulty in implementing this research strategy is that while these comments appear to be relevant to specific individual markets, the implication for aggregates is not so clear.

This is especially true if there are small but detectable differences in the phases of the constituent time series, or if the series being considered have close but distinct frequencies and what we observe is the beat frequency of the combination.

Before leaving this section, these notions can be tied into the concept of identification. The conditions for the identification of a subsystem can be restated as requiring two sets of conditions. The first is that the transformation from the exogenous variables of the system to the observed endogenous variables of the system be unique up to inessential scale transformations. The second requirement, not usually emphasized in econometrics, is that the implicit dynamical system represented by the time path of the exogenous variables be the flow of a corresponding differential equation system that describes the equations of motion of the market or economic system.

The identifying condition in econometrics is usually stated in terms of the rank of the matrix of exogenous variables, but my previous statement emphasizes the dynamical nature of the data. Identification is achievable in reality when the path of the exogenous variables, say $\overleftarrow{z}_t$, is a flow of some dynamical system. The observed behavioral relations to be identified have to be nonsingular transformations of the dynamical system path described by the time path of the vectors $\overleftarrow{z}_t$.

The conditions for the identification of the equation of a single endogenous variables are less stringent but similar in spirit to the ideas just discussed. That is, if the "identifying omitted variables" do not produce a unique path, then their omission is irrelevant to the identifiability of the equation.

The conclusion of this subsection is that as a first step and as a device for learning about the qualitative properties of the dynamical system, the analysis of a single representative "variable," or coordinate, is a useful approach. Clearly, having established the nature of the dynamical system, further work would require the determination of the structural links between the various economic variables of theoretical interest. Such an examination would now be cast within the context of known properties of the dynamical system.

4.4. The Data Used for Illustrative Examples

The data to be used for an extensive but preliminary analysis of these ideas are described in this section. The financial data series include: post-World War II observations on the "supply of money" (M1 and M2), weekly observations on the stock market obtained from the Center for Research in Security Prices (CRSP), and by contrast, economic data on monthly pig iron production since 1877.

The money supply data are the figures produced by the Federal Reserve Board, not Barnett's Divisia indices that some researchers (including myself) have previously used. The money supply observations are monthly figures from January 1959 to November 1987 on M1 and M2. The source is the Federal Research Report, H.6, *Money Stock Measures and Liquid Assets*.

Scheinkman and Le Baron used the CRSP data. These data are value-weighted daily stock returns, with a sample size of 5200 daily returns. Weekly returns were obtained by the simple compounding of the daily returns; the details are contained in Scheinkman and Le Baron [1986]. There are 1227 weekly averaged observations that begin in July 1962 and end in August 1985.

For a contrast, I have also included economic data—in this case—the production of pig iron since 1877 on a monthly basis to 1964. The data series are in two parts; the first part goes from 1877 to 1941 and the second series from 1941 to 1964. The first series was collected by R. F. Macaulay and is stored on the National Bureau of Economic Research (NBER) data tapes. The second set was obtained through the NBER, but the data originated from the American Iron and Steel Institute. The two series overlap for 12 months in 1941. The series were spliced by the simple expedient of averaging the difference in the overlap values and adding the difference to the second series.

Further details can be obtained from the NBER, New York.

4.5. An Empirical Description of Some Economic and Financial Data

The intent of this section is not meant to be in the least definitive, but to indicate some of the tools available and to give some idea of the evidence in favor of nonlinear models in economic and financial data. An essential element in understanding this analysis is that widely differing nonlinear models may have the same autocorrelation function and as a special case may have an autocorrelation function that is identically zero. Consequently, the description of data by auto-correlation functions is irrelevant to the analysis of the nonlinear structure.

However, an issue of some importance is the stationarity of the data. The usual nonlinear analysis of physical or biological data starts with the assumption that the data are, or have been transformed to, stationarity. Further, the most common models of nonlinearity yield steady states that can be described statistically by stationarity. Economic and financial data are not by any means stationary. Economists have become used to transformations to induce first-order stationarity, but until recently have tended to stick to transformations that induced only first-order stationarity, for example, taking log first differences. It is now common knowledge that both economic and financial data are not even second-order stationary. See for example, Bollerslev and Engle with associated references in the bibliography. The data may be nonstationary to an even higher degree, but that is an unexplored issue at the moment.

As a consequence of this discussion, the pig iron production data were transformed to be at least second-order stationary. The procedure used, in the absence of any theoretical information as to the form of the nonstationarity, was to deflate the first-order stationary data by a local approximation of the standard deviation. The approximation to the local standard deviation is obtained by calculating a moving average variance of the first-order stationary data and then deflating each observation by the square root of the approximate variance so found. This procedure adds to the degree of auto-correlation in the data. But in any event, the observed auto-correlation in the transformed data is allowed for in the analysis to follow.

There are two statistical tools to be discussed in the remainder of this article. First is the concept of dimension, or rather, the various concepts of dimension. Second is the notion of time irreversibility and a new procedure to test for its presence.

4.5.1. Dimensional Analysis in Economic and Financial Data

At this point some of the concepts of dimension have become familiar to economists, even if some of them are not well understood. The correlation dimension, a measure of the relative rate of scaling of the density of points within a given space, permits a researcher to obtain topological information about the underlying system generating the observed data without requiring *a prior* commitment to a given structural model. If the time series is a realization of a random variable, the correlation dimension estimate should increase monotonically with the dimensionality of the space within which the points are contained. By contrast, if a low correlation dimension is obtained, this provides an indication that additional structure exists in the time series—structure that may be useful for forecasting purposes. In this way, the correlation dimension estimates may prove useful to economists wishing to scrutinize uncorrelated time series or the residuals from fitted linear time series models for information on possible nonlinear structure.

The appendix contains a brief but intuitive discussion of the various concepts of dimension that appear in the literature of physical sciences as well as economics. The basic idea of calculating dimension from a single time series of a dynamical system is that it is fundamentally the first piece of qualitative information about the system that is needed; namely, how many essential variables are needed to model the system, or to discover what in fact is the order of the underlying differential equations defining the dynamical system. The concept of fractal dimension has tended to confuse the perception of the basic idea and has added a complexity that, while important in its own right, inhibits a clear understanding of the basic notion of dimension. *Dimension*, by indicating the order of the defining differential equation, when there is one, indicates the number of variables that are involved in the system. A similar result holds for maps.

The calculation of dimension, if it ever became effective for economic or financial data, would be of inestimable value in econometrics. A major difficulty in any attempt to model a market or even an economy is the fact that we have no theory to limit the number of variables and equations that must be included in any empirical analysis. Current theory leaves us with an unmanageable host of variables to consider so that the decision is made *ad hoc* and is always treated as an empirical issue.

Whether or not the data have a fractal dimension is in light of this discussion irrelevant. The first step is to limit the set of possible variables. Unfortunately, in economics, no one has yet been successful in isolating any low dimensional systems.

This may be due in part to the fact that economic and financial data require a different modeling approach than is true for physical or biological data. Randomness in its many forms is an obvious hazard to any formal attempts at modeling. Economic systems are very open, even relative to biological systems, they are subject to constant tinkering by economic agents. Whenever those agents learn more about the operation of the system, they alter their behavior and as a consequence alter the structure of the observed dynamical system. Nonetheless, it still seems to be reasonable to assume that the system is not completely random and that once a suitable modeling approach has been acquired further insight can be obtained.

By this time, a substantial number of economists have attempted to discover low dimensional attractors in economic or financial data, Frank and Stengos [1987a, 1987b], Brock and Sayers [1988], Barnett and Chen

[1988], Hsieh [1987], Scheinkman and Le Baron [1986], and even this author in some unpublished earlier work. The data series that have been examined by these researchers include gold and silver prices, GNP, stock returns, various definitions of the money supply, work stoppages, and numerous foreign exchange rates. The list is not complete, but is illustrative.

The outcome of all this research is that as yet there is little evidence for the presence of low dimensional attractors in economic and financial data. This somewhat depressing claim is substantiated in Ramsey, Sayers, and Rothman [1988]. Part of the difficulty is that economic and financial data contain much more noise than physical data and that the length of the data runs is minuscule by the standards in physics. Consequently, the procedures are not really adopted to the economic and financial environment. However, the results do indicate that there is some evidence of nonlinearity. The reader is referred to Ramsey and Yuan [1988, 1989] as well as Ramsey, Sayers, and Rothman [1988] for further details; besides, the case for nonlinearity in economic and financial data has been made most ably by a remarkable series of papers by Patterson and Hinich (see the bibliography under these two names).

There exists yet another set of problems that are particularly severe in a nonexperimental discipline like economics. These problems involve the extended maintained hypothesis that is needed in economic analysis. In the problems examined to date in physics and chemistry, the simple dichotomy—either an attractor, or the data are merely (high dimensional) noise—has been considered to be appropriate. This is not the case in economics. The extended maintained hypothesis must include as alternatives the options that the data come from ARIMA or nonlinear stochastic processes.

Even more damaging to a simplistic version of dimension calculation is the realization that often researchers mistakenly perform dimensional analysis on data that are highly autocorrelated; this procedure vitiates any conclusions that might possibly be made. This is so because dimension is a topological concept and at certain scales of magnification of some stochastic processes, the dimension is in fact quite low. For example, the dimension of a geometric random walk is at intermediate scales, about 1.1; a geometric random walk can be regarded at such scales as a highly convoluted line, giving it a topological structure that is of dimension slightly higher than that of a line. What is worse is that if the data are generated by a simple ARMA process with long auto-correlation lag, that is, a long period before the auto-correlations die to zero, then dimension calculations with such data will produce, over a range of scaling values, low dimensional results.

The problem for all experimental data, even if there were a perfectly well defined and recoverable attractor, is that at small enough scales the dimension is that of noise. Thus, the practical problem of trying to distinguish between attractors, autocorrelated processes, and nonlinear stochastic processes is a real one.

The conclusion is that, while the concept of dimension is of potentially great interest to econometricians, the current approach has not yet discovered how to disentangle low dimensional results from the inevitable noise and large scale aperiodic shocks that seem to beset all economic and financial data.

Indeed, the actual situation is much more of a puzzle. If the current econometric wisdom is correct, then the seemingly universal absence of economic and financial theory to relate this vast array of low order AR or MA processes, and sometimes just random walks, is the real challenge. If economic theory is to be resuscitated for economic and financial time series, it will only be by pursuing alternative lines of enquiry.

4.5.2. Tests for Time Irreversibility in Economic and Financial Data

The concept of time reversibility is discussed in some detail in Ramsey and Rothman [1988]. The definition of time reversibility was given above. The procedure used in Ramsey and Rothman to characterize and to test for the presence of time irreversibility in the context of stationary time series is as follows. The statistics G_{ij}^k are defined by:

$$\begin{aligned} G_{ij}^k &= T^{-1}\Sigma[X_t^i X_{t-k}^j - X_t^j X_{t-k}^i], \\ &= T^{-1}\Sigma[X_t^j X_{t+k}^i - X_t^j X_{t-k}^i]. \end{aligned} \tag{4.25}$$

can be used both to characterize and to test for the presence of time irreversibility. The second way of writing G_{ij}^k is valid only under the assumption of stationary of the time series, but does stress that G_{ij}^k depends on the difference in covariance relationships expressed forward in time and backwards in time. Under the null hypothesis that the series is time reversible, the expectation of G_{ij}^k is zero for all $\{i, j, k\}$. Of course, a zero expectation is always obtained for $i = j = 1$ as in that case G_{ij}^k is simply the auto-correlation function. Intuitively, the time irreversible result can be easily understood from the alternative version in equation 4.25; the covariance between X_t^2 and X_t forward in time is not the same as the same covariance expressed backwards in time.

In practice, Ramsey and Rothman have found that $i = 2$ and $j = 1$ are sufficient for discovering time irreversibility in a wide assortment of data. As discussed in Ramsey and Rothman [1988], the statistic G_{ij}^k expressed as a function of k can be regarded in a similar light to an auto-correlation function. How large k can be allowed to be depends on the statistical properties of the time series and on sample size. The larger k, the larger the corresponding standard errors. Standard errors are also increased when the data are highly correlated. As discussed in Ramsey and Rothman [1988], the shape of the plot of G_{ij}^k as a function of k is indicative of the type of time irreversibility that is exhibited in the data. For example, if the time series are characterized by "cycles" that are slow up and fast down, then the general shape of the plot of G_{ij}^k is also a cycle of the same period, but different phase. The distinction is that for a cycle characterized by slow up and fast down, as opposed to the opposite situation, the G_{21}^k values tend to be negative and the opposite is true for the reverse cycle. The important aspects of the plots of the G_{ij}^k values are the size of the coefficient estimates relative to the estimated standard errors and even more importantly the shape of the plot for all k. The advantage of this approach to nonlinearity as compared to the use of the bispectrum used by Hinich and Patterson is that one can more easily infer the properties of the underlying model.

Figures 4–8 show the time series of the M1 definition of the money supply and figure 4–9 shows the log first differences of that series; the period of maximum amplitude is in the middle of the "Volker experiment" from 1979 to 1981. M1 is definitely nonlinear and time irreversible. From figure 4–10, one sees that after an initial negative effect, the presence of time irreversibility does not reveal itself until about 62 months and the effect lasts up to 80 months; that is, the main nonlinear effects for M1 seem to be concentrated in a time period of between 5 and 6½ years.

The confidence intervals are estimated 95% intervals based in part on the theory underlying the distribution of the G_{ij}^k, supplemented by Monte Carlo simulations to determine the effect of an auto-regressive structure on the standard errors of the estimates. The procedure is described more fully in Ramsey and Rothman [1988].

While the raw time series plot for M2 is very similar, the plot of the log first differences is quite different, see figures 4–11 and 4–12. However, due in part to the much stronger AR effects that seem to hold for M2 as compared to that for M1, the standard errors for the estimation of G_{21}^k in figure 4–13 are very large and seem to increase at a fast rate. There does not seem to be any strong evidence for time irreversibility in the M2 data.

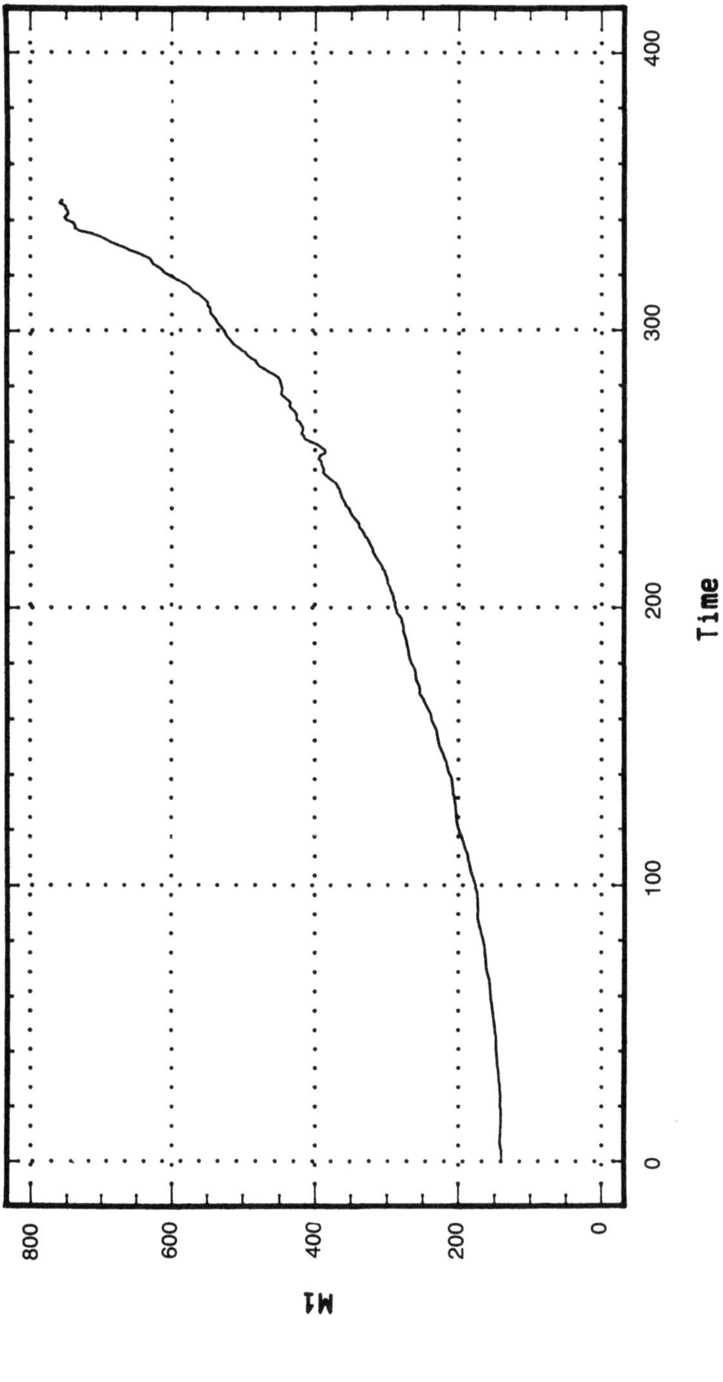

Figure 4–8. Time Sequence Plot: Monthly M1 Data (January 1959–November 1987)

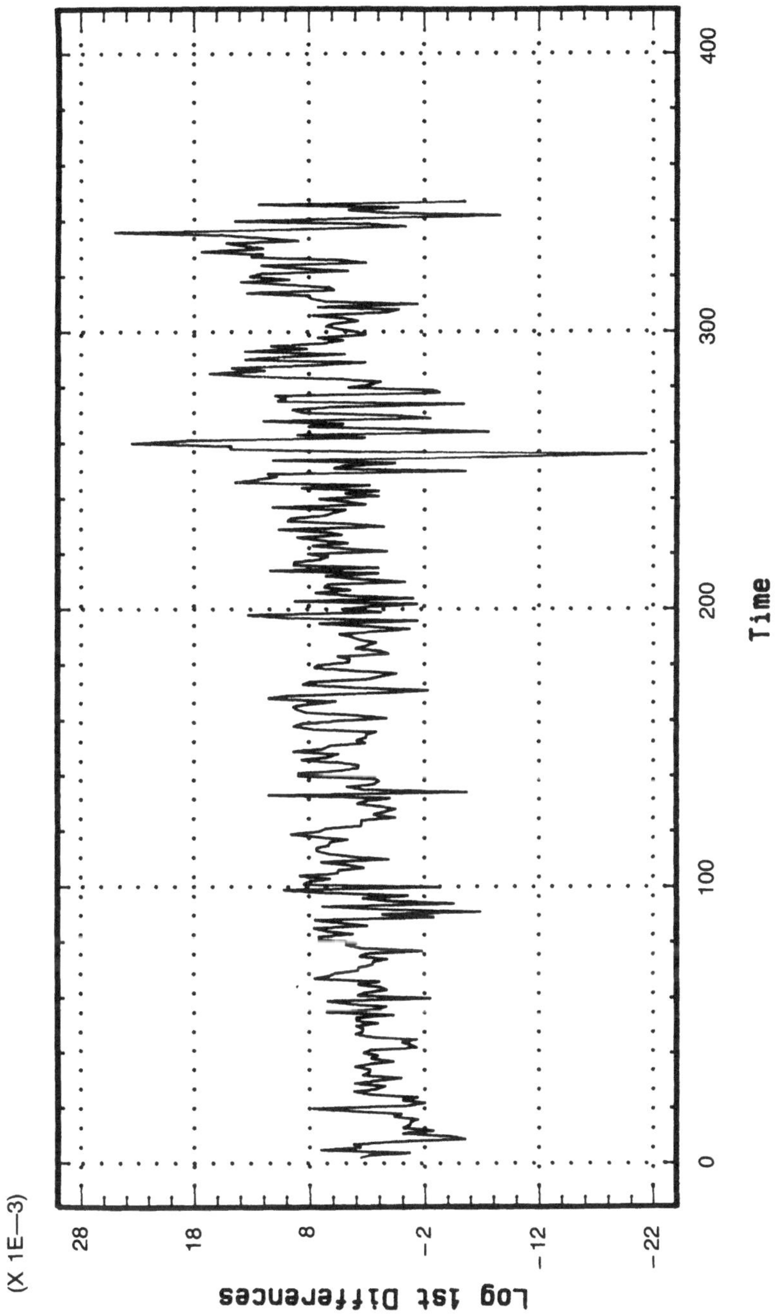

Figure 4–9. Time Sequence Plot: Log First Differences of M1 Data (January 1959–November 1987)

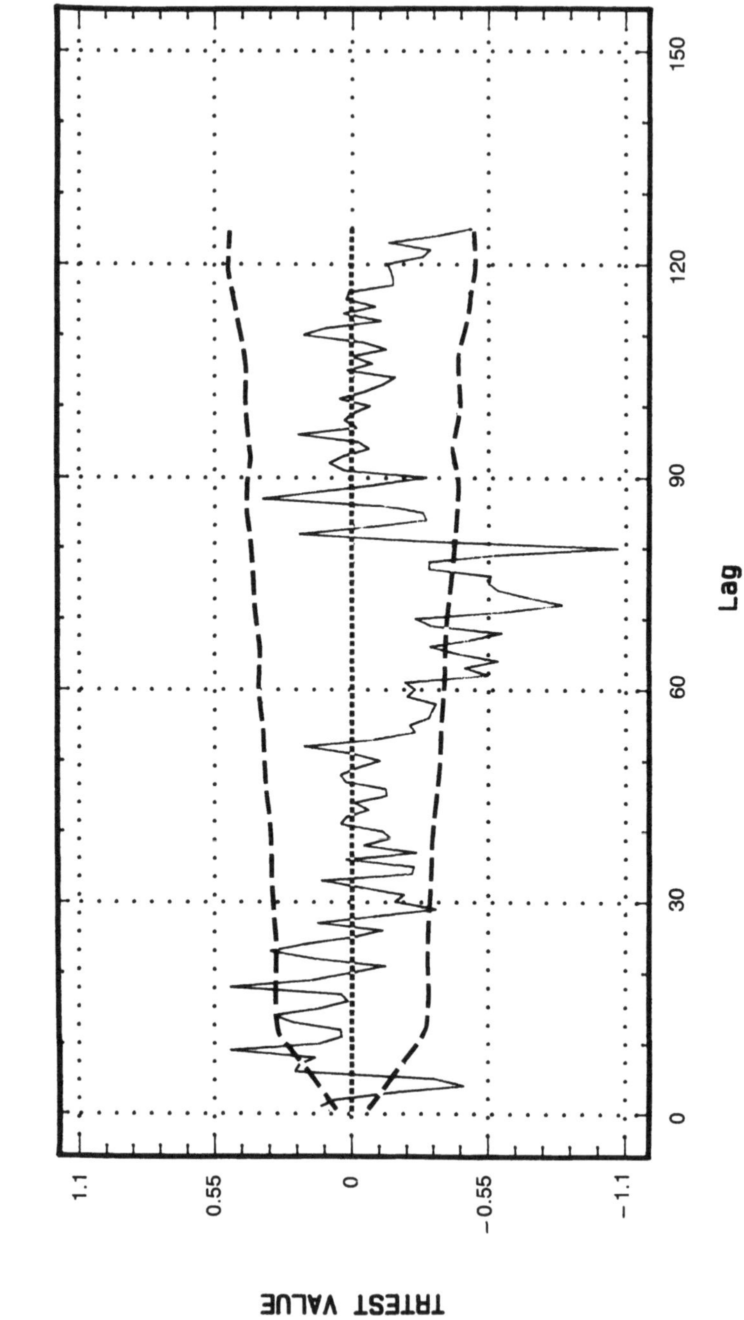

Figure 4–10. Plot of the Trtest Coefficients for the Log First Differences of Monthly M1 Data

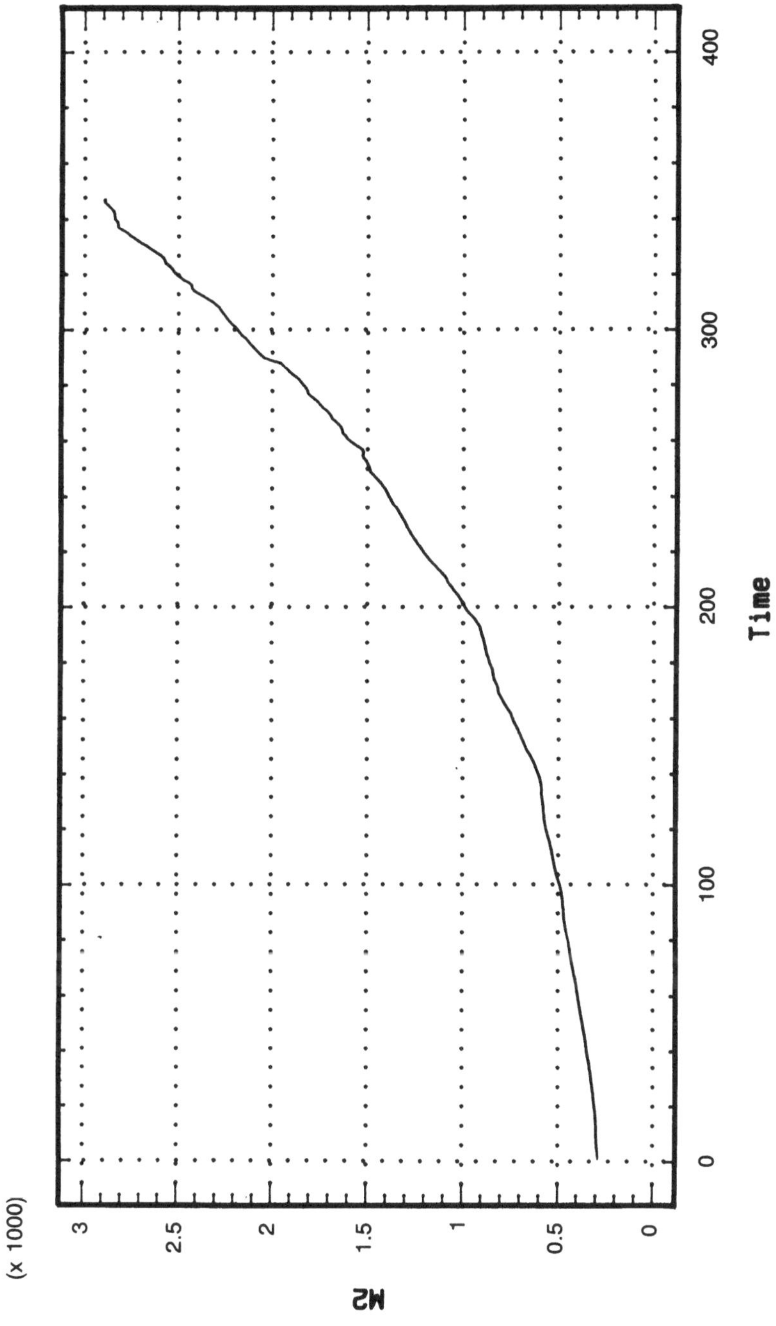

Figure 4–11. Time Sequence Plot: Monthly M2 Data (January 1959–1987)

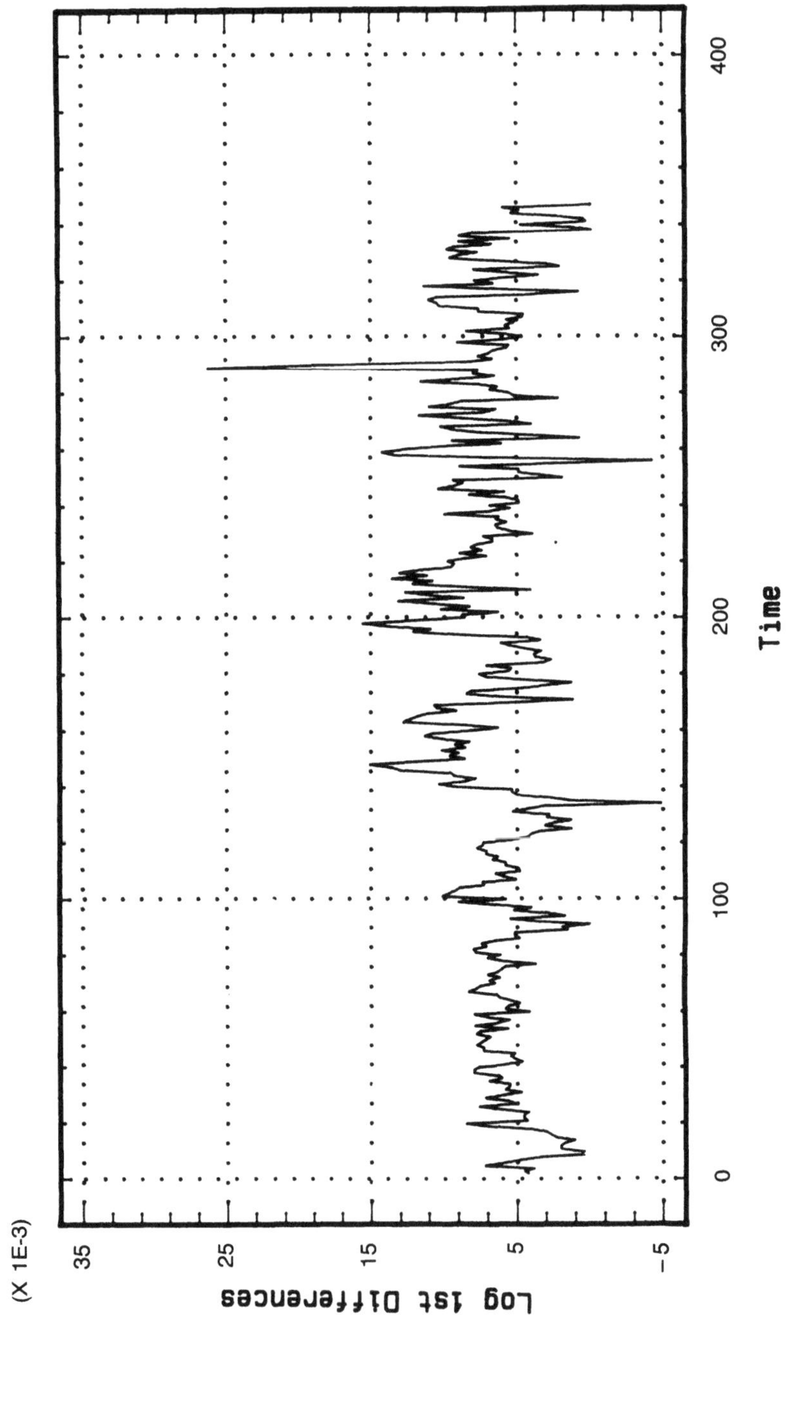

Figure 4–12. Time Sequence Plot: Log First Differences of M2 Data (January 1959–1987)

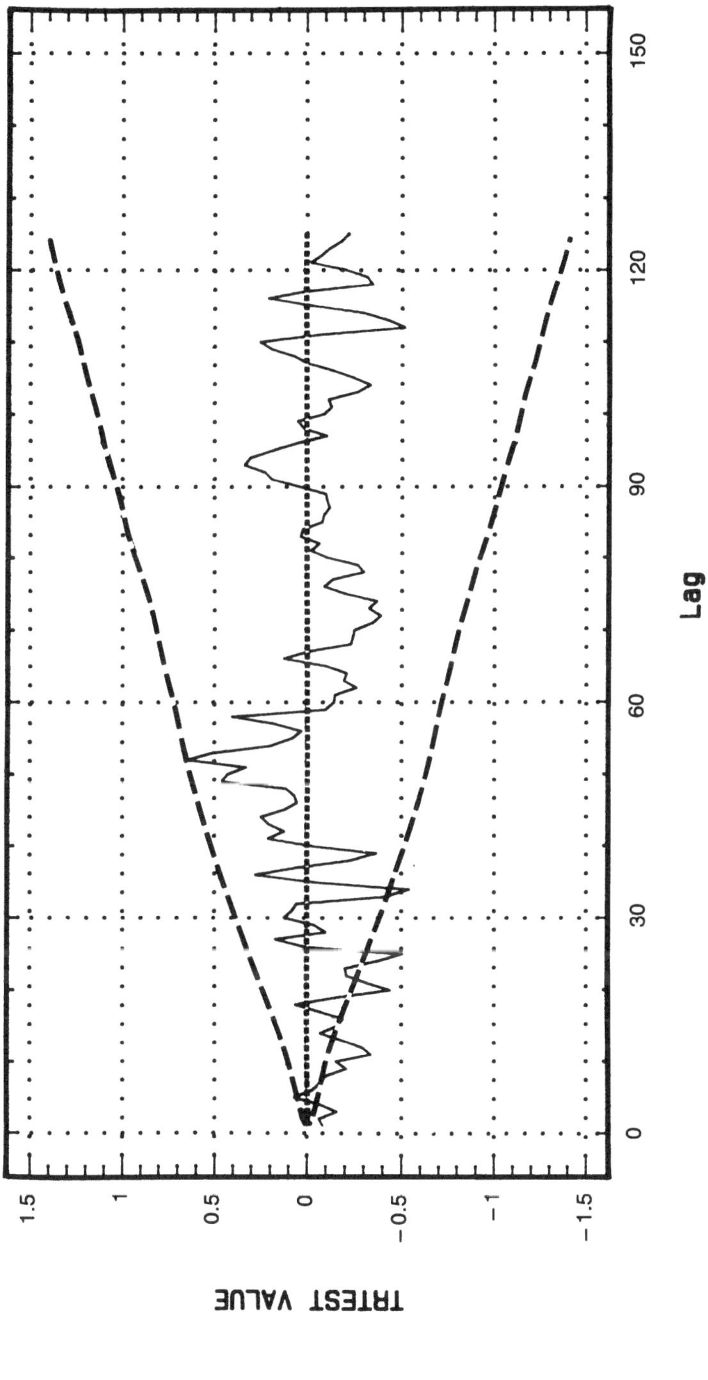

Figure 4−13. Plot of the Trtest Coefficients for the Log First Differences of Monthly M2 Data

Certainly, the presence of strong nonlinearity over a time period of 60 to 80 months is missing.

Figure 4–14 shows the raw time series for the Scheinkman-Le Baron stock return data. The evidence for any type of ARMA process in these data is very weak so that the nonlinearity test for time irreversibility was applied directly to these data. Figure 4–15 shows clearly strong evidence of time irreversibility; in this case the effect is concentrated in the first 20 weeks.

The claim is often made that financial data are different from economic data. However, both types of data evidence in their raw state exponential growth in the series. This statement is substantiated by the plot of monthly pig iron production from 1877 in figures 4–16 and 4–17. Within year variations of the data series had to be smoothed before any other analysis could be usefully performed. The data were subsequently differenced in the logs; the remaining steady increase in the amplitude of the oscillations is still apparent. Figure 4–18 shows the plot of the G_{12}^{k} function for these series from which we see that time irreversibility is clearly present. But in this case, the effect is a sharp positive peak at a lag of about 26 months.

A related, but different approach to the analysis of economic time series is discussed in detail in Ramsey and Montenegro [1988]. This idea can be used whenever the time series can be represented as an *MA* process. The basic idea is that corresponding to any $MA(q)$ process there exist 2^q different models with the same auto-correlation function; that is, all 2^q models belong to an equivalence class that is defined by the auto-correlation function. The alternative members of this equivalence class are defined by the set of roots $\{\lambda_i^{\pm 1}\}$, where $\{\lambda_i, i = 1,2,\ldots,q\}$ are the roots of any one of the alternative models, say, the invertible one. The invertible model is the only one of the set of alternative models that can be estimated by the usual procedures of either least squares or maximum likelihood. The invertible model is the one that can be expressed as a convergent sum of past values of the observed time series.

In Ramsey and Montenegro [1988] it is shown that, provided the innovations in the MA(q) process are not *normally* distributed, the true model can be distinguished from the other members of the equivalence class. The approach uses the higher order cumulants, which are identically zero for the *normal* distribution. Given that the actual model's coefficients can be identified, it is also possible to estimate the innovations generating the observed process.

The minimum mean square error type of forecast is not enhanced by the use of noninvertible models, although the appropriate confidence interval is modified by this approach. The real gain is in evaluating the timing of

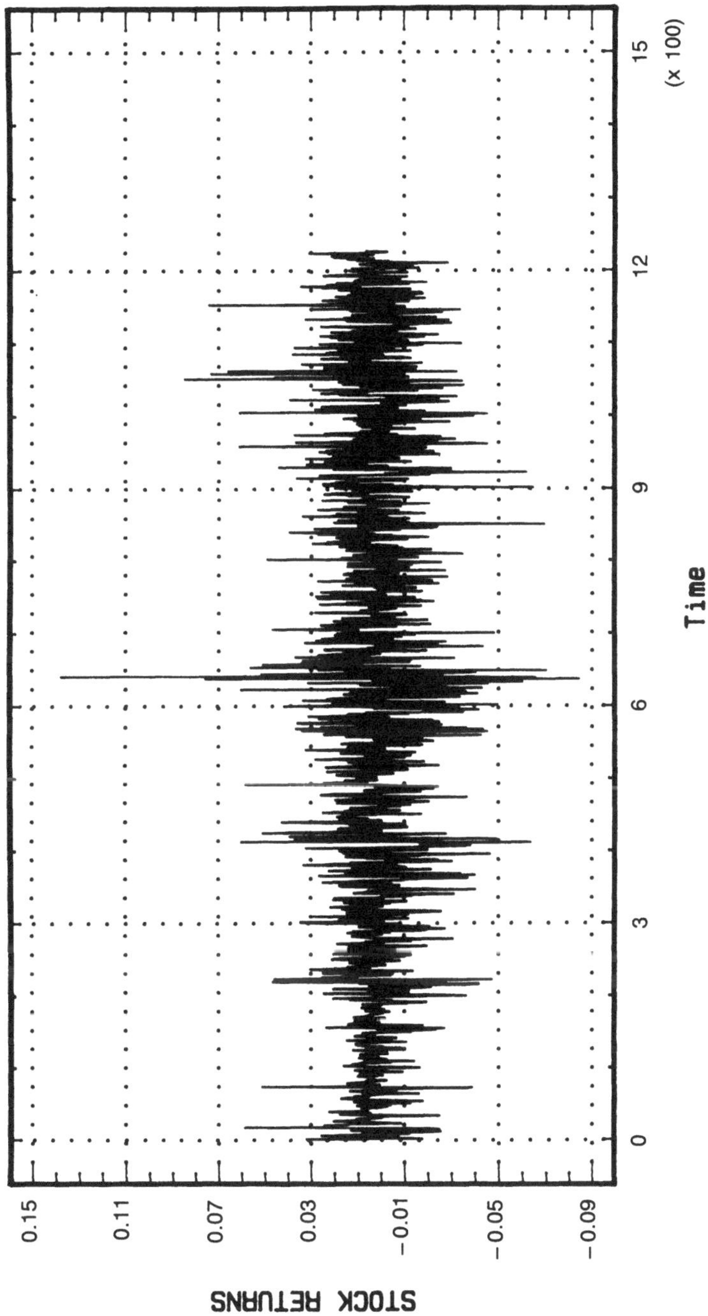

Figure 4–14. Time Sequence Plot: Stock Market Data (July 1962–August 1985)

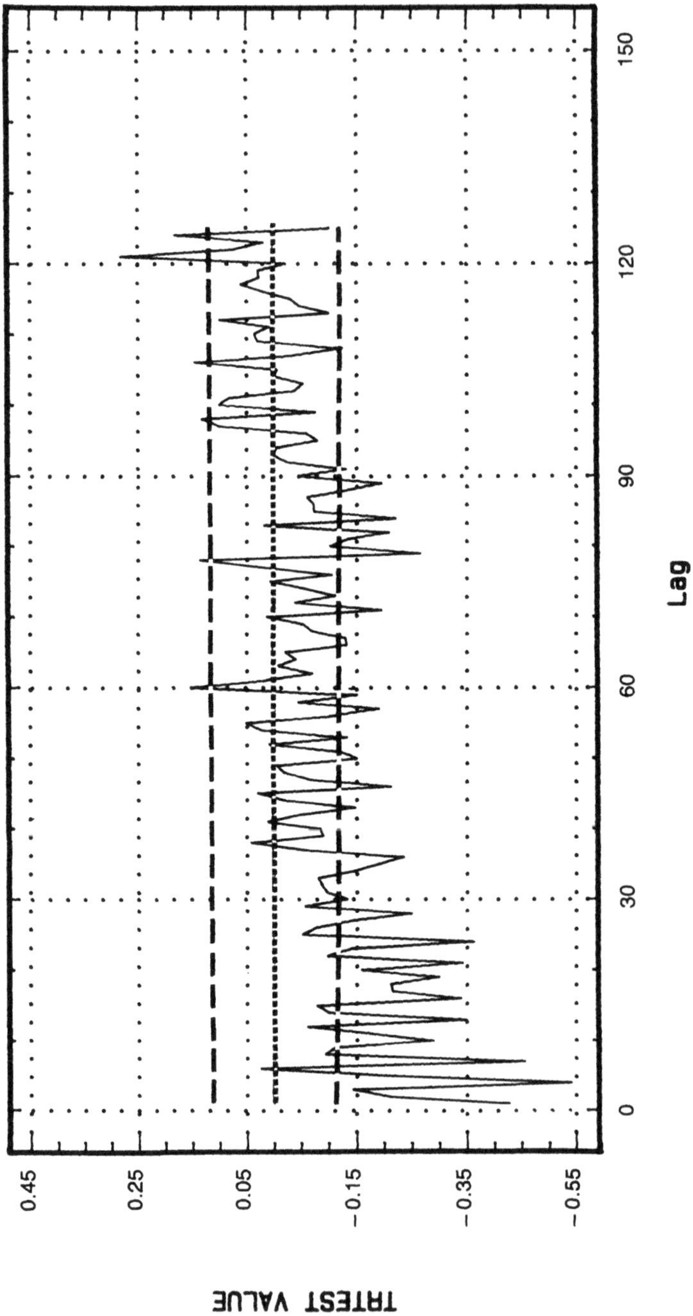

Figure 4–15. Plot of the Trtest Coefficients for the Stock Market Data

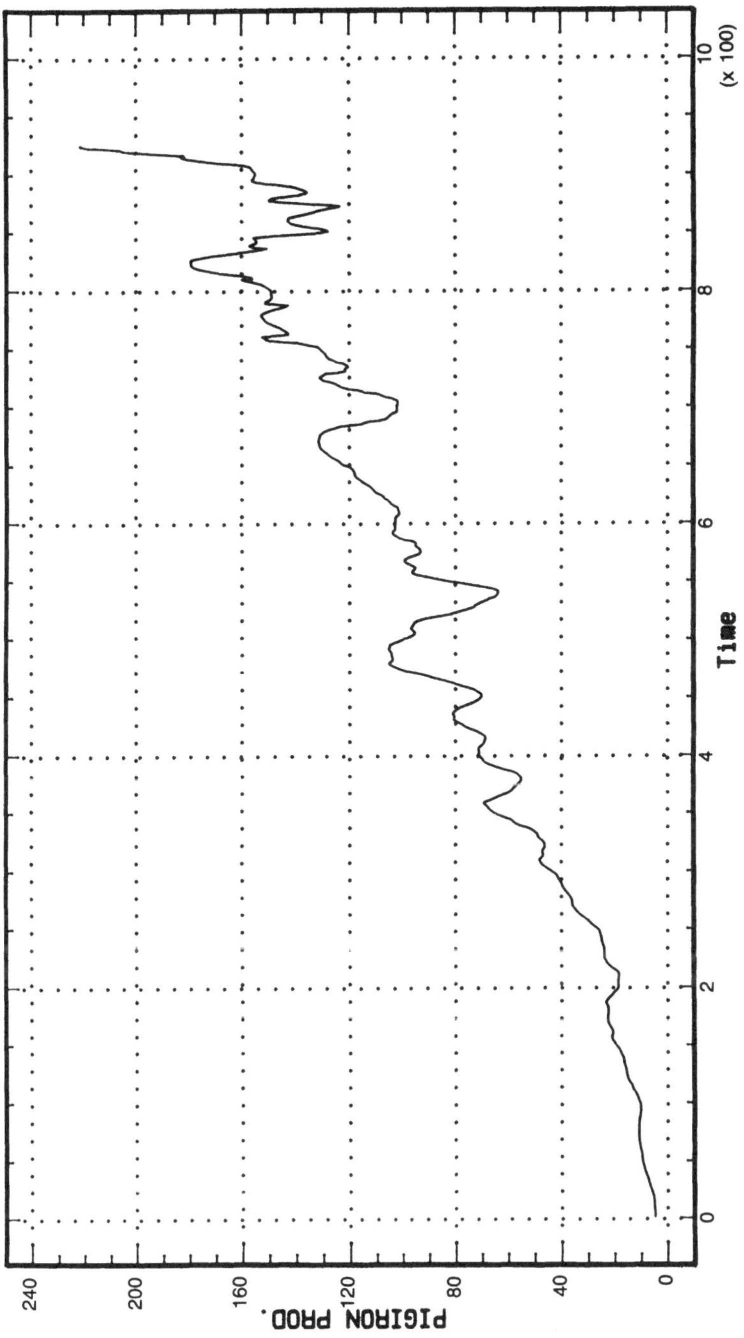

Figure 4–16. Time Sequence Plot: Pig Iron Data Smoothed (13) Monthly (1877–1964)

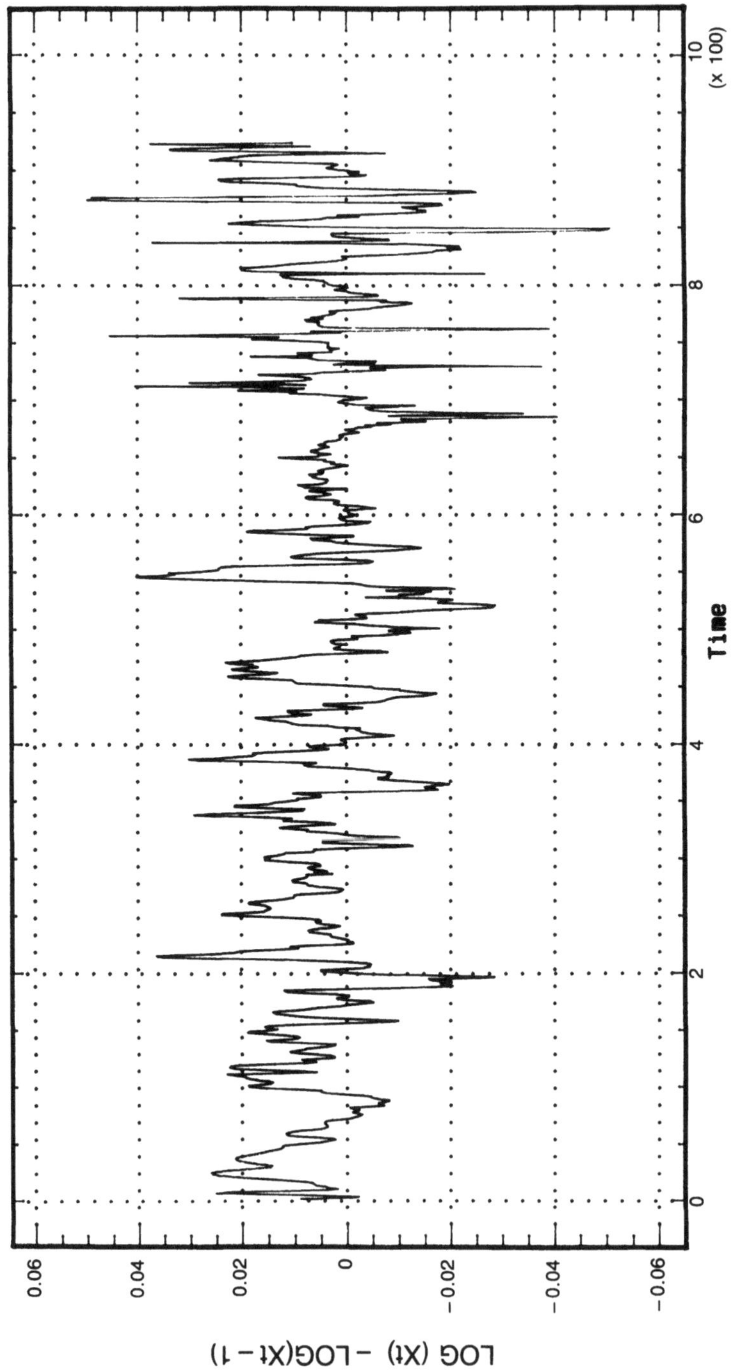

Figure 4–17. Time Sequence Plot: Pig Iron Data Log First Differences of the Smoothed Data

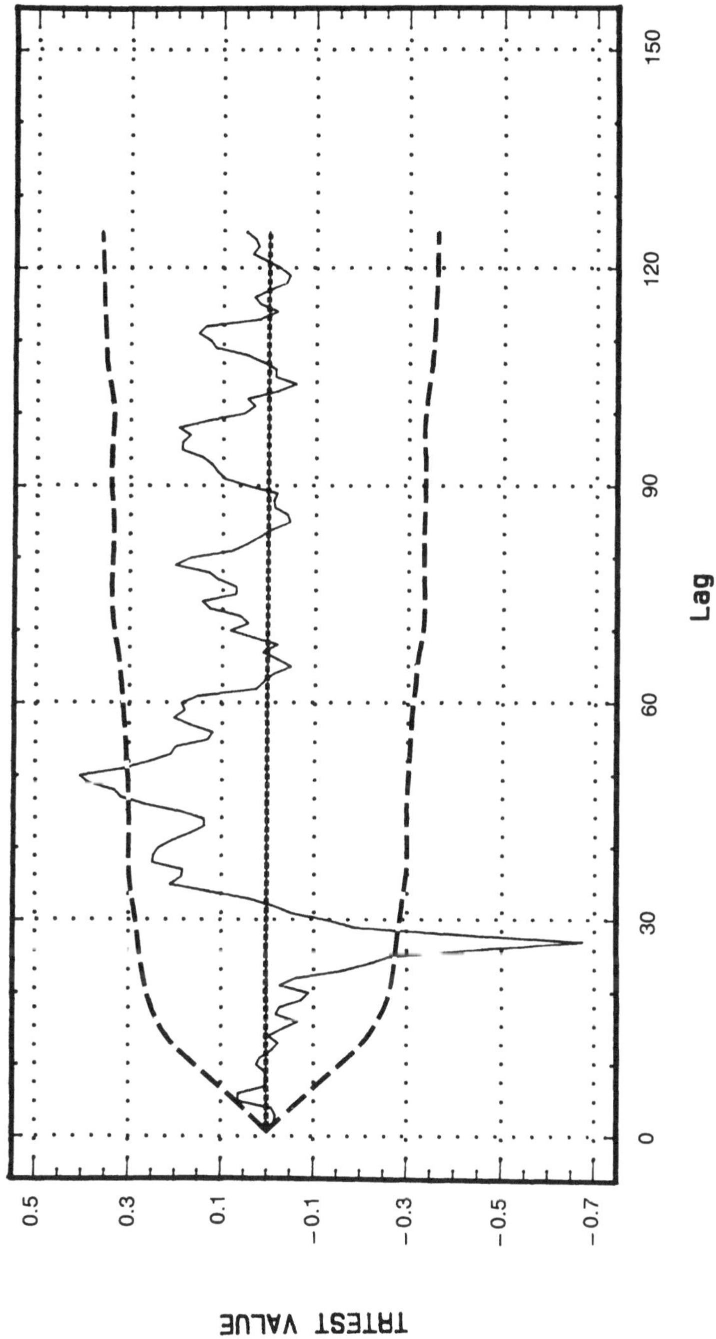

Figure 4–18. Plot of Trtest Coefficients for the Standardized Log First Differences of Pig Iron

the effects of shocks and that the effects of a deliberate, nonrandom, intervention can be correctly assessed.

In Ramsey and Montenegro [1988] several time series were examined. Of those that were found to be low-order MA, two series in particular gave clear evidence of being generated by a noninvertible process: the prime rate and expenditures on plant and equipment. Following Mehra [1986] the prime rate was included in a demand for money equation that has well-recognized antecedents; the objective was to compare the effects of using the prime rate itself in the demand for money equation, the usual estimates of the innovations, and those innovations generated from the chosen noninvertible model. The results are most encouraging. While further work is needed to verify the conclusions reached so far, the clear implication is that the innovations from the noninvertible model are the preferred explanatory variable in the cited demand for money equation.

4.6. Conclusions and Speculations

The main conclusion is easily stated. Economic systems are clearly nonlinear. The evidence is not only from the research cited above, but also from the extensive work of Hinich and Patterson. Even in the case of stock market returns data at low levels of time aggregation for which the case for a random walk model is strongest, the presence of nonlinearities is clear in the work of both groups of researchers.

However, the work above also indicates that the appearance of that nonlinearity may not be apparent until after a considerable lag that is measured in years. The implications for policy are serious if this result is even only partially true, because under these conditions the implementation of policy based on linear models will inevitably be in ignorance of the nonlinear effects. Worse is the fact that these circumstances will inhibit the discovery of the nonlinearity; the policy will seemingly work for awhile and then, apparently at random, break down. Imagine a myopic dog trailing a random walk rat. He will always think that he is hot on the trail and that next time he will at last catch the rat. But the next time never comes unless someone tells the dog what the underlying nonlinear mechanism is so that he can anticipate the rat's next move and the rat's reaction to his own moves.

Linear policy in a nonlinear world with delays is destabilizing at least some of the time and probably most of the time. Linear analysis in a nonlinear world is an analysis that is characterized by models that are constantly being adjusted. The coefficients are unstable over subperiods, and the models frequently break down without warning. While it may be true that any economic model's coefficients will alter over time, there is a better chance of obtaining relatively stable coefficients with nonlinear models.

A question that Professor Brock has often raised with me concerns the forecasting benefits of nonlinear models. For if nonlinear models can do no better than that which we now have, then there is no point in adding useless nonlinear burdens. The answer depends on the criterion for success and the objective.

If we retain the usual minimum mean square error criterion (mmse) and wish merely to observe the future without taking action, then nonlinear models will do little for us. The only source of improvement is a more accurate estimate of the confidence interval that we will place on our forecasts. For example, even in the case of the noninvertible $MA(q)$ models, knowledge of the correct model does not improve our mmse forecast, except in improving the accuracy of the statement of the standard errors. One might as well use the tried and true invertible version.

Further, even if there were a chaotic model underlying economic data, the forecast improvement potential is strictly limited to the very short run. Indeed, the real gain here is to know that no matter how much data one has, there are very strict limits on the forecasting period for a given level of accuracy. If additionally we add noise, as is likely, then the benefit of nonlinear models becomes problematic at best.

These highly negative comments are conditional on the choice of a mmse criterion and the objective that we wish merely to observe. If we relax either of these restrictions, the situation is changed dramatically. In order to focus attention on the essentials, let us imagine that we have a nonlinear model or alternatively a noninvertible $MA(q)$ model, that has the exact same auto-correlation function as an invertible $MA(q)$ model. As a very special case, the invertible model might be simply uncorrelated random variation.

Let us change our objective. We no longer wish merely to observe, but also to implement policy. The implementation of policy in terms of our model is to assume that we will modify the path of our variable of interest, say the money supply, by imposing our own impulse onto the system in addition to whatever random variation occurs simultaneously. Now knowledge of the "true model" is vital if we wish to evaluate the likely effect of our policy. In effect our policy action has changed the model. Next period's output will not be the result of the same mechanism as before; we have modified it to include our own impulse to the system. The average effect will be what we would have obtained in the absence of our impulse, plus the "true model's" processing of our nonrandom impulse. Evaluating the policy action on the basis of the "incorrect model" will be misleading.

Let us now change our criterion from the averaging of squared errors to consider the time path of the reaction of the system to any specific impulse. Knowledge of the correct model is crucial to meeting this expanded criterion function. For example, the noninvertible $MA(q)$ model will give very different results to those predicted by the corresponding invertible model with the same autocorrelation function. This may indicate that the main response will be delayed beyond the initial period. In contrast, the dissipative systems with random shocks, that economists traditionally assume, may have the same expectational properties as a chaotic attractor, but the dynamical paths will differ substantially.

Further, if we add to our set of criteria a concern for the stability of the system and a recognition that stability may be state-dependent, then once again the nonlinear model is needed and the linear approximation is no longer a useful tool. Indeed, questions of stability can only be posed in the context of nonlinear models. Within a linear system, stability is essentially an uninteresting question as linear models produce either fixed points or diverge; we can ignore the practically unimportant two period oscillations produced by negative eigenvalues.

Moving into the realm of speculation, the analysis above seems to lead to the following ideas about an appropriate modeling structure. Some modest but encouraging attempts have already been made along the lines to be suggested. The economic system must be modeled as a dynamical system, so that we need to begin to discover the appropriate equations of motion. Economic systems also contain noise that is embedded in the dynamic itself, that is, the noise term enters the solution of the underlying differential equation system; these effects must be taken into consideration as well. There may also be observational noise that will lower the precision of our estimates, but should have no other serious effects.

A much more difficult phenomenon to model is that economic systems are subject to episodic shocks that reinitialize the system. By *episodic* I mean shocks that occur every so often, but with no detectable underlying probability distribution.

It is also likely that over time the parameters of the system are changing with technology and population, but with a little bit of undeserved luck these changes can usefully be assumed to be changing slowly.

Finally, as economists well know but tend to forget, increased understanding of the system will inevitably change the system, because we are dealing with the actions of rational optimizing agents, no matter how bounded that rationality may be.

Appendix

The idea of this appendix is to provide a quick intuitive introduction to some of the language used in the chaos and qualitative dynamics literature; the various references that are cited can be pursued to good effect.

Three terms that are frequently used in this literature are *attractor*, *embedding dimension*, and *orbit* and should be at least intuitively defined in this paper. Attractors can be strange or chaotic or both.

Embedding dimension is the topological dimension of the space in which the attractor is situated; loosely stated the embedding dimension is the number of axes needed to portray the attractor. Topological dimension specializes in vector spaces to the usual notion of Euclidian dimension.

Orbit is essentially a synonym for the dynamical path, but also implies the notion that the dynamical path revisits any given part of the attractor infinitely often.

A dynamical system may be characterized as either a map or a flow. Maps are discrete; flows are continuous. In either case, an orbit or path of the dynamical system is defined by the solution of the system to yield the sequence $\{x_1, x_2, x_3, x_4, \ldots\}$, for maps, and $\{x(t)\}$, for flows.

An attractor is a compact set, A, such that the limit set of the orbit, $\{x_n\}$ *or* $\{x(t)\}$, as n or $t \to \infty$ is A for almost all initial conditions within a neighborhood of A.

An attractor is the set of points of the path that represents the long-term behavior of the dynamical system; it is that subset of points towards which any dynamical path will converge; that is, the dynamical path is attracted to a subspace of the space containing the paths of the dynamical system from any initial condition. Attractors can be very simple sets such as single points that represent equilibria, or limit cycles, such as the cobweb cycle. But attractors can be much more complex. An attractor can be quasiperiodic, chaotic, or strange. All but the last can be defined on a manifold.

An example of a quasi-periodic attractor is an orbit on a torus, (a doughnut shape), generated by the cosines of a pair of incommensurate frequencies. A chaotic attractor is one that is characterized by exponential divergence of paths within the attractor. Because the attractor is compact, the exponential divergence means that the path is constantly folded over onto the attractor. A strange attractor is one that is characterized by a fractal dimension; the attractor set is a fractal, that is, it has a very fine structure such as is obtained from the Cantor set construction by omitting a sequence of "middle thirds" from the unit interval. An attractor can be both chaotic and strange. Indeed, most of the examples with which economists are by now familiar are both strange and chaotic, but there are examples of attractors that are either chaotic or strange, but not both.

Dynamical orbits have dynamical properties and attractors have topological properties. For strange attractors we can define also measure theoretic properties. Dimension is mainly a topolotical concept, but some concepts of dimension have measure theoretic components.

Dimension concepts indicate

1. the amount of information needed to specify the position of a point on an attractor;
2. the lower bound on the number of essential variables that are needed to model the attractor, or rather, the dynamical system when within the attractor;
3. the relative density of the points on the attractor.

The natural probability measure of an attractor is the relative frequency with which the different regions of an attractor is visited by the orbit.

There are many definitions of dimension used in the literature on nonlinear dynamics. The reader should be warned that sometimes dimension is used in its purely topological sense, that is, dimension is merely a generalization of the Euclidian notion with which all economists are very familiar. In this sense the dimension is always an integer and represents the number of degrees of freedom, or the number of axes needed to represent the attractor.

The other definitions of dimension can be put into three classes of concepts: those that are purely metric, those based on the natural probability measure of the attractor, and those based on the dynamical properties of the orbit within the attractor. Our discussion will be restricted to the first two classes of concepts.

The purely metric concepts include the notion of capacity, d_c, and Hausdorff dimension, d_h.

The capacity measure is formally defined by

$$d_c = \lim_{\varepsilon \to 0} \frac{\ln N(\varepsilon)}{\ln(1/\varepsilon)},$$

where $N(\varepsilon)$ is the minimum number of ε diameter cubes needed to cover the attractor. d_c is nothing more than a measure of the relative rate of increase in the number of coverings of an attractor to the number of coverings needed to cover the unit interval. For a fixed point, an equilibrium point, $d_c = 0$; for a simple cycle $d_c = 1$; but for strange attractors d_c can be noninteger to represent the fractal structure of strange attractors.

For example, the capacity measure of the Cantor set created by deleting middle thirds is $(\ln 2)/\ln 3 = 0.63$.

Hausdorff dimension is defined with respect to the concept of Hausdorff measure, which in turn is a generalization of Lebesgue measure. Hausdorff measure enables one to assign a nonnegative number to many nonempty sets that under Lebesgue would have zero measure.

The Hausdorff α measure of a set A is

$$HM\alpha = \lim_{\varepsilon \to 0} \underset{\{A_i\}}{(\inf)}\ \Sigma\delta(A_i\alpha), \quad A \subseteq \cup A_i$$

where the A_i are covering sets, $\delta(A_i)$ is the diameter of the ith set, and δ is an exponent. If a set has a nonzero Lebesgue measure, then the Hausdorff measure is the same when the choice of α is the same as the topological dimension of the set.

Hausdorff dimension is given by α_0, where α_0 is defined

$$\alpha_0 = \inf\{\alpha : HM_\alpha(A) = 0\}$$

α_0 is merely that scale variable such that the sum of volumes to cover the attractor is finite and nonzero. If $\alpha > \alpha_0$, then $HM\alpha = 0$, and if $\alpha < \alpha_0$, then $HM_\alpha \to \infty$. If the attractor is not strange, say, for example, that it is a simple cycle, then α_0 will be an integer. Whenever Lebesgue measure is positive, Hausdorff dimension will be an integer; Hausdorff dimension will be noninteger when the attractor is strange and has Cantor set characteristics.

The problem with these purely metric concepts is that they treat all parts of the attractor equally, no matter how infrequently some part of the attractor is visited by the orbit. Such measures are enormously data extensive. Two measures that incorporate the relative frequency of visit by the orbit are information dimension, d_I, and pointwise dimension, d_p. We will assume in the sequel that there exists a natural probability measure in that any probability measure defined on the attractor is invariant to the initial conditions.

Information dimension, d_I, is defined:

$$d_I = \lim_{\varepsilon \to 0} \frac{I(\varepsilon)}{\ln(1/\varepsilon)},$$

where $I(\varepsilon)$ is Shannon's Information measure and is formally defined:

$$I(\varepsilon) = -\Sigma_{i=1}^{N(\varepsilon)} P_i \ln(P_i).$$

$N(\varepsilon)$ is the same measure of the number of coverings of the attractor as occurred in the definition of capacity. If all coverings are equally likely, that is, $P_i = N(\varepsilon)^{-1}$, then $d_I = d_c$; in general, d_I is not greater than d_c.

To define pointwise dimension, d_p, we have to define $\mu(B_\varepsilon)$ as the natural probability measure of a ball of radius ε. Pointwise dimension is:

$$d_p(x) = \lim_{\varepsilon \to 0} \frac{ln\,\mu(B\varepsilon(x))}{\ln(\varepsilon)}.$$

If $d_p\ (x)$ is independent of x for almost all x on the attractor, then the common value of d_p is the pointwise dimension of the attractor. Pointwise dimension is that concept of dimension that the Grassberger-Procaccia procedure measures. Pointwise dimension measures the relative rate of scaling of the probability measure of a ball of diameter of radius ε as the diameter approaches zero; compare this measure with that of capacity.

Reviews of the correlation dimension procedures that are written with the economist in mind include Brock [1986], Brock, Dechert, and Scheinkman [1987], Brock and Sayers [1988], Barnett and Chen [1988a, 1988b], and a more detailed evaluation of the details with a guide to the relevant physics literature is Ramsey and Yuan [1989]. The basic idea underlying the calculation of dimension is relatively easily stated.

Any sequence of points, $\{x_t\}$, generated by some mechanism, whether random, chaotic, or otherwise, can be transformed into a sequence of d-tuples, $(x_{t1}, x_{t2}, \ldots, x_{td})$. These d-tuples, regarded as points in a d-dimensional Euclidian space, can be plotted, and properties of the cloud of points so created examined. The choice of the value of d is the choice of embedding dimension; it is the size of the Euclidian space into which the original sequence is being fitted. If the generated points are from observations on a random variable, then as d, the embedding dimension is increased without bound and assuming an unlimited sample size, the size of the space into which the d-tuples will fit is d for all values of d; that is, random variables are space filling. But if the points are generated by a mechanism that is deterministic, or at least one that produces a shape that requires only k dimensions, then as the embedding dimension is increased without limit, the dimension of the points will not increase beyond k. Imagine, for example, an ellipse, which is an object of dimension 1, that requires at least Euclidian dimension 2 to be observed, but no more; consider embedding an ellipse in a 3 or 4 dimensional space; the dimension of the ellipse is still 1.

Unfortunately, the objects of interests to us involve more complicated structures. The simplest intuitive example is to imagine a mechanism that produces points that are best described as the Cartesian product of the unit interval and a Cantor set. A Cantor set is obtained by deleting middle thirds from the remainder of the unit interval obtained by deleting middle thirds at a previous iteration. This idea can be extended to any number of Cartesian products.

The Grassberger-Procaccia [1983 a,b,c] algorithm is a procedure to measure pointwise dimension. Let the ordered sequence $\{X_t\}$, $t = 1, \ldots, N$, represent the observed time series. Then, for a given embedding dimension d, create a sequence of d-histories, $\{(x_t, x_{t+r}, \ldots, x_{t+(d-1)r})\}$.

Here, r stands for the time delay parameter. The sample correlation integral is given by

$$C_r^N = N^{-2} \sum_{i,j} \theta(r - |X_i - X_j|),$$
$$r > 0,\ X_i = (x_i, x_{i+1r}, \ldots, x_{i+(d-1)r}).$$

$\theta(.)$ is the Heaviside step function which maps positive arguments into one, and nonpositive arguments into zero. Thus, $\theta(.)$ counts the number of points which are within distance r from each other. r is the scaling parameter. The calculation of C_r^N is useful because

$$\lim_{\substack{N \to \infty \\ r \to 0^+}} C_r^N \to C_r,$$

and $d \ln C_r / d \ln r = D_2$,
whenever the derivative is defined, Guckenheimer [1984]; D_2 is a member of a general class of dimensions D_q, $q = \{0, 1, 2, \ldots\}$, defined by:

$$D_q = -\lim_{r \to 0} K_q(r)/\ln(r)$$
$$K_q = (1-q)^{-1} \ln \Sigma_{i=1}^{N(r)} P_i(r)^q$$

where $P_i(r)$ is the probability of a point of the attractor being within r of the ith point, $N(r)$ is the number of such boxes needed to cover the attractor, and K_q is the Kolmogorov-Sinai (metric) entropy: details are in Badii and Politi [1985], for example. D_2 will be designated dc to stand for correlation dimension. dc is a measure of pointwise dimension, dp. Pointwise dimension, see Farmer, Ott, and Yorke [1983], measures the relative rate of change in the number of points on the attractor as the diameter of the covering sets is decreased. A first problem in determining the appropriate d-dimensional vectors to analyze is the choice of r, the delay parameter. Where there are, in fact, attractors, the choice is fairly simple; choose r such that the auto-correlations are zero, or more sophisticatedly, so that the mutual information is minimized, Fraser [1986]. In either case, the basic idea is the same, one seeks on average an approximate orthogonal set of basis vectors so as to provide the clearest representation of the attractor. When the data are from an ARMA process, the achievement of "zero-autocorrelation" between the d-tuples is even more important in that, if correlated vectors are used, false conclusions about the presence of low-dimensional attractors can be drawn.

Correlation dimension is usually estimated from experimental data by a linear regression of the observed values of ln C_r^N on $\ln r$ over a suitably chosen subinterval of the range of r, (0, 1). The estimated slope coefficient of this regression, designated hereafter as $d\hat{c}$, is the usual estimator of correlation dimension cited in the literature. However, there are a number of important qualifications to this seemingly simple procedure. First, an important practical issue involves the appropriate choice of the scaling region r actually used to calculate dc. While the theory discusses the properties of C_r as $r \to 0$, the reality is that the range of r used is far from zero and inevitably increases away from zero as embedding dimension is increased. Smaller values for r require substantial increases in sample size at any given embedding dimension in order to be able to determine a logarithmic linear relationship between C_r and r. In fact, the relationship between $\ln C_r$ and $\ln r$ is only approximately linear over a relatively narrow range of values for r. For large values of r, C_r saturates at unity so that the regression of $\ln C_r$ on $\ln r$ is zero. Further, as the value of r declines towards zero even with very large data sets, two complications arise: One is due to the limited precision of the data series and the other is due to the inevitable presence of noise. The former problem sets a practical lower bound on r before C_r collapses to zero and the latter difficulty offsets the decline in values of C_r when r reaches the level of the noise scales. Consequently, the negative slope of $\ln C_r$ on $\ln r$ starts at zero, increases first at an increasing rate, then may remain constant for a short range before increasing again and then falling very sharply.

References

Abraham, N. B., et al. 1986. "Calculating the Dimension of Attractors from Small Data Sets." *Physics Letters* 114A:217.

Arnold, V. I. 1985. *Ordinary Differential Equations* Cambridge, MA: The MIT Press.

Ashley, R. A.; Patterson, D. M.; and Hinich, M. J. 1986. "A Diagnostic Test for Nonlinear Serial Dependence in Time Series Fitting Errors." *Journal of Time Series Analysis* 7(3):165–178.

Badii, R., and Politi, A. 1985. "Statistical Description of Chaotic Attractors: The Dimension Function." *J. Stat. Phys.* 40:725.

Baek, E. G., and Brock, W. 1988. "A Nonparametric Test for Temporal Dependence in a Vector of Time Series." Social Systems Research Institute. Madison: University of Wisconsin.

Baek, E. G., and Brock, W. 1988. "The Theory of Statistical Inference for Nonlinear Science: Gauge Functions, Complexity Measures, and Instability Measures." Social Systems Research Institute. Madison: University of Wisconsin.

Baillie, R. T., and Bollerslev, T. 1987. "The Message in Daily Exchange Rates: A Conditional Variance Tale." Econometrics and Economics Theory Paper No. 8702. East Lansing Michigan: Department of Economics.

Barnett, W., and Chen, P. 1988a. "The Aggregation-Theoretic Monetary Aggregates Are Chaotic and Have Strange Attractors." In *Dynamic Econometric Modelling, Proceedings of the Third International Symposium on Economic Theory and Econometrics*, ed. W. Barnett, E. Berndt, and H. White. Cambridge: Cambridge University Press.

Barnett, W. and Chen, P. 1988b. "Determinstic Chaos and Fractal Attractors as Tools for Nonparametric Dynamical Econometric Inference: With an Application to the Divisia Monetary Aggregates." *Mathematical Computer Modelling* 10:275.

Baumol, William J. 1957. "Speculation, Profitability, and Stability". *The Review of Economics and Statistics*. 39(3):263–271.

Baumol, William J. 1961. "Pitfalls in Contracyclical Policies: Some Tools and Results." *The Review of Economics and Statistics* 43(1):21–26.

Baumol, W. J., and Benhabib, J. 1988. "Chaos: Significance, Mechanism, and Economic Applications." *Journal of Economic Perspectives* November.

Ben-Mizrachi, A., et al. 1984. "Characterization of Experimental (noisy) Strange Attractors." *Physical Review A* 29:975.

Bergé, P.; Pomeau, Y.; Vidal, C. 1984. *Order Within Chaos: Towards a Deterministic* Approach to Turbulence. Paris: John Wiley & Sons, Inc.

Blatt, John M. 1983. *Dynamic Economic Systems* Armonk, NY: M. E. Sharpe, Inc.

Bollerslev, T. 1986. "Generalized Autoregressive Conditional Heteroskedasticity." *Journal of Econometrics* 31:307–327.

Bollerslev, T. 1987a. "A Conditional Heteroskedastic Time Series Model for Speculative Prices and Rates of Return." *Review of Economics and Statistics*, forthcoming.

Brandstater, A., and Swinney, H. L. 1986 "A Strange Attractor in Weakly Turbulent Couette-Taylor Flow." University of Texas, Department of Physics and the Center for Nonlinear Dynamics.

Brock, W. A. 1986. "Distinguishing Random and Deterministic Systems: Abridged Version." *Journal of Economic Theory* 40:168.

Brock, W. A. 1987. "Introduction to Chaos and Other Aspects of Nonlinearity." Forthcoming in *Differential Equations, Stability, and Chaos in Dynamic Economics* New York: North Holland.

Brock, W. A., and Dechert, W. D. 1988. "Theorems on Distinguishing Deterministic From Random Systems." In *Dynamic Econometric Modeling*. Cambridge: Cambridge University Press.

Brock, W. A., and Sayers, C. 1988. "Is the Business Cycle Characterized by Deterministic Chaos?" *Journal of Monetary Economics* 22:71–90.

Brock, W. A.; Dechert, W. D.; and Scheinkman, J. A. 1988. "A Test for Independence Based on the Correlation Dimension." In *Dynamic Econometric Modelling, Proceedings of the Third International Symposium on Economic Theory and Econometrics*, ed. W. Barnett, E. Berndt, and H. White. Cambridge: Cambridge University Press.

Caputo, J. G., et al. 1986. "Determination of Attractor Dimension and Entropy for Various Flows: An Experimentalist's Viewpoint." In *Dimensions and Entropies in Chaotic Systems, Quantification of Complex Behavior*, ed. G. Mayer-Kress. New York: Springer-Verlag.

Chou, R. Y. 1987. "Persistent Volatility and Stock Returns—Some Empirical Evidence Using GARCH." UCSD, Dept. of Economics, working paper.

Engle, R. F. 1982. "Autoregressive Conditional Heteroskedasticity with Estimates of the Variance of U.K. Inflation." *Econometrica* 50:987–1008.

Engle, R. F., and Bollerslev, T. 1986. "Modelling the Persistence of Conditional Variances." *Econometric Reviews* 5:1–50.

Engle, R. F.; Lilien, D. M.; and Robins, R. P. 1987. "Estimating Time Varying Risk Premia in the Term Structure: The ARCH-M Model." *Econometrica* 55:391–407.

Farmer, J. D.; Ott, E.; and Yorke, J. A. 1983. "The Dimension of Chaotic Attractors." *Physica*, 7D: 153.

Frank, M., and Stengos, T. 1987a. "Measuring the Strangeness of Gold and Silver Rates of Return." Department of Economics, University of Guelph.

Frank, M., and Stengos, T. 1987b. "Some Evidence Concerning Macroeconomic Chaos." Department of Economics, University of Guelph.

Fraser, A. M. 1986. "Using Mutual Information to Estimate Metric Entropy." In *Dimensions and Entropies in Chaotic Systems*, ed. Gottfried Mayer-Kress. New York: Springer-Verlag.

Frisch, Ragnar. 1933. "Propagation Problems and Impulse Problems in Dynamic Economics." *Economic Essays in Honor of Gustav Cassel*. London: Allen and Unwin.

Gennottee, G., and Marsh, T. 1976. "Variations in Ex ante Risk Premiums on Capital Assets." Berkeley Business School, University of California.

Goodwin, R. M. 1951. "The Nonlinear Accelerator and the Persistence of Business Cycles." *Econometrica* 19:1–17.

Grassberger, P. 1985. "Generalizations of the Hausdorff Dimension of Fractal Measures." *Physics Letters* 107A:101.

Grassberger, P., and Procaccia, I. 1983a. "Characterization of Strange Attractors." *Physical Review Letters* 50:346.

Grassberger, P., and Procaccia, I. 1983b. "Estimation of the Kolmogorov Entropy from a Chaotic Signal." *Physical Review A* 28:2591.

Grassberger, P., and Procaccia, I. 1983c. "Measuring the Strangeness of Strange Attractors." *Physica* 9D:189.

Grebogi, C., et al. 1984. "Strange Attractors That Are Not Chaotic." *Physica* 13D:261.

Greenside, H. S., et al. 1982. "Impracticality of a Box-counting Algorithm for Calculating the Dimensionality of Strange Attractors." *Physical Review A* 25:3453.

Guckenheimer, J. 1984. "Dimension Estimates for Attractors." *Contemporary Mathematics* 28:357.
Gumowski, Igor, and Mira Christian, 1980. *Recurrences and Discrete Dynamical Systems*. New York: Springer-Verlag.
Halsey, T. C. et al. 1986. "Fractal Measures and Their Singularities: The Characterization of Strange Sets." *Physical Review A* 33:1141.
Hinich, M., and Patterson, D. 1985a. "Evidence of Nonlinearity in Daily Stock Returns." *Journal of Business and Economic Statistics* 3(1):69–77.
Hinich, M., and Patterson, D. 1985b. "Identification of the Coefficients in a Nonlinear Time Series of the Quadratic Type." *Journal of Econometrics* 30:269–288.
Hinich, M., and Patterson, D. 1987. "Evidence of Nonlinearity in the Trade-by-Trade Stock Market Return Generating Process." Working Paper, Univ. of Texas at Austin, July.
Hinich, M., and Patterson, D. 1987. "Fitting a Quadratic Moving Average Model to Data." Technical Report, Applied Research Laboratories, University of Texas at Austin.
Hinich, M. J. 1982. "Testing for Gaussianity and Linearity of a Stationary Time Series." *Journal of Time Series Analysis* 3:169–176.
Holzfuss, J., and Mayer-Kress, G. 1986. "An Approach to Error-free Estimation in the Application of Dimension Algorithms." In *Dimensions and Entropies in Chaotic Systems, Quantification of Complex Behavior*, ed. G. Mayer-Kress. New York: Springer-Verlag.
Hsieh, D. 1987. "Testing for Nonlinear Dependence in Foreign Exchange Rates: 1974–1983." Graduate School of Business, University of Chicago.
Hurewicz, W., and Wallman, H. 1948. *Dimension Theory*. Princeton: Princeton University Press.
Kalecki, M. 1943. *Studies in Economic Dynamics*. New York: Allen and Unwin.
Kawakami, H. 1984. "Strange Attractors in Duffing's Equation—50 Phrase Portraits of Chaos." University of Tokushima, Dept. of Electronics, preprint.
Mackey, M. C., and Glass, L. 1977. *Science* 197:287.
Mehra, Yash. 1986. "Recent Financial Deregulation and the Interest Elasticity of M1 Demand." Federal Reserve Bank of Richmond *Economic Review* 72:4.
Mitchell, Wesley C. 1913. *Business Cycles*. Berkeley, CA: NBER.
Phillips, A. W. 1954. "Stabilization Policy in a Closed Economy." *Economic Journal* 64:290–323.
Priestly, M. B. 1981. *Spectral Analysis and Time Series*, Vols. 1, 2. New York: Academic Press.
Ramsey, J. B., and Montenegro, A. 1988. "The Identifiability and Estimability of Non-invertible MA(Q) Models." C. V. Starr Center Working Paper No. 88–08.
Ramsey, J. B., and Yuan, H. 1987. "The Statistical Properties of Dimension Calculations Using Small Data Sets." C. V. Starr Center Working Paper No. 87–20.
Ramsey, J. B., and Rothman, P. 1988. "The Characterization of Time Irreversibility: Estimates and Test Statistics." C. V. Starr Center Working Paper, New York University, September.

Ramsey, J.B., and Yuan, H.J. 1989. "Bias and Error Bars in Dimension Calculations and Their Evaluation in Some Simple Models." *Physics Letters-A*, 134:287–297.

Ramsey, J. B., and Yuan, H. J. 1988b. "The Statistical Properties of Dimension Calculations Using Small Data Sets." Submitted to *Nonlinearity*.

Ramsey, J. B., Rothman, P., and Sayers, C. L. 1988. "The Statistical Properties of Dimension Calculations Using Small Data Sets: Some Economic Applications." Submitted to *The International Economic Review*.

Ruelle, D. 1979. "Sensitive Dependence on Initial Conditions and Turbulent Behavior in Dynamical Systems." *Annal. N. Y. Acad. Sci.* 316:408–416.

Ruelle, D., and Takens, F. 1971. "On the Nature of Turbulence." *Commun. Math. Physics* 20:167–192.

Samuelson, Paul A. 1939. "Interactions Between the Multiplier Analysis and the Principle of Acceleration." *Review of Economics and Statistics* 21(May):75–78.

Sayers, C. L. 1986. "Work Stoppages: Exploring the Nonlinear Dynamics." Department of Economics, University of Wisconsin.

Sayers, C. L. 1987. "Diagnostic Tests for Nonlinearity in Time Series Data: An Application to the Work Stoppages Series." Department of Economics, University of North Carolina—Chapel Hill.

Scheinkman, J. A., and LeBaron, B. 1986. "Nonlinear Dynamics and Stock Returns." Department of Economics, University of Chicago.

Scheinkman, J. A., and LeBaron, B. 1987. "Nonlinear Dynamics and GNP Data." In *Economic Complexity, Chaos, Sunspots, Bubbles, and Nonlinearity*, ed. W. Barnett, J. Geweke, and K. Shell. Cambridge: Cambridge University Press.

Takens, F. 1980. "Detecting Strange Attractors in Turbulence." In *Dynamical Systems and Turbulence*, ed. D. A. Rand and L.-S. Young. Springer Lecture Notes in Mathematics, Vol. 898. New York, Heidelberg, Berlin: Springer-Verlag.

Tong, Howell. 1983. "Threshold Models in Nonlinear Time Series Analysis." In *Lecture Notes in Statistics*. New York: Springer Verlag.

Whitney, H. 1955. "On Singularities of Mappings of Euclidian Spaces I, Mappings of the Plane onto the Plane." *Ann. Math.* 62:374–410.

Whitney, H. 1944. "The Self-Intersections of a Smooth *n*-Manifold in 2*n*-Space." *Ann. Math.* 45:220–246.

COMMENTARY

by W. Davis Dechert

Recently there has been a great deal of interest in applying the ideas of the branch of nonlinear dynamics known as chaos theory in an effort to model economic and financial systems. A working definition of chaos for our purposes is a dynamical system (necessarily nonlinear) that gives rise to observations that have the characteristics of random data, and yet nevertheless are deterministically generated. Professor Ramsey explores several issues that pertain to the application of the theory of chaos to economic and financial data. First, he introduces an approach to modeling time series as nonlinear dynamical systems that are chaotic; second he raises some empirical difficulties that are involved in estimating the structure of those systems; and third, he discusses a test for non-stationarity and applies it to stock market prices, pig iron production data, and money supply aggregates.

In the first part, Professor Ramsey takes as a starting point a simple differential equation (known as Duffing's equation)

$$\ddot{x} + \delta\dot{x} - \beta x + x^3 = \gamma\cos(\omega t) \tag{4C.1}$$

which for certain ranges of values of the parameters β, γ, δ, and ω has chaotic solutions. Although he explains how each of the terms can be intepreted in an economic context, his main interest is in adapting equation 4C.1 to economic and financial time series, much in the same way as an autoregression

$$x_t = \sum_{k=1}^{N} \alpha_k x_{t-k} + \varepsilon_t \tag{4C.2}$$

is fit to time series data. There is a parallel of methodology that is worth emphasizing for these two equations. Equation 4C.2 is not in general derived from a dynamic economic model, but rather it is used to test the time series for an auto-regressive structure. A well-known limitation of this approach is that forecasts based on fitted values of the coefficients $\hat{\alpha}_k$ are rarely accurate.

Forecasting on the basis of equation 4C.1 is even more tenuous. The difficulty is that any equation whose trajectories are chaotic, exhibits sensitive dependence on initial conditions. This means that even if the data are generated by equation 4C.1, and even if we know the exact values of the constants, a slight error in the initial condition $(x_0, \dot{x}_0)$ is quickly magnified so that the solution to the differential equation is no longer close to the data. This is exacerbated when the parameters in equation 4C.1 are estimated. This lack of stable trajectories poses an impediment to identifying the structural form of the process that is generating the data. Model fitting in the classical sense is virtually a futile exercise for chaotic data.

In the second part, several empirical issues are raised that relate to the estimation of parameters in the presence of chaos. The author's focus is on the calculation of the dimension of the data set. If the data are generated by a process that is either nonstationary or highly autocorrelated, the estimated dimension can be severely biased. There can also be a "small sample" problem as well. The Grassberger-Procaccia correlation dimension is given by

$$C_{m,n}(\varepsilon) = \binom{n}{2}^{-1} |\{(s,t) \mid 1 \leq s < t \leq n,\ d(x_t^m, x_s^m) < \varepsilon\}| \tag{4C.3}$$

where $|S|$ denotes the number of elements of the set S, $x_t^m = (x_t, x_{t+1}, \ldots, x_{t+m-1})$, and $d(x,y) = \max_{1 \leq i \leq m} |x_i - y_i|$. The dimension of the data set at embedding dimension m is defined by

$$d_m = \lim_{\substack{n \to \infty \\ \varepsilon \to 0}} \frac{\ln(C_{m,n}(\varepsilon))}{\ln(\varepsilon)} \tag{4C.4}$$

where the limit on n is taken first. It was shown that when the dimension of the data set is based on the Grassberger-Procaccia correlation dimension [1988b] this estimate is biased because of the following small sample problem: With a finite data set the value of ε in equation 4C.4 cannot be too small for otherwise $C_{m,n}(\varepsilon)$ will be 0 and d_m is undefined. The smaller the number of observations, the larger ε has to be, and the more biased the estimate of the dimension, d_m, will be. What is perhaps foreign to analysts of economic and financial data is that their data sets are small relative to those used in the physical sciences. Dimension calculations from experimental data often are based on upwards of 50,000 observations. Data sets with less than 1,000 observations are small by comparison. Thus dimension estimates for economic and financial data are likely to be substantially biased.

Another issue that Professor Ramsey raises in this article is that economic and financial data sets often do not exhibit time reversibility.

$$G_{ij}^k = \frac{1}{n} \sum_{t=1}^{n} [(x_t)^i (x_{t-k})^j - (x_t)^j (x_{t-k})^i] \tag{4C.5}$$

is used to test for the presence of time reversibility [1988a]. This statistic is used to test monthly M_2 data, daily stock market data, and monthly pig iron production data for time reversibility. In all three time series evidence of time irreversibility is found. As an extension of this research, it would be useful to know how the time irreversibility of a time series might affect the estimation of the dimension of the data set.

Professor Ramsey notes in his conclusion that "economic systems are clearly nonlinear...and also contain noise that is embedded in the dynamic itself." He concludes that we need to improve our understanding of an "appropriate modeling structure" for economic and financial data. Currently there is another line of research that is being pursued based on the premise that it is important to develop methods to detect the presence of nonlinearities, and to discover the effects that randomness has on the observability of the system. While some researchers in economics have attempted to discover a low dimensional attractor (notably [Barnett]), others (e.g., Brock, Frank, Hsieh Sheinkman) have been testing economic and financial data for the presence of nonlinearities. These tests use the BDS statistic, [Brock, 1987] and are based on the following idea: If the sequence of data, $\{x_t\}$ is independent and identically distributed (IID), then the statistic

$$W_{m,n}(\varepsilon) = C_{m,n}(\varepsilon) - C_{1,n}(\varepsilon)^m \tag{4C.6}$$

converges to zero with probability one, and furthermore $\sqrt{n}W_{m,n}(\varepsilon)$ is asymptotically normal. In [Brock 1988] the use of the BDS statistic as a specification test is developed. There it was shown that if the true model is

$$x_t = f(x_{t-1}, x_{t-2}, \ldots) + u_t \tag{4C.7}$$

where $\{u_t\}$ is IID and one specifies the model as

$$x_t = g(x_{t-1}, x_{t-2}, \ldots) + v_t \tag{4C.8}$$

then one can use the estimated residuals to test for model misspecification. This test goes as follows: One estimates equation 4C.8 on a sample of length n with

$$x_t = g_n(x_{t-1}, x_{t-2}, \ldots) + v_{t,n} \tag{4C.9}$$

where $\{v_{t,n}\}$ are the estimated residuals. As long as the estimated model in equation 4C.9 satisfies $g_n \rightarrow g$, then $v_{t,n} \rightarrow v_t$ where

$$v_t = f(x_{t-1}, x_{t-2}, \ldots) - g(x_{t-1}, x_{t-2}, \ldots) + u_t. \tag{4C.10}$$

It follows that if $f = g$ then $\{v_t\}$ is an IID sequence. Under certain regularity conditions on f and g it was shown that the converse is true [Brock 1988]. This is the basis for a test of model misspecification: Estimate a model and then test the residuals for IID. If it fails the test, then this is evidence that there is additional structure in the data that is not captured by the model.

The usefulness of the test sketched above is determined by the power of the test against various alternatives. Extensive tests are run with the BDS statistic [Hsieh and LeBaron, 1988a, b, c]. The general conclusion is that not only does the statistic have good power against low-dimensional chaos (after all the test is based on the concept of dimension), but also against many stochastic models. Included in this latter group are data that are uncorrelated, yet nevertheless not independent.

In conclusion, it is not clear to me that estimating nonlinear models that give rise to chaos such as Duffing's equation is the right approach to understanding economic and financial time series data. In my view the best attitude to take is to use the methods of other disciplines (in this case those of the mathematical and physical sciences) wherever they seem to fit; however one must tailor their usage to one's own discipline.

References

Barnett, W. A., and Chen, P. 1988. "The Aggregation Theoretic Monetary Aggregates Are Chaotic and Have Strange Attractors." In *Dynamic Econometric Modeling: Proceedings of the Third International Symposium in Economic Theory and Econometrics*, ed. W. A. Barnett, E. R. Berndt, and H. Whit. Cambridge: Cambridge University Press.

Brock, W. A., and Dechert, W. D. 1988. "A General Class of Specification Test: The Scalar Case." Forthcoming in the *Proceedings of the American Statistical Association*.

Brock, W. A.; Dechert, W. D.; and Scheinkman, J. A. 1987. "A Test for Independence Based on the Correlation Dimension." SSRI Working Paper, Department of Economics, University of Wisconsin.

Brock, W. A., and Sayers, C. 1988. "Is the Business Cycle Characterized by Deterministic Chaos?" *Journal of Monetary Economics* 22:71–90.

Frank, M., and Stengos, T. 1987. "Measuring the Strangeness of Gold and Silver Rates of Return." Department of Economics, University of Guelph.

Hsieh, D. 1987. "Testing for Nonlinear Dependence in Foreign Exchange Rates: 1974–1983." Graduate School of Business, University of Chicago.

Hsieh, D, and LeBaron, B. 1988a. "Small Sample Properties of the BDS Statistic, I." Graduate School of Business, University of Chicago.

Hsieh, D., and LeBaron, B. 1988b. "Small Sample Properties of the BDS Statistic, II." Graduate School of Business, University of Chicago.

Hsieh, D., and LeBaron, B. 1988c. "Small Sample Properties of the BDS Statistic, III." Graduate School of Business, University of Chicago.

Ramsey, J. B. "Economic and Financial Data as Nonlinear Processes," this volume.

Ramsey, J. B., and Rothman, P. 1988. "The Characterization of Time Irreversibility: Estimates and Test Statistics." C. V. Starr Center Working Paper, New York University, September.

Ramsey, J. B., and Yuan, H. J. 1988. "The Statistical Properties of Dimension Calculation Using Small Data Sets." New York University.

Scheinkman, J. A., and LeBaron B. 1986. "Nonlinear Dynamics and Stock Returns." Department of Economics, University of Chicago.

5 STATISTICAL ANALYSIS OF PRICE AND BASIS BEHAVIOR: OCTOBER 12–26, 1987, S&P 500 FUTURES AND CASH

Eugene Moriarty,[1] J. Douglas Gordon[2], Gregory Kuserk[3] and George Wang[4]

5.1. Introduction

In analyzing the behavior of the stock market and stock-index futures during October 1987, some observers noted the large discounts of futures to the cash index. While the effects of delayed openings on October 19 and trading halts on October 20 on futures discounts were noted by some, the effect of price-adjustment delays on stock indices generally was not highlighted in interpreting the events of October 19. However, the temporal relationship between the prices of the S&P 500 futures contract and the

---

The views stated here are those of the authors and do not necessarily reflect those of the Commodity Futures Trading Commission, the Treasury Department, or their staffs.

[1] President, Evergreen Financial Management, INC.

[2] Senior Financial Economist, Office of Thrift Supervision, U.S. Department of Treasury

[3] Agricultural Economist, Division of Economic Analysis, Commodity Futures Trading Commission

[4] Senior Financial Economist, Division of Economic Analysis, Commodity Futures Trading Commission, and Visiting Professor of Finance, School of Business, George Mason University.

stock index itself is important in assessing the effect of stock-index futures trading. According to some, the large negative basis that existed implies a transmission effect from the futures market to the stock market via a revelation of stock index values on the floor of the Chicago Mercantile Exchange. Such an interpretation regarding the effects of futures trading is affected by the statistical properties of the price series and the presence of a significant nontrading affect.

5.2. Methodology

To assess the degree to which futures lead cash prices and the extent of the nontrading effect during the October market break, research staff of the Commodity Futures Trading Commission (CFTC) estimated a proxy for the S&P 500 index made up of the more actively traded stocks in the index for each day during the period October 14, 1987, through October 26, 1987. The purpose of constructing the proxy index was to estimate the change in value of stocks, which was being revealed on the floor of the New York Stock Exchange (NYSE), and relate those changes to futures price changes. The approach taken did not separate the various sources of the nontrading effect such as the lag in transaction prices reflecting quotation adjustments, market-maker continuity effects, execution of large orders in smaller transactions, or the triggering of "stale" limit orders. Also, any differential in negative serial correlation in the index versus the futures contract price due to market-making activities or differential reporting lag were not removed from the data.

For each day during the October 14 through 26 period, the trade-by-trade transaction records of 480 of the 500 stocks in the S&P 500 Index were examined from a NYSE consolidated audit tape. Those stocks that traded at least once in 90% of the five-minute intervals contained in a given trading day were included in that day's proxy trading portfolio. The number of stocks in the proxy portfolio from October 14 through October 26 were 108, 127, 140, 110, 123, 127, 54, 93, and 101 respectively. The transaction price used for each stock in a given five-minute interval was the one closest to the end of the interval. A five-minute time interval was chosen for the analysis as a compromise between a shorter interval, which would decrease the staleness of any transaction prices contained in the interval, and a longer period, which would allow the inclusion of more stocks in the proxy portfolios.

The futures data were taken from the time and sales records of the Chicago Mercantile Exchange (CME). The reported index used was that captured by the CME from ADP Corp. and disseminated to the trading floor. During the crash week the frequency of capture of the S&P 500 index generally ranged from every fifteen to thirty seconds.

The five-minute time interval chosen for the analysis makes it less likely that longer-term causes of positive serial correlation, such as information lumpiness and market-maker inventory rebalancing will be captured.

The trading proxy index value was calculated on a capitalization-weighted basis. The trading proxy index for a given day was normalized to the S&P 500 index by setting the proxy index equal to the S&P 500 during a five-minute interval that contained relatively little price change (and was preceded and followed by such a period) in both the S&P 500 index and the Chicago Mercantile Exchange's December S&P 500 future. The normalizing interval was also chosen with the consideration that a large proportion of the stocks in the S&P 500 index and the proxy index traded during that interval. The long-term betas of the proxy portfolios relative to the S&P 500 were calculated, and they ranged from 1.03 to 1.10 with an average of 1.06.

For each five-minute period the reported basis was calculated by subtracting the S&P 500 index from the December S&P 500 futures price. The futures transaction price selected in a five-minute interval was the one closest in time to the capitalization-weighted average transaction time of the stocks included in that day's proxy portfolio.

5.3. Results

The estimates of the leads or lags of the S&P 500 futures price changes relative to the S&P 500 index changes were obtained by calculation of cross-correlations and Granger-type regressions. The autocorrelation function of the December S&P 500 futures price sampled at two-minute intervals did not exhibit significant autocorrelation structure either during the week of October 12 or the week of October 19. The S&P 500 index exhibited significant (at the 95% level) autocorrelations at 2 lags (4 minutes) during the week of October 12 and at 7 lags (14 minutes) during the week of October 19. The trading proxy index did not exhibit significant autocorrelation structure for the week of October 12 or the week of October 19 over the five-minute intervals at which the proxy index was calculated.

To assess the lag structure between the December 1987 S&P 500 future and the index, the cross-correlations of log price changes of the future and the whitened residuals of the S&P 500 index were calculated after removal

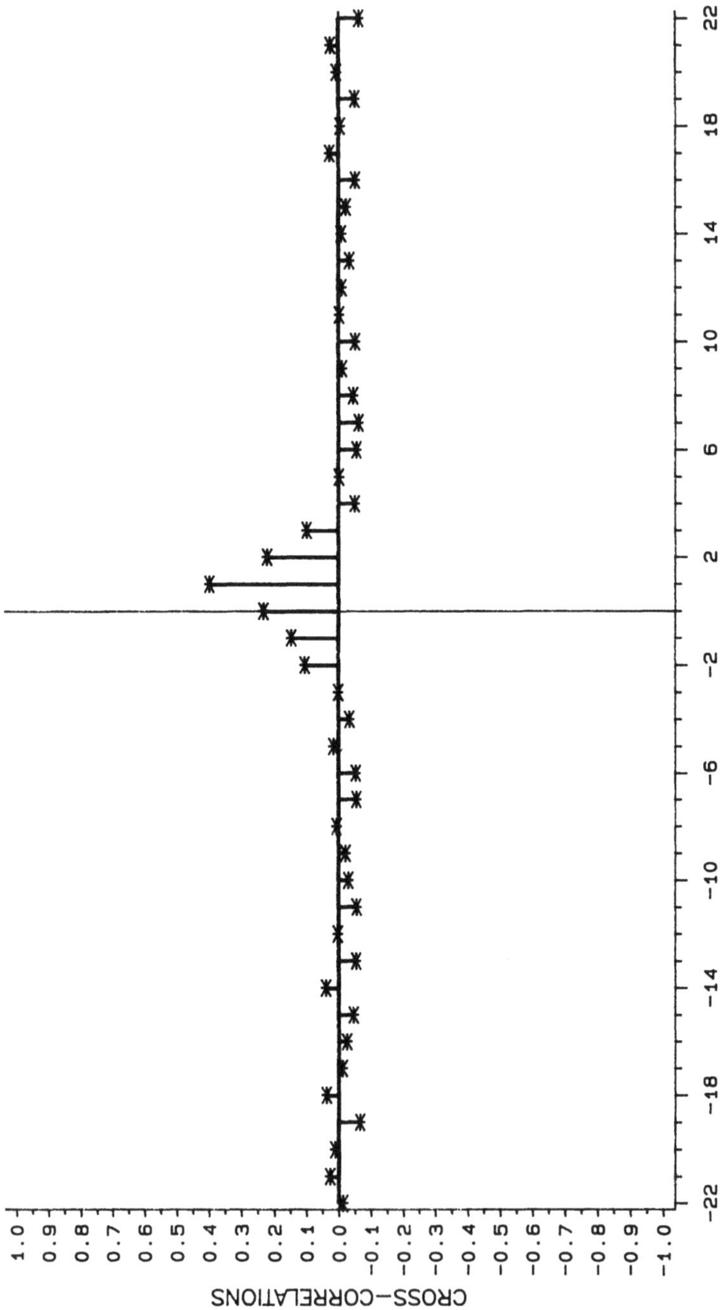

Figure 5–1. Cross-Correlation of Log Price Changes of December Futures and the Whitened Residuals of the S&P 500 Index (Week of October 12, 1987)

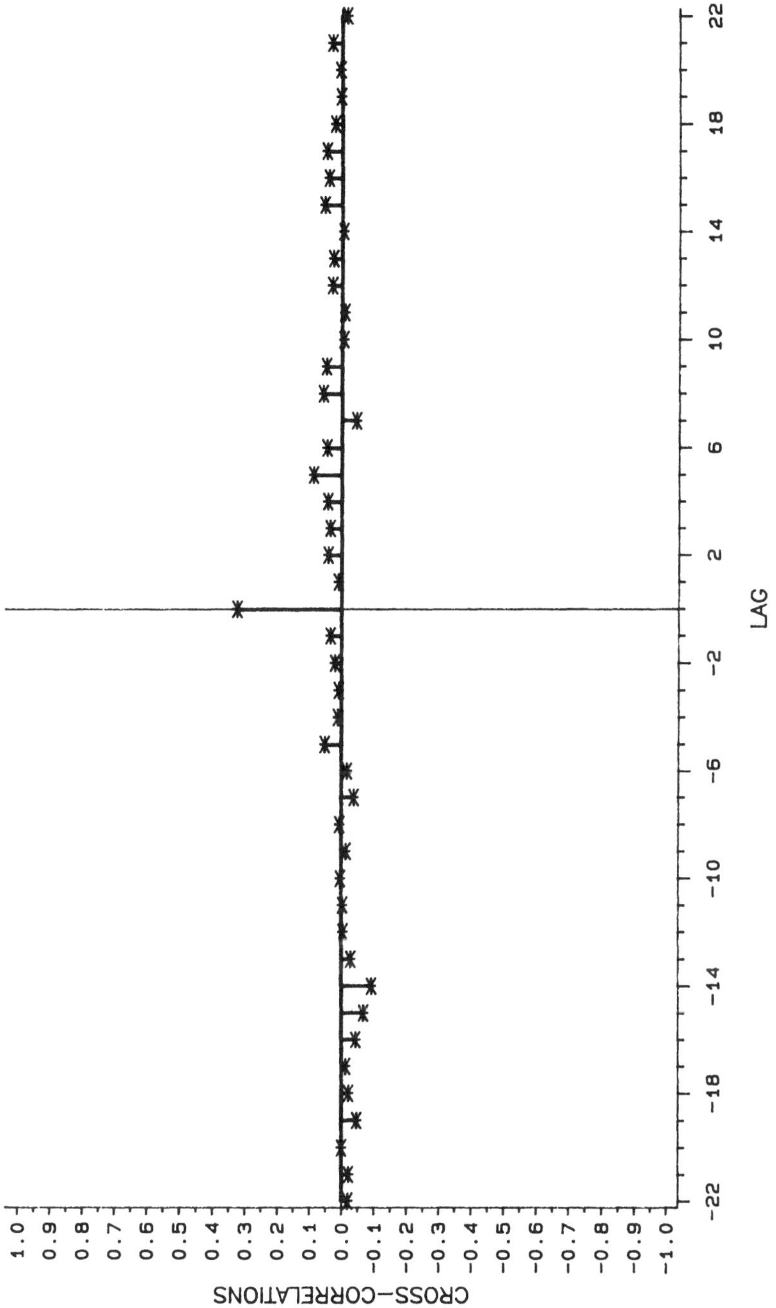

Figure 5–2. Cross-Correlation of Log Price Changes of December Futures and the Whitened Residuals of the S&P 500 Index (Week of October 19, 1987)

of the autocorrelation structure of the S&P 500 index log price changes. Those cross-correlations showed that during the week of October 12 the future and cash markets were related, with the future showing a one-period (two minutes) lead over cash and significant simultaneity during the week of October 12 (see figure 5–1), as well as less positive and negative temporal relationships between futures and the index. However, figure 5–2 shows a significant change in the character of the relationship, showing only a simultaneous relationship between futures and cash price changes. The Granger regressions corroborated these cross-correlation results.

Thus, the significant lead of up to 14 minutes of futures price changes over S&P 500 index price changes is reduced to 4 minutes during the week of October 12 and to zero lead during the week of October 19 when the serial correlation is removed from the S&P 500 index.

Another approach to interpreting the temporal structure between futures and stock price change can be achieved by examining the role of the nontrading effect in the cash-futures basis relationship.

The S&P 500 index, the proxy index, and the December S&P 500 futures contract are plotted in exhibits 5–1 through 5–9 for each day from October 14 through October 26 for those five-minute intervals during which the trading proxy index estimates were most reliable. When there were large price changes, the exhibits show that the S&P 500 index tended to lag the December S&P 500 future's price change. However, the lag is significantly reduced or eliminated when the December S&P 500 future is compared with the proxy index rather than the reported S&P 500 index. This also indicates that the value of stocks actually being traded during the market crash from moment to moment on the N.Y.S.E. floor and the concurrent value of the December S&P 500 future moved on a more simultaneous basis than was reflected by the reported S&P 500 index. Such a result would be expected when the last transactions differ significantly from current quotations.

Exhibits 5–10 through 5–18 plot the basis of the December S&P 500 future relative to the reported S&P 500 index (reported basis) and the nontrading effect (proxy index level minus S&P 500 index level) from October 14 through October 26 for the same five-minute intervals. The difference between these two plots provides an indication of the futures discount or premium not explained by the estimated nontrading effect. For example, if the reported basis were a negative ten points and the estimated nontrading effect was a negative eight points, then a negative two point discount would be indicated using the value of stocks being traded on the NYSE floor instead of using the reported S&P 500 index value.

On October 14 through 16 a significant nontrading effect was absent

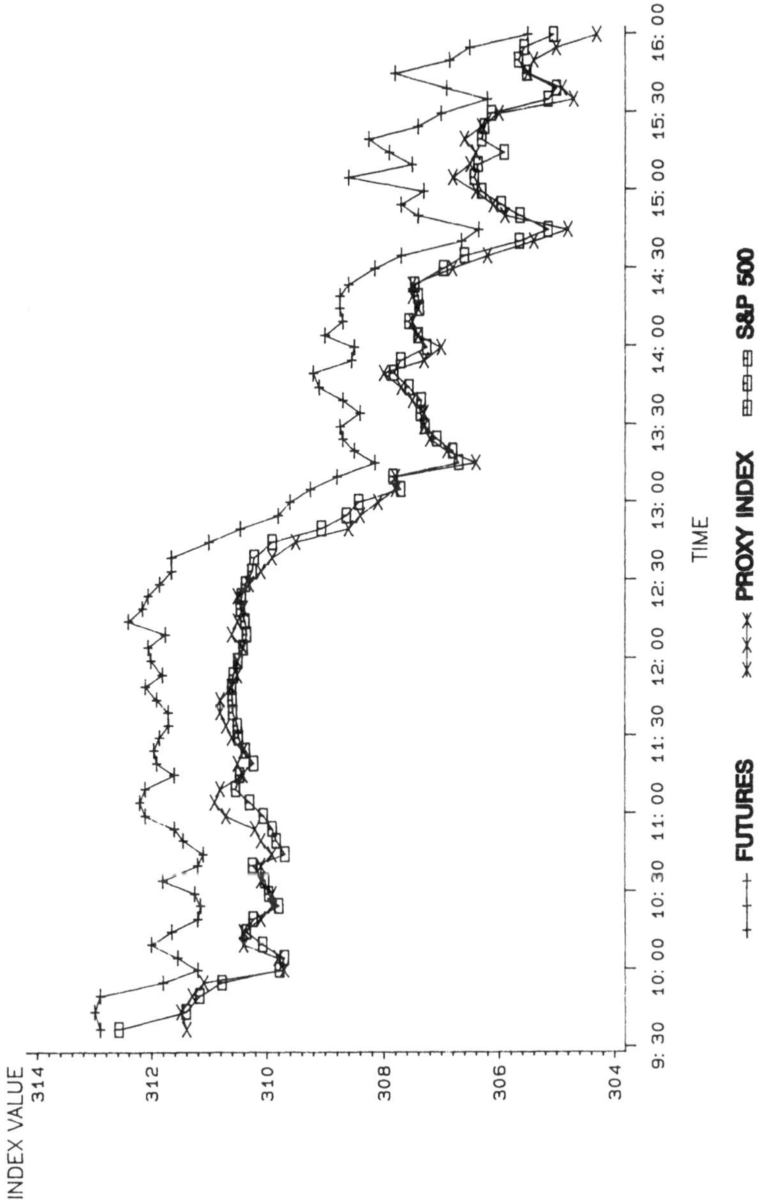

Exhibit 5–1. S&P 500 Index, Trading Proxy Index, and December Futures (October 14, 1987)

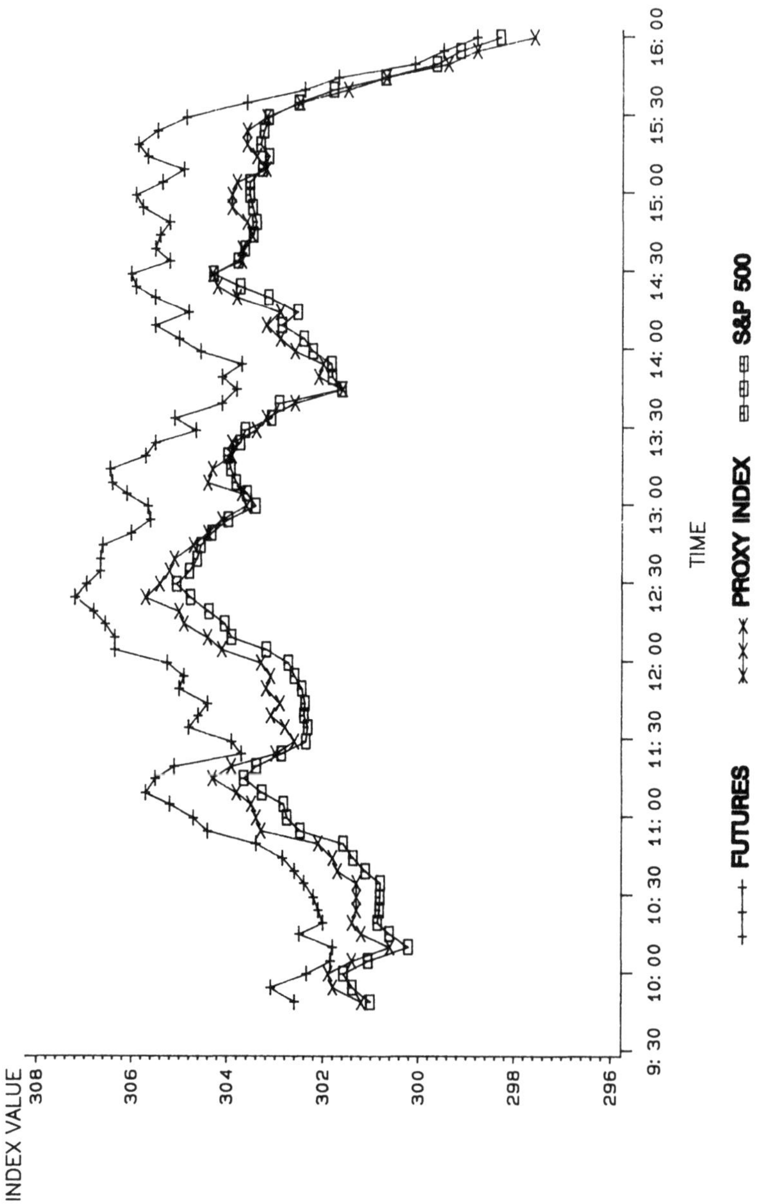

Exhibit 5–2. S&P 500 Index, Trading Proxy Index, and December Futures (October 15, 1987)

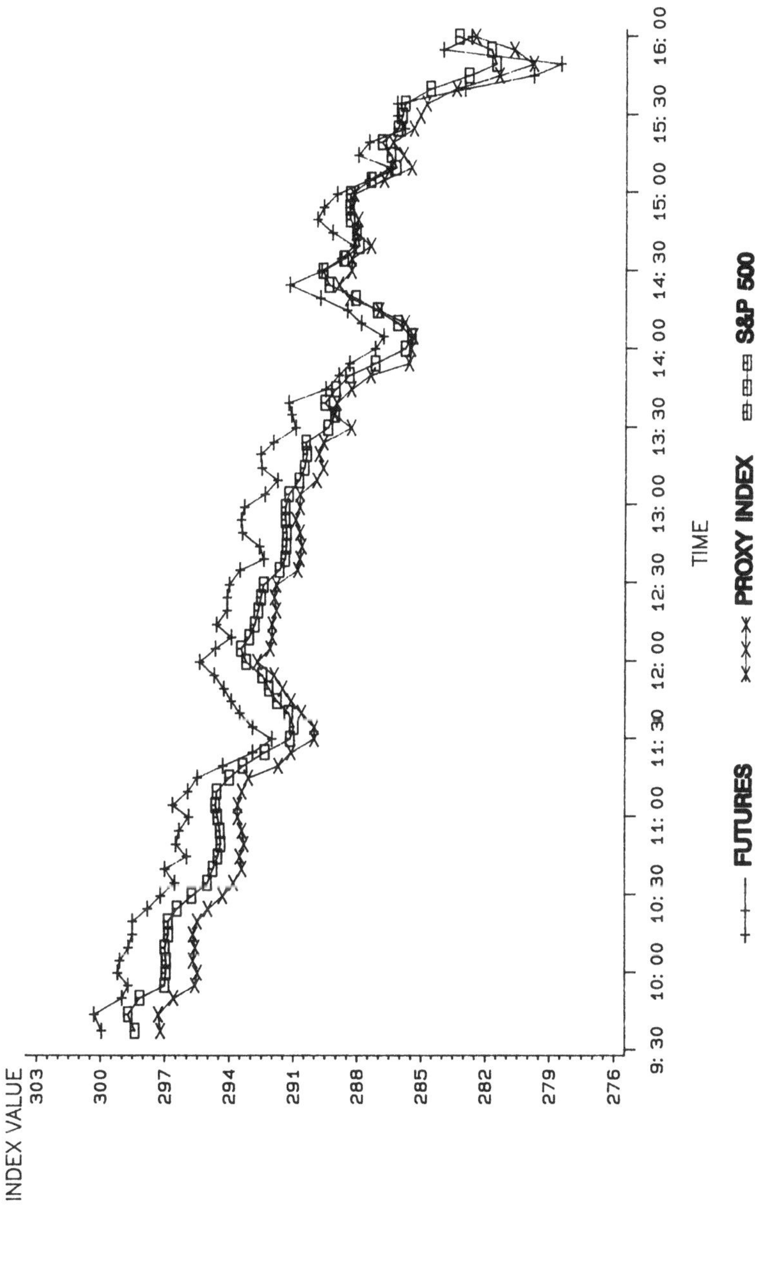

Exhibit 5–3. S&P 500 Index, Trading Proxy Index, and December Futures (October 16, 1987)

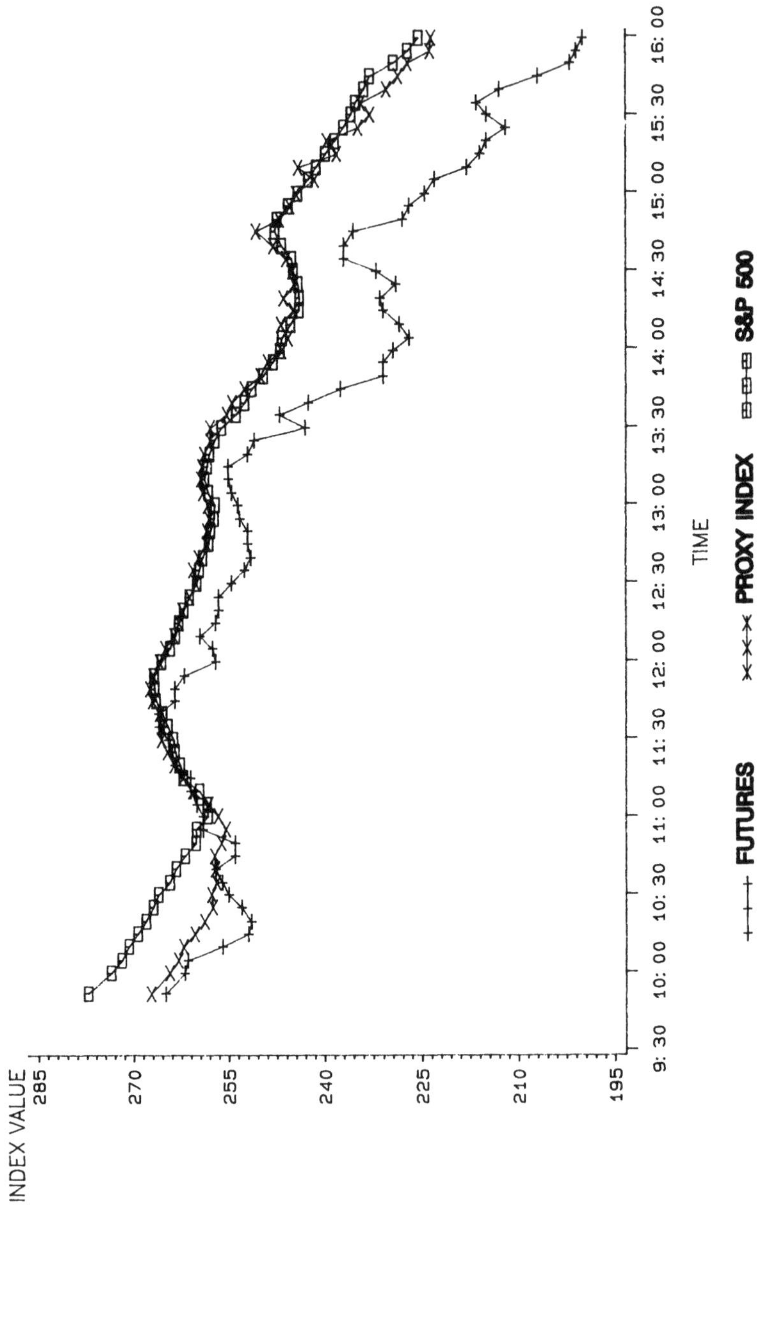

Exhibit 5–4. S&P 500 Index, Trading Proxy Index, and December Futures (October 19, 1987)

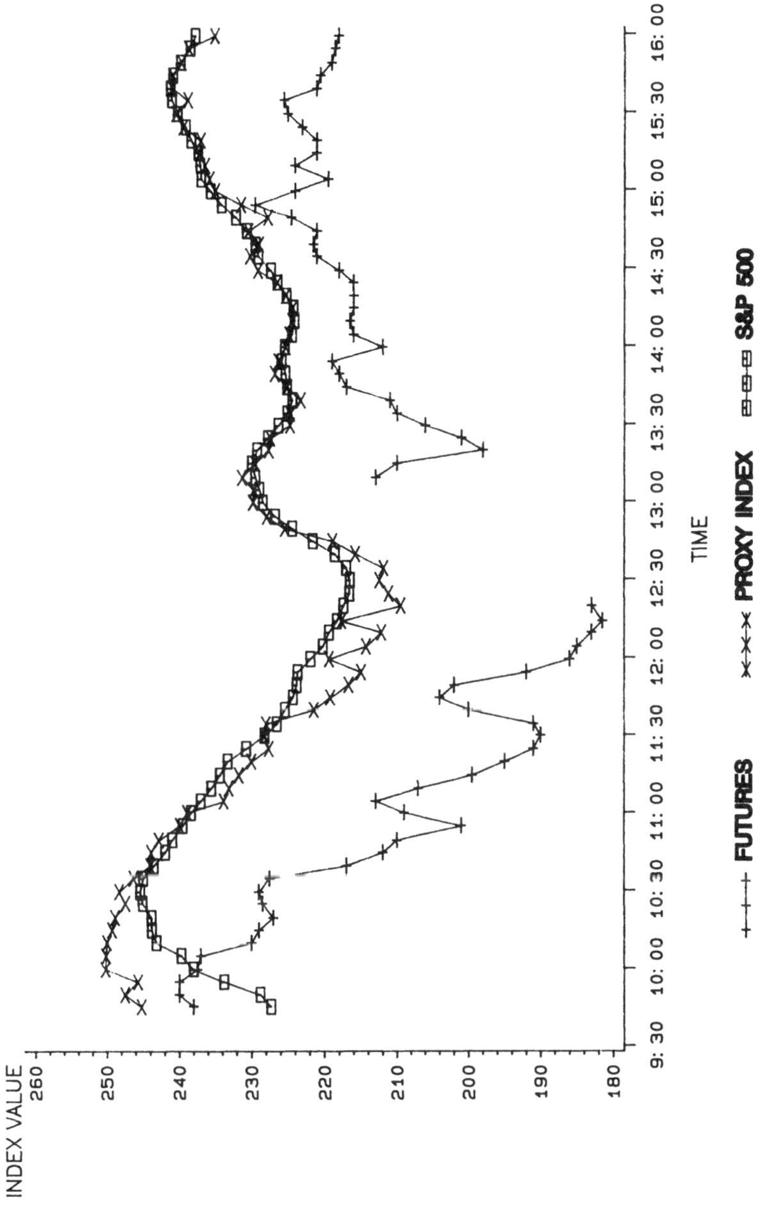

Exhibit 5–5. S&P 500 Index, Trading Proxy Index, and December Futures (October 20, 1987)

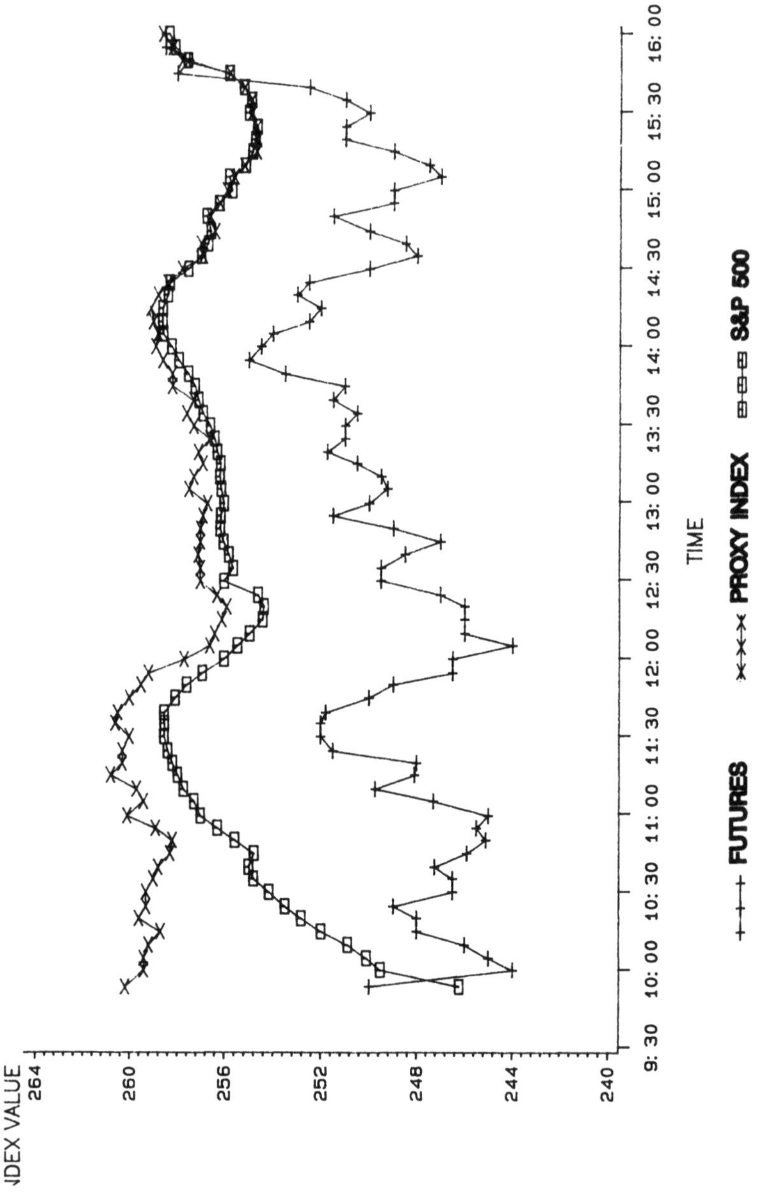

Exhibit 5–6. S&P 500 Index, Trading Proxy Index, and December Futures (October 21, 1987)

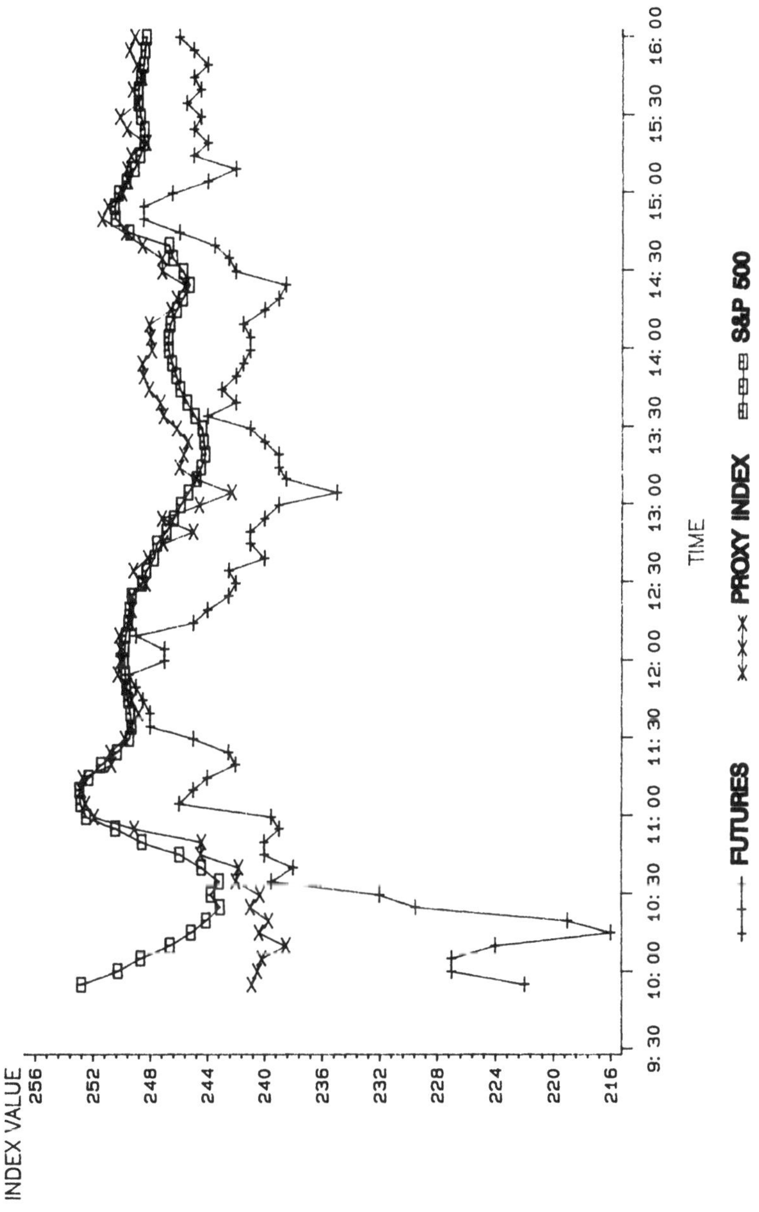

Exhibit 5–7. S&P 500 Index, Trading Proxy Index, and December Futures (October 22, 1987)

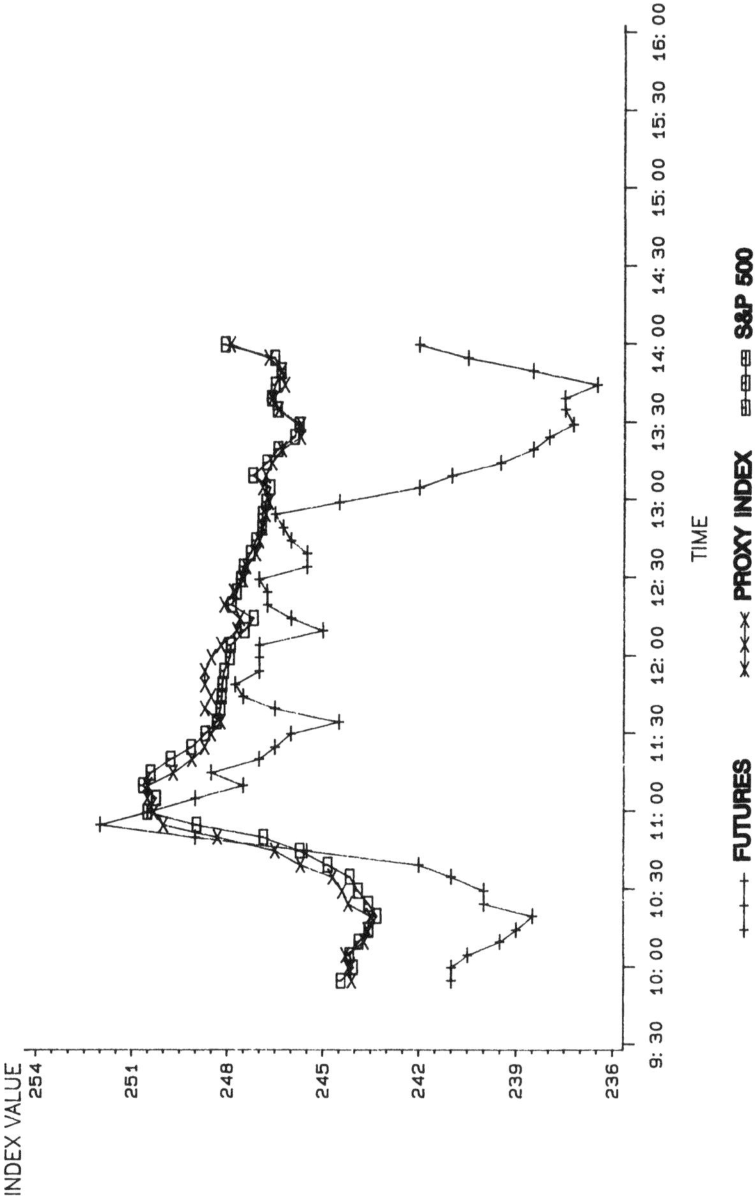

Exhibit 5–8. S&P 500 Index, Trading Proxy Index, and December Futures (October 23, 1987)

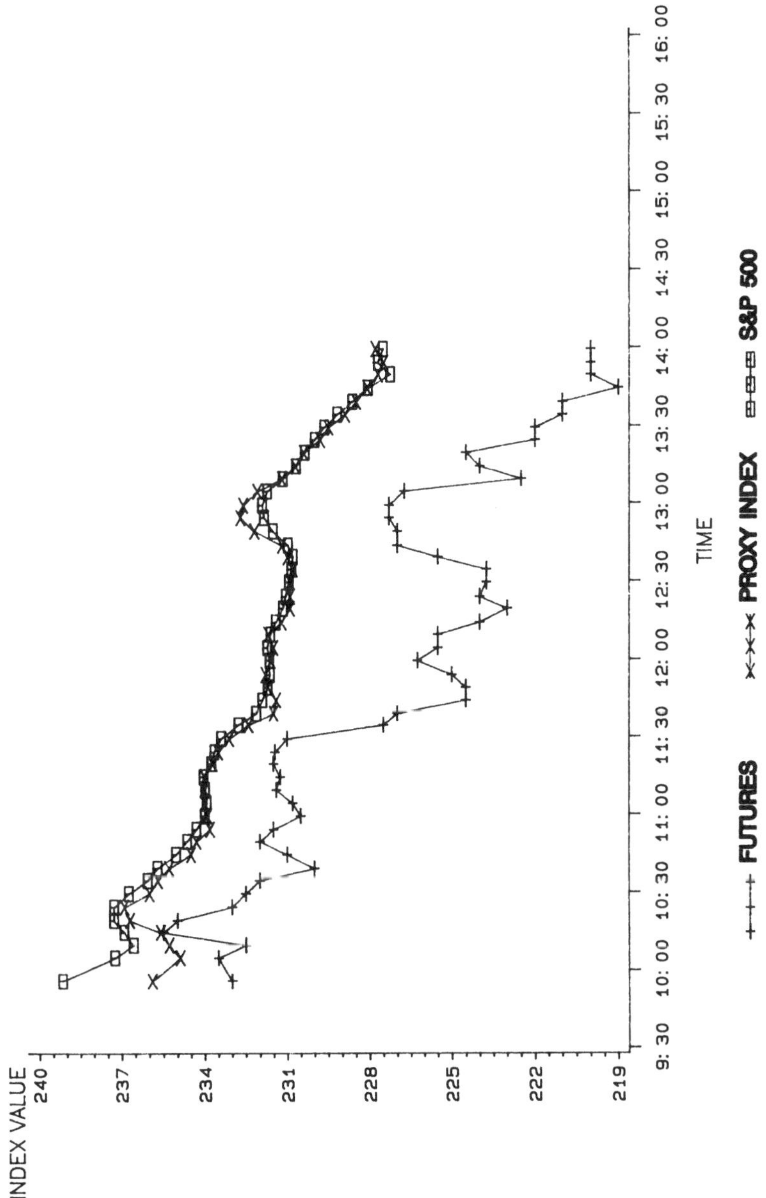

Exhibit 5–9. S&P 500 Index, Trading Proxy Index, and December Futures (October 26, 1987)

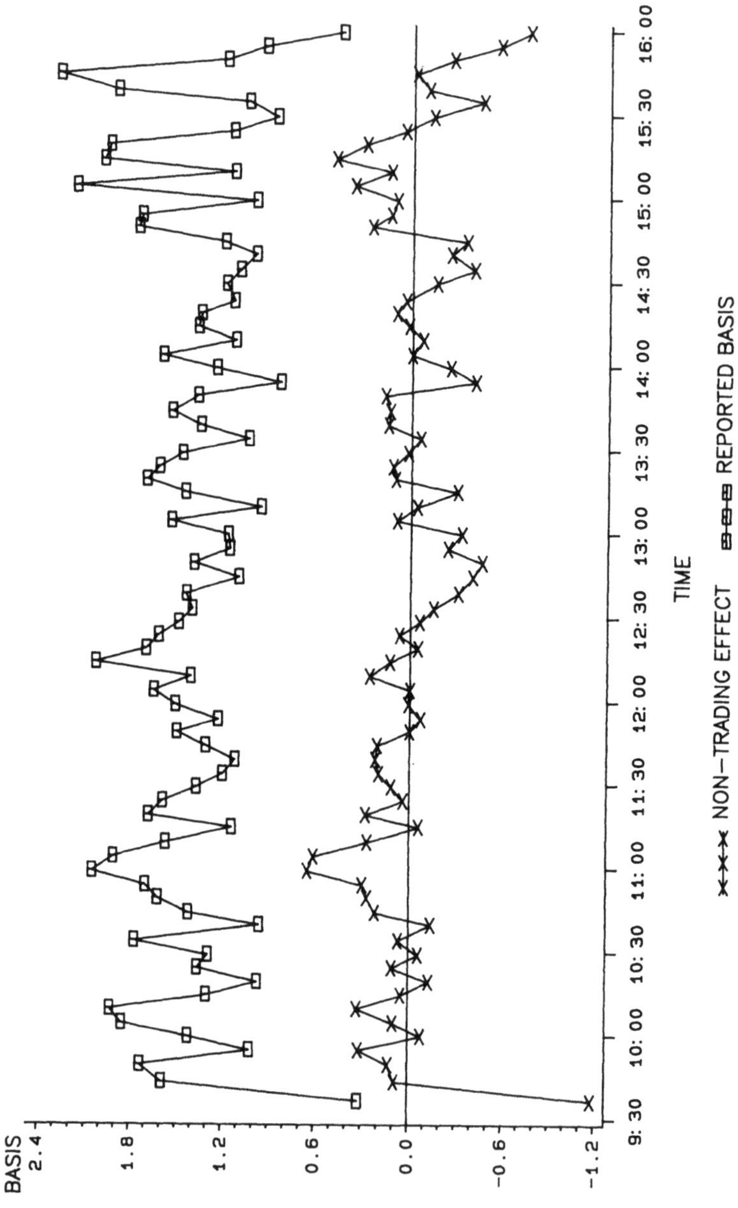

Exhibit 5–10. S&P 500 Stock Index Reported Basis and Nontrading Effect (October 14, 1987)

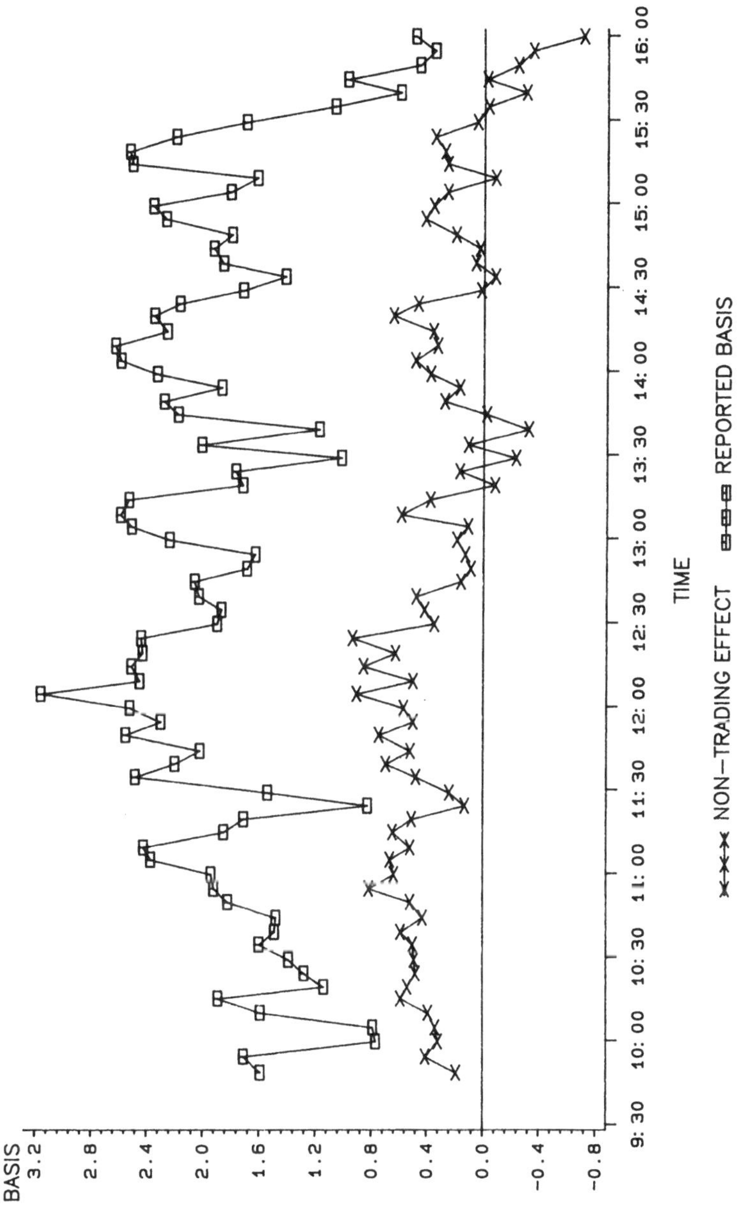

Exhibit 5–11. S&P 500 Stock Index Reported Basis and Nontrading Effect (October 15, 1987)

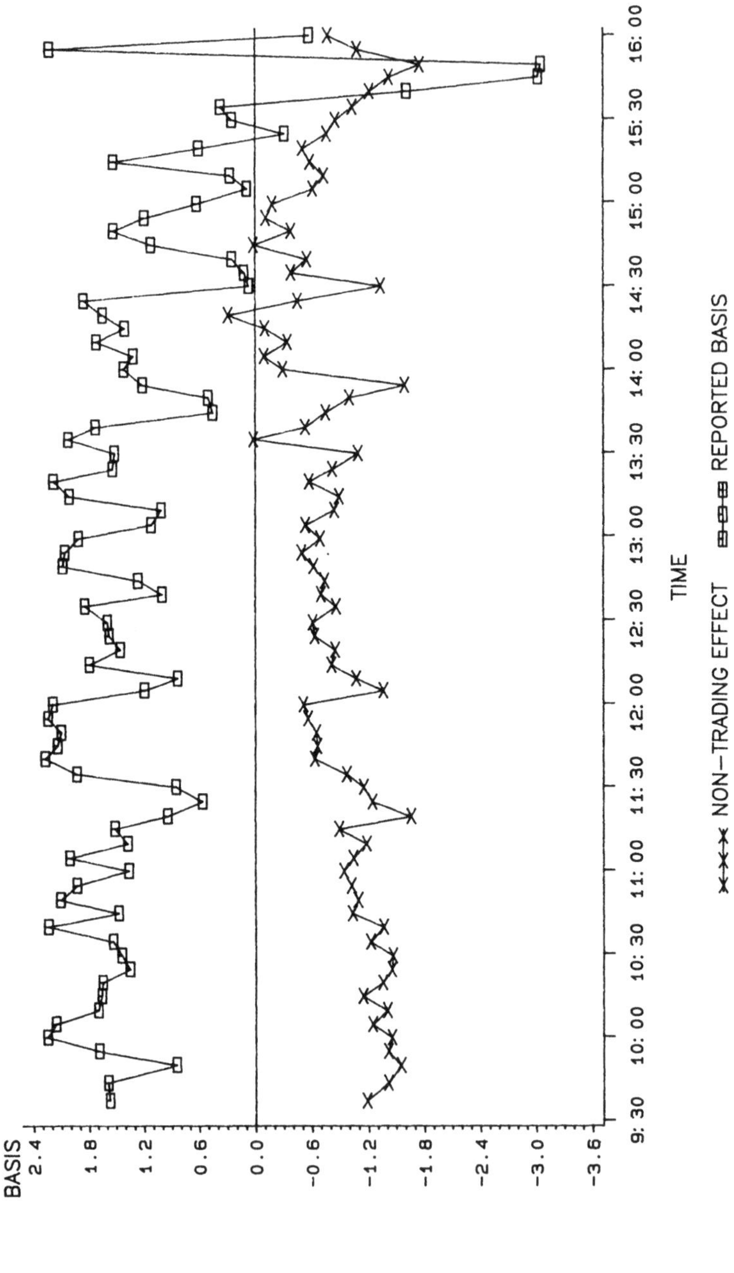

Exhibit 5–12. S&P 500 Stock Index Reported Basis and Nontrading Effect (October 16, 1987)

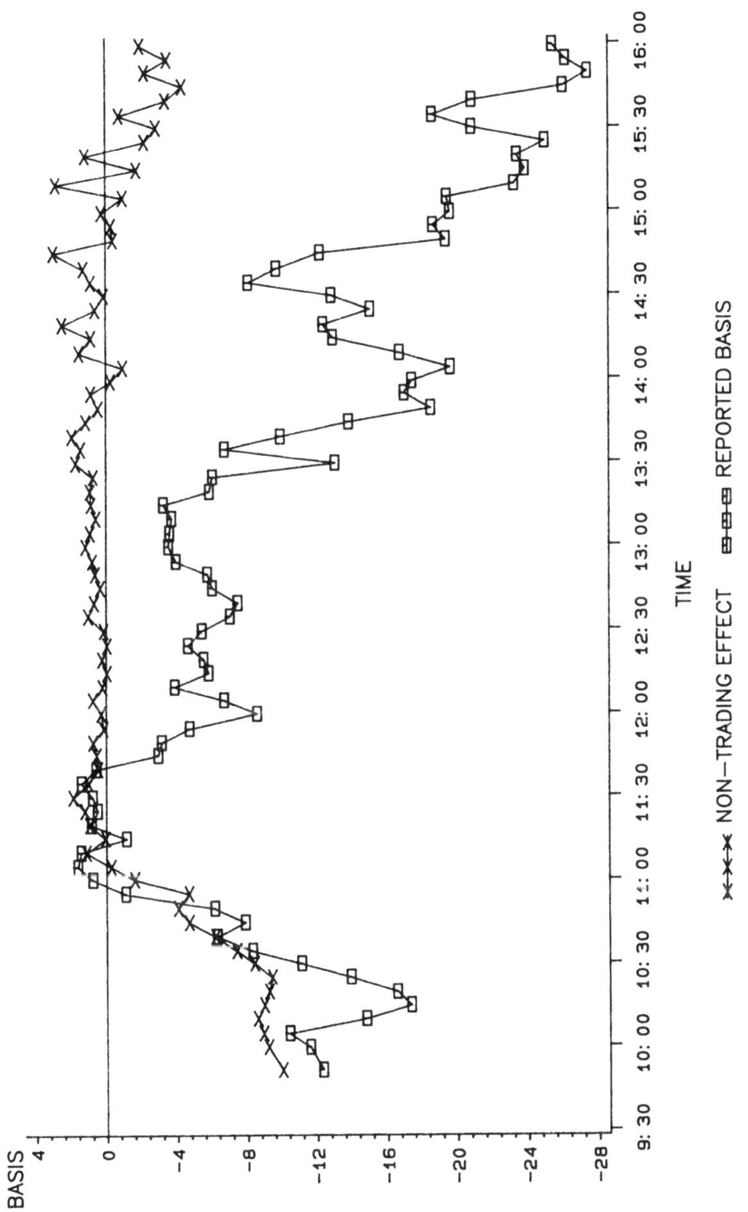

Exhibit 5–13. S&P 500 Stock Index Reported Basis and Nontrading Effect (October 19, 1987)

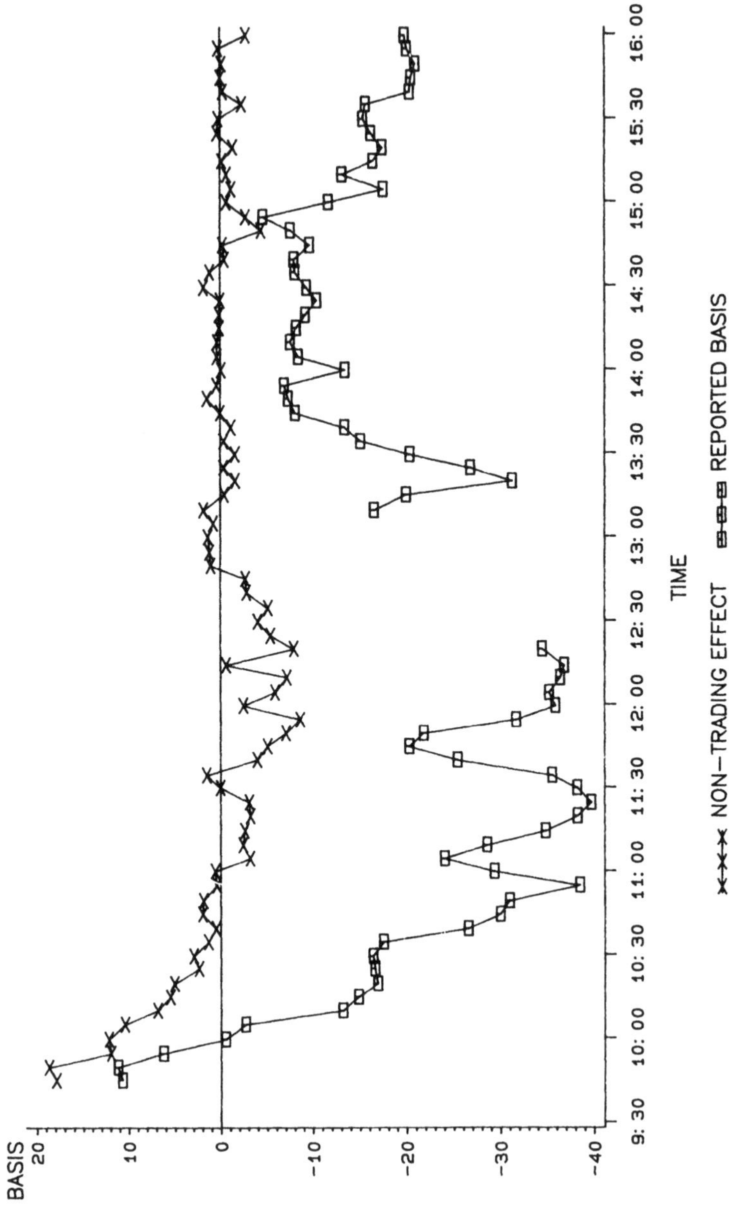

Exhibit 5–14. S&P 500 Stock Index Reported Basis and Nontrading Effect (October 20, 1987)

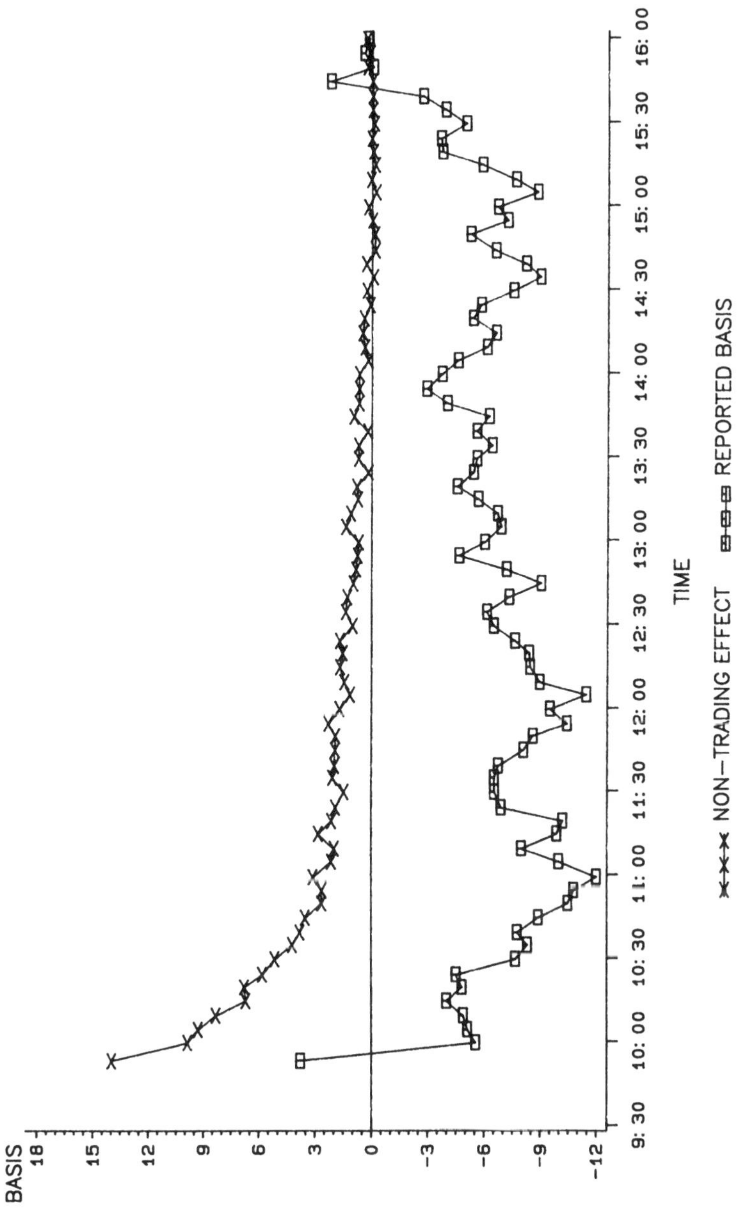

Exhibit 5-15. S&P 500 Stock Index Reported Basis and Nontrading Effect (October 21, 1987)

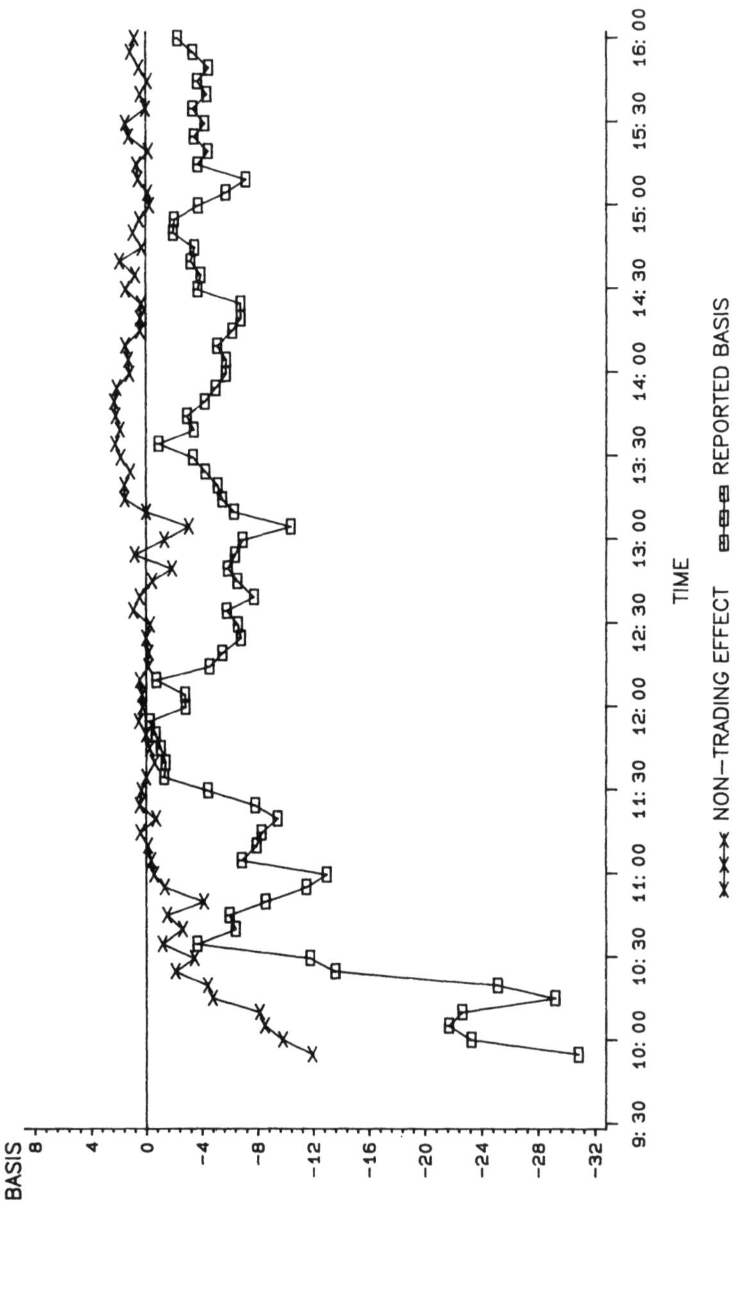

Exhibit 5–16. S&P 500 Stock Index Reported Basis and Nontrading Effect (October 22, 1987)

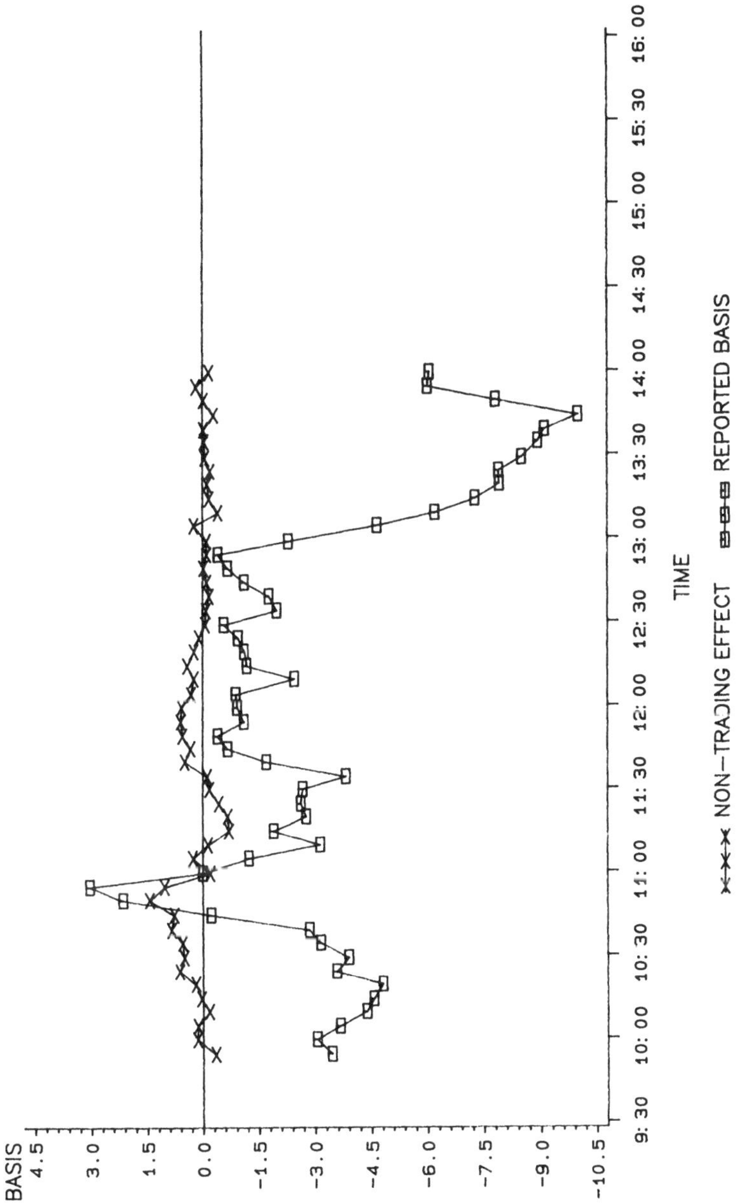

Exhibit 5–17. S&P 500 Stock Index Reported Basis and Nontrading Effect (October 23, 1987)

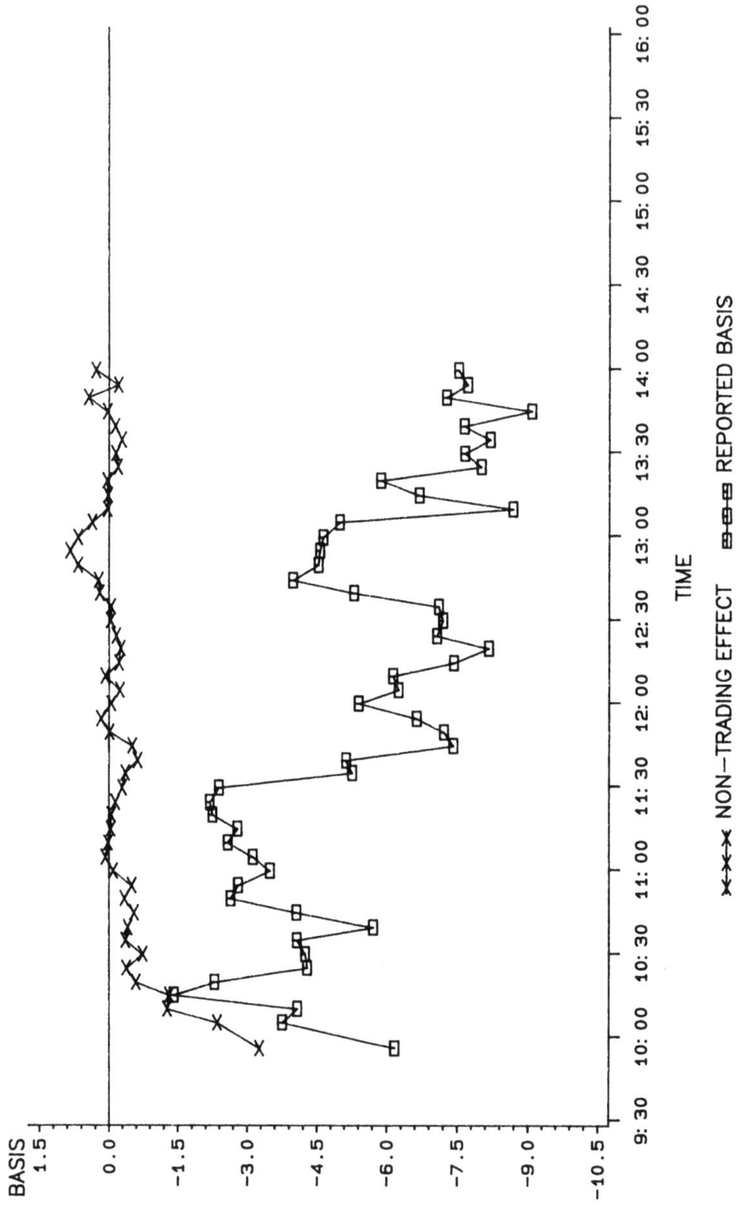

Exhibit 5–18. S&P 500 Stock Index Reported Basis and Nontrading Effect (October 24, 1987)

with the exception of the late afternoon of October 16. On October 19, however, the stock and futures markets opened significantly lower, and the December S&P 500 future's reported basis ranged between a 10- and 20-point discount from 9:30 to 10:00 A.M. EDT (all times are Eastern Daylight Time). Nevertheless at 10:00 A.M., for example, the estimated proxy basis was nearly zero, while the reported basis was at approximately a 10-point discount (equal to approximately 3½% of the then current value of the reported S&P 500 index). The plot of the nontrading effect indicates that the sharp decline in the futures opening price did not significantly lead the stock market down, but rather reflected the decline that was occurring in those stocks trading contemporaneously on the NYSE floor. The reported S&P 500 basis remained at a large discount for most of the period from 9:55 to 11:55 A.M., but substantial portions of that discount reflected the nontrading effect. During that time interval larger deviations between the proxy index and the futures contract tended to be corrected towards zero quickly.

From 12:00 to 1:30 P.M. on October 19, the reported basis was at a negative average discount ranging from approximately 4 to 8 points, while the estimated nontrading effect was close to zero, consistent with a wider arbitrage band and a weakened arbitrage link between the two markets. Beginning around 1:30 P.M., the reported basis began to fall to much deeper discounts, which persisted through the close of trading that day, indicating a likely weakening of the arbitrage link between the two markets, while there was no significant nontrading effect present.

To better estimate the basis for the opening intervals on October 19, the same estimation methodology was employed using a portfolio of those stocks that traded in a least five of the six five-minute intervals in the first half hour of trading on October 19. Exhibits 5–19 and 5–20 show the results from that 29-stock portfolio estimate. The results show that from 9:35 A.M. to 10:00 A.M., the future's discount was almost equal to the estimated nontrading effect, reinforcing the analysis that indicates the futures price level reflected the actual trading on the NYSE floor. This analysis indicates that the unadjusted comparison of S&P 500 index prices and the prices of the S&P 500 December future was contaminated by a nontrading effect equal to approximately 10 points on the S&P 500 index during the early trading on October 19.

On October 20, there was a noticeable positive nontrading effect around 10:00 A.M. and a negative nontrading effect during the period immediately preceding the S&P 500 futures trading halt of up to 8 points. However, after 10:00 A.M. and for most of the remainder of the day, the reported basis was at a significant discount with little nontrading effect, indicating a lack of a significant arbitrage link between the two markets.

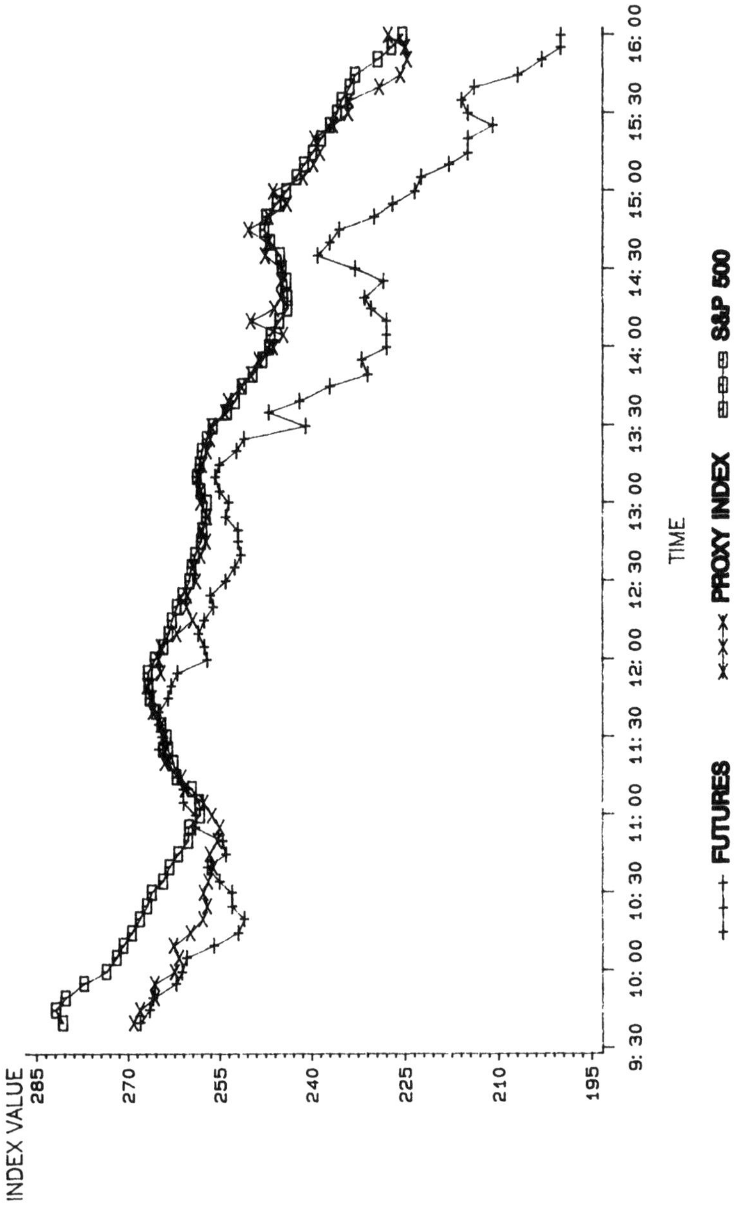

Exhibit 5–19. S&P 500 Index, Trading Proxy Index, and December Futures (October 19, 1987) Small Portfolio

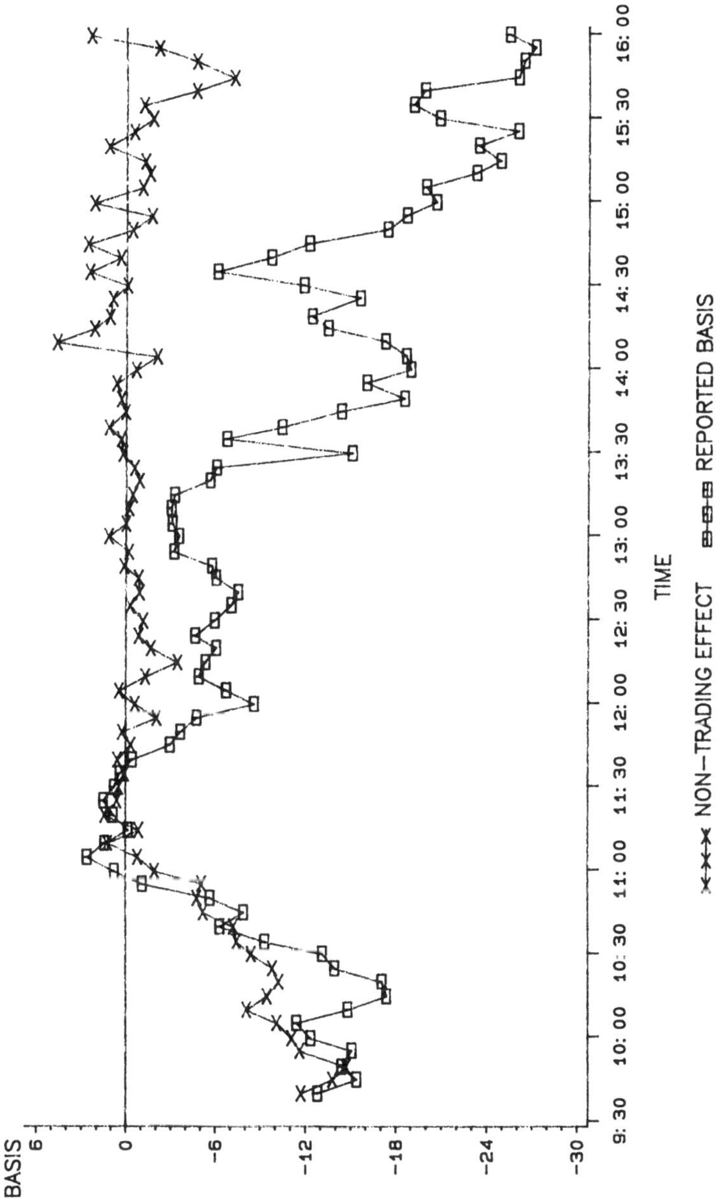

Exhibit 5–20. S&P 500 Stock Index Reported Basis and Nontrading Effect (October 19, 1987) Small Portfolio

On October 21, the stock and futures markets opened higher with a positive reported basis. However, the level of the trading proxy index indicates that, due to a substantial nontrading effect, the reported stock index was understating the extent of the market increase, and that the future basis relative to the proxy index was at a discount nearly equal to that which existed during the afternoon of October 20. From approximately 11:15 A.M., the reported basis was at a discount to cash index values, and the nontrading effect was small. The discount diminished until approximately the last hour of trading when it was eliminated completely.

On October 22, the S&P 500 December future opened sharply lower while the reported S&P 500 index remained relatively unchanged, resulting in a huge reported discount that reached 63 points (approximately 25% of the then-current value) by 9:35 A.M. The plot of the reported basis in exhibit 5–16 indicates that as late as 9:45 to 9:50 A.M., when the reported basis has been reduced to a 32-point discount, the estimated nontrading effect was approximately one-third of the discount. A significant nontrading effect was present in the reported S&P 500 index until approximately 10:15 A.M.

On October 23, there was no evidence of a significant nontrading effect, and the levels of the reported basis through 10:30 A.M. were similar to their levels during the afternoon of October 22. The basis reached both a 3-point positive and a 10-point negative value during the day, indicative of very poor linkage between the stock and futures markets.

Exhibit 5–18 indicates that on October 26 the nontrading effect accounted for about 50% of the reported discount at 9:55 A.M. By 10:15 A.M., the nontrading effect was nearly eliminated, and the discount in the basis widened gradually for the remainder of the day, indicating a continuing absence of significant arbitrage activity between the two markets.

5.4. Conclusions

The existence of a significant deviation between reported index prices and contemporaneous futures prices have led some to conclude that futures price changes during the October market break were more violent than those in the cash market, and that there were substantial billboard or cascade effects operating during that period. The analysis of the statistical properties of the S&P 500 futures and index price changes indicate that the lead of futures prices over stock price during the weeks of October 12 and 19, 1987, are significantly overstated if the nontrading effect is not removed from the S&P 500 index.

Indeed, during the week of October 19 the cash and futures markets appear to have reacted simultaneously to factors affecting the valuation of stock prices. Also, as the analysis of the S&P 500 index and proxy index basis and the estimated level of the nontrading effect indicates, interpretations of temporal comparisons between stock and futures market behavior are fraught with pitfalls. After explicit correction for the nontrading effect, the picture that emerges again from the trading surrounding October 19 is one of nearly simultaneous price discovery in both markets, before the afternoon of October 19, with a significant deterioration in the arbitrage linkage between the two markets for most subsequent periods, as evidenced by the persistence of moderate-sized real futures discounts. Intervals during the mid-October period when the nontrading effect was not prevalent were the afternoons of October 19 through 22 and October 23 and 26.

Such results do not lend great credence to the interpretation of the events surrounding October 19 as being significantly exacerbated or caused by changes in valuation of stock index futures.

References

Atchison, Michael D.; Butler, Kirt C.; and Simonds, Richard R. 1987. "Nonsynchronous Security Trading and Market Index Autocorrelation." *Journal of Finance* 42(1):111–118.

Cohen, Kalman, J.; Hawawini, Gabriel; Schwartz, Robert A.; and Whitcomb, David K. 1986. *The Microstructure Of Securities Markets*. Englewood Cliffs, New Jersey: Prentice-Hall.

Cohen, Kalman J.; Maier, Steven F.; Schwartz, Robert A.; and Whitcomb, David K. 1979. "On the Existence of Serial Correlation in an Efficient Securities Market." *TIMS Studies in the Management Sciences* 11:151–168.

Harris, Lawrence. 1987. "Nonsychronous Trading and the S&P 500 Stock-Futures Basis in October 1987." University of Southern California Working Draft, December.

Kawaller, Ira G.; Koch, Paul D.; and Koch, Timothy W. 1987. "The Temporal Price Relationship between S&P 500 Futures and the S&P 500 Index." *Journal of Finance* 42(5):1309–1329.

Perry, Philip R. 1985. "Portfolio Serial Correlation and Nonsynchronous Trading." *Journal of Financial and Quantitative Analysis* 20(4):517–523.

Stoll, Hans R., and Whaley, Robert E. 1987. "The Dynamics of Stock Index and Stock Index Futures Prices." Owen Graduate School Management at Vanderbilt University working paper, October.

Shanken, Jay. 1987. "Nonsynchronous Trading and the Covariance-Factor Structure of Returns." *Journal of Finance* 42(2):221–231.

COMMENTARY

by Lawrence Harris

Introduction

Moriarty, Gordon, Kuserk, and Wang (MGKW) have written an interesting and important study about the relation between the S&P 500 index futures market and the underlying cash S&P 500 market. The article is interesting because it provides a partial explanation of the unprecedentedly large basis observed during the October 1987 stock crash. It is important because the basis is the key to understanding the pricing relation between the two markets.

The basis is normally calculated by subtracting the futures price from the most recent value of the S&P 500 index. The result, however, may not be the best measure of the true price relation between the two markets when values change quickly. The S&P 500 index, which is computed from the last observed price of each of the 500 stocks, will lag the underlying value of the index portfolio if some of the stocks have not recently traded. If the futures price is contemporaneously correlated with the underlying aggregate S&P 500 stock value, the index will appear to lag behind the futures price. Failure to recognize this problem can lead to spurious conclusions about the relation between the index futures market and the stock market. Traders who ignore the problem will falsely identify arbitrage opportunities.

Errors in computing the index due to stale prices are greatest when prices are analyzed over short time intervals, such as are examined in studies of intraday data, and when trading is thin. Both conditions apply to detailed studies of market performance during the October 1987 crash.

The crash probably will be best understood by studying intraday data, and, due to institutional factors and/or investor behavior, trading became thin at precisely those times when timely information would be most useful. These considerations suggest that better measures of the underlying value of the S&P 500 stocks be constructed and used. MGKW construct such a measure and use it to analyze the relation between the two markets.

Method and Relation to Other Work

The MGKW method computes an index of actively traded stocks for each day in the sample. The index is computed using only those stocks that traded in 90% of the five-minute intervals during that day. The level of the comparison index is set equal to the level of the S&P 500 index during a five-minute interval when a large fraction of the S&P 500 traded but around which there was little price change.

The results suggest that some of the unusual basis can be explained, especially on the morning of October 19, but that in general, the two markets became disconnected.

The MGKW method is not the only method by which this problem can be addressed. Given data that identify the time and price of every trade, a model of the index can be constructed and estimated that would directly solve the stale price problem. This is the approach that I took in related work [Harris 1989].

In that study, each transaction price change is decomposed into a systematic component and a nonsystematic component. The systematic component is further decomposed into a sum of systematic price changes, one for each time interval spanned by the transaction price change. The systematic price changes, which are assumed to be common to all transaction price changes spanning a given interval, are estimated as parameters using a weighted sum of squares method. The results are used to estimate what prices would have been observed had all securities traded. These are then used to compute an adjusted index. In effect, the estimation method obtains information from those stocks that did trade to determine the implied value of the underlying index. The method yields results that are quite similar to the MGKW results.

Consider now how the MGKW method and my method complement each other. The MGKW method is an intuitively simple method of inference. It yields results that are easy to understand, but which one fears may not be reliable because the method is ad hoc. In particular, fixing the level of the comparison index to the level of the S&P 500 index when the underlying stocks most frequently traded can introduce substantial error if the index at that time poorly represents underlying value. My method captures all possible information given the model, but one fears that if the model is not correct, so might be the inference. Fortunately, the two methods yield the same results. This suggests that the MGKW method captures sufficient information to be of value, and that my method is based on a sound model.

Additional Interpretations

A full analysis of why and how the crash occurred requires much broader studies than those presented by MGKW and myself. However, the partial elimination of stale prices as an explanation for the large basis reduces the set of possible causes and clarifies the problem. A reasonable interpretation of the results suggests that the crash might not have been as large as it was had more orderly trade mechanisms been maintained. In particular, the partial elimination of futures arbitrage due to exchange regulation, to congestion in the order and confirmation systems, and to other difficulties associated with executing sale orders in the cash market, removed a potentially significant flow of buy orders from the futures market. Moreover, these same difficulties may have increased the number of sell orders coming into the futures market that otherwise would have been sent to the cash market. Taken together these two factors may have caused larger drops in the futures than might otherwise have been observed. This may have had a very significant effect on the overall performance of the two otherwise integrated markets, especially if traders looked to the relatively uncongested futures market to determine index values.

This interpretation of the results suggests that the future problems can be at least partially avoided if capacity limits to the flow of information are raised. In particular, orders, confirmations, and transaction reports on the ticker tape should all arrive at their destinations instantly.

Also, the requirement that specialists maintain continuous markets should be relaxed somewhat in the direction of broad market moves. Freedom to change prices more quickly would make the specialists less vulnerable to losses due to arbitrage-generated orders and would allow them to find the market more quickly when values change quickly. It is quite possible that had the specialists been able to lower price more quickly, they might have been able to generate more buying interest by value-motivated traders. This interest probably did not materialize during the crash because value-motivated traders looked to the futures market to determine value. Seeing the futures trade at a large discount to the cash probably greatly decreased their enthusiasm for buying stock.

In practice, the continuity relaxation could be accomplished by monitoring the difference between the percentage price change in the specialist's stock and the percentage change in some market index over the same time interval. Currently, only the size of price changes in the stock is monitored. The relaxation of the continuity requirement should be offset by paying greater attention to the size of the spreads quoted by specialists.

References

Lawrence Harris. 1989. "The October 1987 S&P 500 Stock-Futures Basis." *Journal of Finance* 44(1).

COMMENTARY

by Bradford Cornell

In his comments Larry Harris dealt with the technical details of the article by Moriarty, Gordon, Kuserk, and Wang, henceforth MWGK. To avoid repeating his comments, therefore, I want to focus on some policy issues lurking behind the question of the behavior of the spot-futures basis during the October 1987 stock market crash. Many commentators and government officials allege that the magnitude of the crash was exacerbated by the futures market. The story, endorsed in part by the Brady Commission, runs roughly as follows. When panic selling began on October 19, the first place traders turned was the futures market. Massive sales of futures by portfolio insurers and other institutional investors drove prices for stock index futures well below levels consistent with cash-and-carry models of futures pricing. As a result, arbitrageurs entered the market to buy futures and sell cash, thereby dragging down cash prices. Implicit in this interpretation is the notion that if the futures market had not provided an easy avenue for "selling the market," the overall decline would have been lessened.

Supporters of this interpretation point to the behavior of the basis as evidence consistent with their view. During the days following October 19, 1987, the basis, which cash-and-carry models predict should be slightly positive, fell to unprecedented levels. In some instances, futures prices as much as 10% below cash prices were observed. Critics of the interpretation were quick to point out that the data on the basis were misleading. Because the cash index is computed using the most recent prices on the underlying securities, the index will not reflect current market conditions unless all the securities in the index trade continuously. Under normal circumstances the time intervals between trades in cash stocks are relatively short, so that the nontrading bias in the basis is small. During the crash, however, there was very erratic trading in the cash securities. In some cases, for instance, the first trade in a stock did not occur until several hours after the market opened. When stock prices are falling, such nontrading causes the index to be biased upward and the basis to be biased downward. Consequently, a debate erupted over what fraction of the decline in the basis was due to nontrading and what fraction was real. Both MWGK and Harris [1989] attempt to answer that question.

MWGK construct an adjusted S&P 500 index by focusing on those stocks that were actively traded in each five-minute interval. When they compare this index to the actual S&P index and the S&P 500 futures price, they find a significant nontrading effect that explains part, but by no means all, of the drop in the basis. The question on which I want to focus is what can we learn from this work.

The MWGK results should clearly be of interest to the New York Stock Exchange. To the extent that nontrading was a problem it indicates that the clearing mechanism used by the Exchange was not able to cope with the chaotic conditions that prevailed during the crash. By comparing the actual index with the adjusted index, Exchange officials can determine those time intervals during which the nontrading problem was most severe.

Can the work be used to cast light on whether the futures market deepened the crash? I think not. To begin, there is international evidence that futures markets had little to do with the crash. Based on a study of 23 national markets, Richard Roll [1988] reports that market prices during the crash fell an average of 23% in the 15 countries with futures markets and 24% in the 8 countries without futures markets. Overall Roll concluded that the dramatic decline in stock prices was a worldwide phenomenon unrelated to the particular market structure in any country.

Given that the crash was coming, it is not surprising that it hit first in the futures market in the United States. Edwards [1988] reports that the cost of clearing the same trade on the New York Stock Exchange (NYSE) is seven to ten times higher than the cost of trading the S&P 500 futures contract on the Chicago Mercantile Exchange (CME). It is reasonable, therefore, that traders who were anxious to sell turned first to the least expensive and most liquid market.

The fact that sellers were initially drawn to the futures market does not explain how the adjusted basis, using MWGK's adjusted index, declined so sharply. One possibility, of course, is that the MWGK adjustment is incorrect. In this case, however, measurement error is not likely to be the culprit. First, the decline in the basis is much larger than could reasonably be attributed to measurement error. Second, Harris [1989] produces almost identical results using a different method to calculate an adjusted index.

If the drop in the basis was real, where were the arbitrageurs? A discrepancy of 10% between the theoretical basis and the actual basis seems to offer unprecedented profit opportunities. One explanation for the absence of arbitrage trading goes back to the chaotic conditions in the cash market. Not only were bid-ask spreads huge, but arbitrageurs could not be confident when a trade would be executed. As one specific example, I called my broker on the morning of October 20 intending to buy IBM stock. She told me that the last trade was at 108 and that I *might* get the stock somewhere between 100 and 118 sometime during the next hour. Such price quotes are hardly the stuff of which arbitrage transactions are made.

Second, the fact that margin requirements were not integrated led to huge margin calls that threatened the integrity of the market place and made it difficult for arbitrageurs to act. To establish a position an arbitrageur had to meet margin requirements in both the cash and the futures market because neither exchange recognized the offsetting nature of the position. Even if the arbitrageur had sufficient cash to meet the margin requirements and was willing to bear the execution risk, he still faced the problem that the exchanges and other counter parties might not be able to honor their commitments. Greenwald and Stein [1988] report that margin calls to member firms by the CME (futures) and Optrows Clearing Corporation (OCC) (options) totaled approximately $5 billion dollars on October 19 and October 20. At the time, it was unclear how some investment firms were going to come up with the cash to meet such unprecedented calls.[1] In the face of all these uncertaintics many arbitrageurs simply shut down operations.

In summary, the behavior of the basis tells us more about the cash market than the futures market. It supports the view that because of lower transaction costs major adjustments are likely to begin with trading in the futures market. It tells us that the basis will appear to widen when prices are changing quickly because of nontrading in cash stocks. It tells us that even after adjustment for nontrading the basis is likely to widen because of the difficulties in executing cash transactions, meeting margin requirements, and checking the credit of counter parties, which make arbitrage trading inordinately expensive.

To the extent that the behavior of the basis can be used to draw conclusions about how the markets should be reformed, the most direct implication is that the clearing mechanism in the cash market should be improved and margin requirements should be altered to take account of cross exchange hedge positions. Unfortunately, the evidence also indicates that neither of these reforms would have prevented the drop on October 19 because institutional arrangements were not responsible for the decline in the first place. In light of the fact that the market functions well most of the time, and because we do not understand why it collapsed in October 1987, comprehensive reform seems premature. Uninformed intervention is more likely to interfere with the normal functioning of the market than to prevent another crash.

Notes

1. Aggressive intervention by the Federal Reserve Board to provide funds for banks to lend to investment firms was most helpful in this regard.

References

Edwards, F. R. 1988. "Studies of the 1987 Stock Market Crash: Review and Appraisal." working paper, Center for the Study of Futures Markets, Columbia University.

Harris, L. 1989. "The October 1987 S&P 500 Stock-Futures Basis." *Journal of Finance* 44(1):77–99.

Greenwald, B., and Stein, J. 1988. "The Task Force Report: The Reasoning Behind the Recommendations." *Journal of Economics Perspectives* 2:2–24.

Roll, R. 1988. "The International Crash of October 1987." *Black Monday and the Future of Financial Markets* ed., Robert W. Kamphuis, Jr., Roger C. Kormendi, and J. W. Henry Watson. Chicago: Mid America Institute.

6 THE SWIFTNESS OF DIVINE RETRIBUTION AND ITS TENDENCY TO MISTAKE ITS TARGET: AN ANALYSIS OF THE BRADY REPORT

David D. Haddock

Standing on the pavement was a big fat man whom Dixon recognized as his barber. Dixon felt a deep respect for this man because of his impressive exterior, his rumbling bass voice, and his unsurpassable stock of information about the Royal Family. At that moment two rather pretty girls stopped at a pillar-box a few yards away. The barber, his hands clasped behind his back, turned and stared at them. An unmistakable look of furtive lust came over his face; then, like a courtly shopwalker, he moved slowly towards the two girls. Welch now accelerated again and Dixon, a good deal shaken, hurriedly switched his attention to the other side of the road, where a cricket match was being played and the bowler was just running up to bowl. The batsman, another big fat man, swiped at the ball, missed it, and was violently hit by it in the stomach. Dixon had time to see him double up and the wicket-keeper begin to run forward before a tall hedge hid the scene. Uncertain whether this pair of vignettes was designed to illustrate the swiftness of divine retribution or its tendency to mistake its target, Dixon was quite sure that he felt in some way overwhelmed. . . .

—Kingsley Amis, *Lucky Jim*

Upon reading the *Report of the Presidential Task Force on Market Mechanisms*, the Brady Report, one gets much the same feeling of being overwhelmed that James Dixon got during his little drive with Professor Welch. The Report was certainly compiled swiftly enough following the events of October 1987, during which securities prices plunged worldwide. That report urges substantial new regulatory machinery in response to the event that has come to be known as the 1987 market break, but a disconcertingly large proportion of the findings, conclusions, and recommendations lodged there are very much off-target from a public interest perspective. In the first place, the market break of 1987 was no big deal if placed in the perspective of the following year and compared with other similar events in the history of securities exchanges. Since World War II, four other declines in the Dow Jones Industrial Average (DJIA) have been of a larger percentage than the 26.1% difference between the peak of 2722 registered on August 25, 1987, and the level of 2011 attained exactly one year later.[1] And all of those declines are minor league by the standards of the 1920s and 1930s.

Moreover, it was the European (not the American) markets that were the first to break [Dwyer and Hafer 1989]. How then can new regulation that is directed solely at the securities markets of the United States, as is implicit in the Brady proposals, prevent a recurrence? This is not merely nitpicking; there exists a serious danger that introspective internal regulation will seriously disable our national securities exchanges in the increasingly competitive world securities market.

Finally, nobody would have protested or called for new regulatory action if the year-long experience had resulted in a 26.1% *increase* in security prices, even if the short-run movements had been equally abrupt. This is not to deny that the rapidity of the decline during a few days of mid-October startled and troubled market professionals, costing some of them substantial sums (but profiting a few handsomely). So did the several transitory rebounds that interrupted the mid-October slide, and the much more permanent one that came after the DJIA had fallen to almost 1700 by October 20, a level that proved to be the lowest point during the year-long span. And, indeed, it does seem that the clearing arrangements in place in the exchanges were severely taxed during the few days of most rapid decline.

But, to my mind the most remarkable features of the market break have been the tenacity of the champions of regulatory proposals that are purportedly designed to solve a problem that seems more of a nonproblem with every passing month, and the continuing highly publicized attention (but inaction) of Congress toward an event of little interest to the general population of voters—even during the period of most rapid price decline. Although commentators frequently claim that common investors *might* become disillusioned and discouraged by a continuing failure by Congress to adopt new controls, the only private citizens who have actually taken the trouble to participate vociferously in the regulatory debate are market professionals, who, of course, have a strong private interest in the outcome.

Although regulatory proposals have arisen from many quarters, the focus of this paper will be on those advanced in the Brady Report (after Nicholas F. Brady, the chairman of the task force). It is difficult to state concisely the views encapsulated in the rather disjointed Brady Report. On a superficial level, panic or even hysteria seems most apt. Perhaps it merely betrays the nature of any authorship by committee. Long passages are devoted to lamenting one inequity or another, with no obvious regulatory correction ever being suggested. Some of the regulatory proposals that *are* advanced in the Report seem hardly to have been foreshadowed by those market failings asserted by the Commission. If the Brady Report were a legal brief, the action might well be dismissed for failure to state a cause of action, with the defense not even being required to present a rebuttal.

6.1. Appropriate Responses to System Failure

6.1.1. The View of the Brady Report

It is implicit in the Brady Report, and in many alternative regulatory proposals, that the options before us are 1) to cope with events similar to the recent market break by increasing governmental regulation, or 2) to do nothing about such events at all. It is also implicit that the second option is profoundly inferior to the first. Finally, it is implicit that the entire episode of the market break represents a conflation of inseparable but confusing events that cannot appropriately be dealt with in a piecemeal fashion.

> Analysis of market behavior during the crucial days in mid-October makes clear an important conclusion. From an economic viewpoint, what have been traditionally seen as separate markets—the markets for stocks, stock index futures, and stock options—are in fact one market [Brady Report, p. 55].

By implication, no aspect of the problem can be dealt with in an arena that is fundamentally different than that in which any other aspect is approached. The report urges a coherent, unified approach instead.[2] It is urged that nonspecialists cannot reasonably hope to understand what has happened in the securities market during the past year.[3] Consequently, nonspecialists cannot understand how the regulatory proposals will help avoid a recurrence of the October terror in the future. Instead, it is necessary to depend on public-spirited specialists to instruct a functionally blind nation regarding appropriate courses of action.

6.1.2. An Alternative Viewpoint

I disagree with virtually everything summarized in the section just concluded. At the very least, I assert that the case to back such views has yet to be made, or even begun. This judgment does not depend on the reason for the market break—a change in fundamentals, the bursting of a speculative bubble, psychological factors, or whatever—nor upon the strength with which the efficient market hypothesis is seen to hold.

In the first place, lots of markets are interrelated, many of them closely, with no particular need for regulation implied: For example, houses, apartments, and offices are closely related markets. Since the majority of such buildings are covered by mortgages, those markets are closely related to financial markets. Since the construction industry produces houses, apartments, and offices, but also produces highways, bridges, television and radio stations, those markets are interrelated as well. The latter items draw a connection with the entertainment industry—films, plays, recordings—and then on to screenplays and books. In fact, if one had nothing better to do, it would be possible to trace out paths to virtually every market in the world, concluding that they all are part of "one market."

And they are! It is called the economy. And no citizen, not even an Adam Smith, completely understands the economy. But while that may justify studying economics, it does not, in and of itself, justify new regulation. Regulators are not some breed of intellectual supermen who can see through matters that are opaque to the rest of us—far from it. Consequently, whether or not we employ regulators, losses will befall society that could have been avoided if foresight were as good as hindsight. So, an observation that such a loss has just occurred justifies employing scarce resources in new regulatory activity, if and only if, the regulator will have some advantage over private actors. The Brady Report nowhere addresses this question of comparative advantage. Instead, the report lists platitudes with great thoroughness. The thoroughness of the listing serves only to distract attention from the list's lack of important implications.

Selecting the appropriate response to a trying event, such as the market break, is considerably more complicated and less obvious than the Brady Report implies.

In fact, it is often wise to respond to highly unsettling events by doing nothing at all. A nonresponse is desirable under at least two sets of circumstances:

1) Highly unsettling events are often inevitable in the workings of markets, as resources are expelled from uses that are less valuable than the alternatives. Such events should ordinarily be ignored. Artificially retain-

ing resources in a present activity denies more valuable activities a full opportunity to expand, a notion known to economists abstractly as a constraint. Congressional inaction in view of the market break will undoubtedly discourage some investors who have been involved in the market in certain ways (playing the market). But that may be all to the good—such people and their funds will not collapse into inaction if they are not playing the market; they will instead turn to other pursuits where they have a comparative advantage. Similarly, brokers will lose income, and some will be forced to find other employment as they lose clients.[4] Again, although brokers will be unenthusiastic about the prospect, the situation frees resources for the expansion of activities that utilize similar inputs.

2) Even if the event cannot (and possibly should not) be ignored, it must be remembered that responses are costly. They are merited, if and only if, the total cost of a response exceeds the total benefit, which *is* the cost borne in the event of nonresponse. Although one easily observes that regulatory responses to anything are vastly expensive propositions, to my knowledge nobody has done even a back-of-the-envelope *empirical* examination designed to determine whether any response to October 1987 is merited.

Moreover, even when the totals indicate some response is warranted, the problem being responded to ordinarily will not be obliterated by an optimal response. The *magnitude* of the optimal response will be determined by the *marginal* cost and benefit of responding. Since the marginal cost is often substantial, the optimal response will equally often be one that retains a substantial probability that some similar events will recur. It is far from clear, particularly with the benefit of hindsight, that October 1987 was anything more than such an "optimal failure" of the system of controls already in place.

Further, even if the marginal empirical analysis (assuming it were attempted) indicated that greater controls on securities exchange mechanisms are desirable, the controls ought to be sought along the least costly avenues. In many instances that will imply private rather than governmental regulatory controls. The notion that adequate incentives may exist to spur private institutions, such as the New York Stock Exchange (NYSE), to continue innovating and developing appropriate exchange controls seems alien to the Brady Report.

Even if a new governmental regulatory approach seems desirable, the requisite powers to implement the approach may already be vested in an existing agency, such as the Securities and Exchange Commission (SEC). Hence, there is a whole array of plausible responses to the market break that involve no major new regulatory legislation. Only in those instances in which each and *every* one of those alternatives is rejected as being inappropriate does it make sense to divert scarce congressional attention from other important matters so that some entirely new regulatory structure can be designed and erected. It seems odd, from a public-interest perspective, that the Brady Report urged just such a revamped regulatory structure without ever seriously considering *any* of the alternatives. And it seems odd that members of the Brady Commission continue to bemoan the failure of Congress to act promptly on their proposals, despite the continuing scarcity of empirical evidence that the proposals are actually related to the problems the commission members claim to have perceived during the market break. Apparently, their preferred hardware for conducting empirical investigations is a newspaper printing press.

6.2. A Public-Interest Analysis of the Regulatory Proposals

The public interest is, of course, a highly ambiguous concept.[5] But for the purpose of determining whether or not the Brady Report can plausibly be represented as a public-interest document, it is informative to adopt the relatively lenient Kaldor-Hicks standard.[6] Even under this loose standard, however, it will be shown that serious failings seem to permeate the Brady Report as a public-interest document. The assertions of the Report to the contrary, the actual events detailed seem to imply no need for additional government regulation. Consider some of the major, albeit disorganized, pieces of the Brady Report in turn.

In retrospect, it seems that the recent securities price decline was especially remarkable only for the speed with which events occurred during the several days beginning with October 19. Although the Brady Report discusses the speed of the price decline unfavorably—a "free-fail"—and at length, I believe the Report perceives neither the mechanism that caused the rapid price decline nor its economic importance.

One hypothesis that could explain the unusually rapid securities price decline is that it was merely a drawing from one tail of a distribution describing a stochastic process. That would mean that the speed of the October segment of the 1987 market break implies nothing about future market breaks, and thus implies nothing new concerning our understanding of the regulatory environment. Consequently, it implies nothing obvious concerning new regulatory initiatives. This hypothesis has not been refuted. Instead, wild inferences are drawn from a sample of one (increasingly unimpressive) observation.

The most obvious alternative hypothesis that might account for the speed of the October securities price drop is more optimistic. That hypothesis would focus on evolutionary changes in the environment of securities exchanges that simply make things work faster now than they formerly did. In other words, perhaps what happened in 1987 was the same general process that had earlier driven the 36% decline in the DJIA from the end of 1968 through mid-1970, but it just got telescoped—we need to deflate our clocks and calendars.

Several examples of evolutionary changes that could plausibly speed market processes were specifically pointed to by the Brady Report. They include the initiation of block-trading and portfolio insurance. As Greenwald and Stein [1988] note, however, such mechanisms seem not to be implicated: Similar market breaks occurred abroad even in markets and for financial instruments for which block-trading and portfolio insurance were absent.

Suppose that Greenwald and Stein are mistaken about the contribution of portfolio insurance to the events of October. Even so, those portfolio insurance sales that occurred in the early part of the break were neither inappropriate from a private nor from a social point of view. In retrospect, it is seen that those sales extricated clients from the lower prices that soon prevailed (privately appropriate), and they drove securities prices more quickly toward a new equilibrium (socially appropriate). If portfolio insurance strategies led to inappropriate mechanical dumping of portfolios late in the market break, that would have contributed to the overshoot that was ultimately observed (socially inappropriate). It also would have contributed to decreasing the wealth of the subscribers (privately inappropriate), so the market will issue retribution to the portfolio insurance firms where suitable (socially appropriate). In fact, portfolio insurance is now approximately one-quarter the size it had attained prior to the market break. There seems to be no task left with respect to portfolio insurance for a regulator to perform.

An alternative example of a suspect evolutionary change that would have compressed market time is a general increase in the rate at which communications of various sorts now proceed, due possibly to advances in electronics, satellite transponders, computer software, etc. Since essentially everyone agrees that the expected profitability of firms at least influences securities prices, if it is not the entire determinant, then increasingly rapid communications that drive the DJIA more promptly toward a new equilibrium in the face of new information is not a social ill at all, but rather a boon. This is not to deny that rapid movements in prices will inevitably prove a problem for certain individuals, but the gains to the winners will exceed the losses of the losers, and I have adopted the Kaldor-Hicks notion of social welfare in this article. Securities prices influence decisions regarding new investment. If new information implies that investment plans should be reconfigured, the quicker that information becomes widely known the fewer the inappropriate projects that are initiated. Given the rate at which new real investment is initiated, even a rather brief delay can lead to serious misallocations in an absolute sense.

Nevertheless, the Brady Report indicates that the rapidity of the decline was one of the problems associated with the market break. Similarly, the report laments the failure of some exchange specialists to "lean against the wind." When the market is moving toward a new equilibrium, as hindsight says it was during most of the market break,[7] specialists serve neither their own nor social purposes by leaning against the wind, although that would of course benefit certain individuals. From a social viewpoint, if specialists know where the market is ultimately headed, they should lean *with* the wind in order to attain that new equilibrium as promptly as possible, and they have private incentives to do just that.

Under the efficient market hypothesis, even in its weak forms, the behavior of those specialists who were buying on net before the market reached a new equilibrium was as injurious as net sales by specialists after the new equilibrium had been passed. Either sort of behavior delays the stabilization at a new equilibrium, so either one prolongs the period of erroneous investment decisions that result. Yet to the Brady Commission the former is good behavior, while the latter is bad.[8] In retrospect one can surely find instances in which specialists were selling at prices below the ultimate, new equilibrium and others in which they were buying at prices above the new equilibrium. That will have proven to be privately costly, and so it indicates only that the foresight of specialists is imperfect, as would have been the foresight of anyone caught in the midst of the decline. There is no externality worth worrying about. Because such trading is privately costly to specialists, one may assume the specialists themselves will undertake any improvements in their techniques that are worth more than they cost. It is doubtful that a regulator could adopt a superior *modus operandi.*

Even if one assumes that the events of October were entirely the result of the bursting of a speculative bubble, and that no new information was implicated at all, the appropriate response would seem to be rather trifling in comparison with the proposals of the Brady Report. The appropriate guard against similar events occurring in the future would seem to be better definition of the mechanism through which the bubble forms and wide distribution of a concise and clear explanation to the public. Maybe "bubble warnings" could be issued by anyone wise enough to foresee one (although one wonders why that person would not simply sell short, make a fortune, and help initiate an early bursting of the bubble while it was still small). Most investors are risk-averse and would simply withdraw into a safe-harbor whenever a credible bubble warning was issued. If some investors are willing to gamble on being better than most at timing a break—and a gamble is exactly what a net long position would imply when a bubble was known to be in existence—it would seem inappropriate to gear the regulatory structure simply to prevent the gamblers from exercising their wishes.

If new and better understanding is the solution to speculative bubbles, no additional regulatory structure is implied. The SEC, for one, already possesses ample authority to undertake and publicize studies of speculative behavior, while universities and investment banks require no authorization in the first place—at least not in this country.

A similar response seems called for to deal with the inappropriate reversals and eventual overshoot of the market during the market break. After all, that is hardly a new phenomena. If such events could be efficiently predicted with greater precision—that is, if there were anything a new regulator could do to prevent them at a cost worth bearing—other people in the market would have taken advantage of the opportunity already and would now be wealthy. Hence, while continued investigation of the phenomena is difficult to oppose in principle, institutions that are already in place seem to possess adequate authority and incentive to continue at an appropriate rate a process long since initiated.

A problem that did arise during the 1987 market break, and that apparently was related to a newfound speed of communication, arose from an imbalance of communications of various sorts. The rate at which the electronic technology at the exchanges could cope with information flowing in from outside was less than the rate at which the outside world could feed in the information. The imbalance contributed to long delays in executing orders, and thus to substantial deviations between price quotations when orders were placed and the transactions prices actually realized when the orders were executed. That, of course, leads to poor investment decisions of another sort—not directly with respect to real investment, but with respect to portfolio management decisions, which are designed to mediate between independently variable consumption and income streams. Moreover, those investors with better access to new communications equipment had better luck at getting their orders executed than those who were still relying on older technologies such as simple telephone conversations (at least early in the break).

The appropriate response to such an inability of the exchanges to cope with a burst of incoming orders would seem to be either none or private. It does not make sense to build storm cellars in counties where tornadoes occur once in a century, even if such a storm has just hit one of the county's towns. And it does not make sense for exchanges to invest in more sophisticated and more expensive electronics if the imbalance discussed in the paragraph above is rare.

If it *does* make sense to update the communications technology of the exchanges, however, and very possibly it does, the planning and implementation can sensibly be made by the exchanges themselves. The exchanges have a profit motive for making good decisions about how much, what kind, and how soon, and about the appropriate level of communications inter-ties to form among independent exchanges. Supplanting markets with regulation is usually rationalized in an abstract setting by hypothesizing external effects that no private individual can internalize profitably, but it is difficult to detect such an externality here.

In contrast, a government regulator will respond to political incentives. Political responses tend to be more episodic than market responses, less expert, less dynamically sensitive to the evolution of the social and technological environment, and more prone to become hostage to special interests and unrelated policy concerns.[9]

Furthermore, in the absence of a revealed Pareto-relevant externality [Buchanan and Stubblebine 1962], a regulatory solution creates rigidities that can frustrate attempts to reach the *best* solution.[10] Anything that a regulation is effective at mandating, a private institution is capable of selecting voluntarily. No option is lost by failing to mandate a specific action. In the absence of an externality that cannot be privately internalized,[11] the profit motive leads individuals to attempt just such a selection unless another option is superior. If the initial choice is mistaken, private parties can quickly revise their selection, and competition among them will promote such a revision by the ultimately successful individual.

In contrast, if a mandated regulatory response is mistaken, private parties are compelled to select it nonetheless, and since regulatory agencies are legal monopolies, proximate competition cannot correct the error. If competition is to play any role at all, it must come via competition for the jobs of elected officials who oversee the agency. That sort of competition will be seriously diluted among all sorts of other political concerns. Legislators rarely if ever win or lose seats because of a failure to keep a tight enough rein on some independent regulatory agency [McChesney 1987].

It is also claimed in the Brady Report that small investors were particularly disadvantaged by communications failures. For substantial periods during the market break small investors, who lacked direct ties to securities markets, simply could not get their orders executed. In the terminology of the Brady Report, investors could not withdraw from the market in a timely fashion.[12] In some instances that phenomenon arose from a straightforward inability of the system to process orders at a rate equivalent to the rate at which investors were trying to execute them. But in the over-the-counter market, the inability of investors to execute orders sometimes arose from another source—the total disappearance of market makers. Because no one in the over-the-counter market has an obligation to make a market, many of those who ordinarily do simply decided not to do so during the market break.

The failure of such individuals to make markets implies that they were trying to evaluate the ultimate impact of the break. Otherwise, they could simply have moved to the new equilibrium price but continued to make markets, thus earning the bid-ask spread on all the transactions that in fact they failed to make.[13] Moreover, investment banking firms most often are those who serve as market makers for over-the-counter securities. Since the opportunity cost of their resources had temporarily increased as the firms scrambled to keep abreast of events occurring on the exchanges, their withdrawal from the typically lower-volume over-the-counter markets may well have represented an efficient reallocation of resources.

With respect to the organized exchanges, where the markets for individual securities continued to function most of the time, the concern for small investors is largely misplaced. According to the Brady Commission a limited number of investors seemed to drive the market down. That observation is an *implication* of the efficient market hypothesis. Most investors place funds in securities because the life-cycle of earnings does not mirror the life-cycle of consumption precisely, or even closely. Parking savings in securities for the stream of dividends and capital gains they yield is superior to parking them under the mattress. Only a few investors play the market, trying to make money more rapidly than the typical investor by buying before a market rises and selling before it falls [Manne 1966].

Such a distribution of investor types is sensible. Efficient pricing is a public good, and so for any one security only a few individuals should make the substantial investments necessary to collect and appropriately process the complex flows of information that arrive into the market. When the information indicates that little change is called for, these information specialists have no incentive to trade, and the trading activity overall will then be dominated by portfolio adjustments that time-function traders make while bringing their fluctuating incomes into balance with their even more variable expenditures.

The activities of time-function traders will be largely unchanged by inflows of new information—they cannot hope to be first to learn of it, so all profit would be drained before they could act [Haddock and Macey, 1986, 1987]. The behavior of those few individuals who specialize in processing information *will* be affected by new information. Since, by definition, they are the first to learn and understand the new information, they can profit by acting on it. Thus, the proportion of transactions that involve information specialists will be positively correlated with the rate of new information inflow. Since those individuals tend generally to be relatively large traders in the securities in which they specialize, an increase in their trading activity in response to a rapid inflow of new information will imply an increase in the Herfindahl index of concentration of trading activity. This only implies that people try to exploit their comparative advantages, not something sinister. And exploitation of comparative advantages ordinarily is taken to be both privately and socially advantageous.

It is claimed in the Brady Report, and I will accept it as fact, that the clearinghouse arrangement in the securities market was threatened by insufficient liquidity until it was rescued by the Federal Reserve system. In particular, since debiting and crediting of accounts takes time, some participants were threatened with insolvency because they were not receiving credit due promptly enough to maintain adequate balances with the clearinghouse to cover margin calls on other positions. This problem is alleged to have been particularly acute because different clearinghouses service different securities market segments, and the different segments maintain interlinks that are too tenuous.

Private institutions operating in the securities markets have an incentive to avoid temporary breakdowns of their clearing arrangements. Their world would not collapse if the clearinghouse became overloaded, but trading would be slowed or halted while the failure was rectified, with a loss of commissions and trading opportunities in the meantime. If a regulator can imagine and implement an alteration that makes such a breakdown less likely, why cannot the private institutions imagine and implement the same alteration?

Perhaps the Brady Commission's concern about the clearinghouse mechanism is, in fact, well placed. Perhaps the private incentives are not strong enough to induce an appropriate revamping. A private revamping of the clearinghouse mechanism would entail private costs, but experience reveals that the Federal Reserve will bail out the clearinghouses at moments of crisis, as it did in October of 1987. If that is the source of a problem, however, the appropriate alteration in public policy would be to direct the Federal Reserve to take a hands-off approach in the future, and to announce such an alteration in policy to the exchanges.[14] That would give exchange institutions full incentive to take efficient advantage of technical opportunities. Contrary to the suggestions of the Brady Report, the "Fed" needs no overarching new regulatory authority over securities exchanges to carry out such a task.

Finally, the Brady Report suggests coordinating margin requirements across exchanges, and coordinating circuit breaker mechanisms—trading halts and the like. These are difficult suggestions to dismiss out of hand [Telser 1989]. *If* it is desirable to have unified margin requirements and unified trading halts, then they will not arise without coordinated action among the various market segments. A high-margin requirement or a trading halt in only one exchange will merely divert transactions onto other exchanges, so that the exchange with the most lenient attributes will determine the de facto attributes for all exchanges. It remains to be shown, however, that this competition among exchanges is socially injurious.

Suppose, however, that one or both can be shown to be injurious to investors. If so, some capital that would otherwise be invested in securities markets will be diverted to other uses. Consequently, firms that wish to use the capital markets to raise funds would like to guarantee that their securities were going to be traded only on exchanges with appropriate margin requirements and/or trading halt protocols, because that will increase the price for which they could sell their securities when they are issued.

If my reasoning is correct, what is wanted is a modification of SEC policy that permits cross-listing of securities by one exchange whenever the security is listed on another exchange.[15] The appropriate modification would require that the firm whose securities are to be cross-listed authorize the cross-listing. In a similar fashion, firms should be enabled readily to delist their securities from an exchange whose trading practices begin to displease them.[16] If the firms issuing securities could confine their listings to the exchange(s) they selected, competition among exchanges would lead to an optimal configuration of margins and trading halts, as well as other improvements in exchange practices. Again, no new regulatory authorization is required, just an alteration of the rules under old authorization.

6.3. Conclusions

If the Brady Report was intended to be a public-interest document, then it seems to be a poorly reasoned and poorly informed one. The recent market break seems indeed to call for substantial changes in public regulatory policy, but seems to require no new regulatory authorization. The desirable new policies would hardly have the form envisioned by the Brady Commission. For instance, the Federal Reserve system should make it clear that, contrary to its behavior during October 1987, it will not intervene in a pinch to save clearinghouses from their own failures to make adjustments in practices as the environment evolves. This will afford the clearinghouses themselves appropriate incentives to undertake any efficient alterations in their operations that are required to speed clearing across exchanges.

Similarly, the Securities and Exchange Commission should take advantage of securities-issuing firms' own incentives to seek efficient securities trading environments for their issues. This can be done by permitting the firms to veto cross-listing of their securities by exchanges they have not selected themselves, and by enabling them to delist more easily than is now possible. Some may counter that such a policy will constrain competition among exchanges. And it will—but in exactly the same way that any other contractual arrangement constrains competition *after the contract is concluded*. That does not constrain exchanges' incentives to compete ex ante. To the contrary, it enhances that competition. As it stands today, exchanges have little incentive to compete for listings by developing better exchange practices from the viewpoint of the listed firms.

Finally, it is possible that the Securities and Exchange Commission should revamp research priorities to provide more emphasis to the study of the growth, bursting, and recognition of bubbles. But there is an opportunity cost to an increase in such research, for other sorts of research must be deemphasized. Hence, that is an empirical issue, and my intuition, which is no better (but I suspect no worse) than the Brady Commission's data, does not support any strong conclusion on this score.

If still other alterations in regulation are indeed appropriate from a public-interest perspective, the logic to justify them will have to come from somewhere other than the Brady Report.

Adopting the public-interest viewpoint that I have used here, an analysis of the Brady Report almost inevitably reads as if it were a professor's corrections written on a mediocre term paper. That, of course, raises the possibility that the Brady Report is not even intended as a public-interest document. Would the Report reflect a more sophisticated understanding of economic reality if one took some different viewpoints? Perhaps it was motivated by special-interest groups who are more interested in rationalizing self-serving proposals to a skeptical public than in increasing social welfare [Peltzman 1976, Stigler 1971], or it may be motivated by some entirely different incentive. Possibly it is best seen as a mere threat to act against certain narrowly defined interests in order to extract concessions from those interests in favor of governmental actors [McChesney 1987]. I investigate the possibility that the Brady Report is better characterized as a special-interest or as a rent-extraction document elsewhere.

Notes

1. For all the declines, the peak level is used as the denominator for the percentage calculation. At least three additional transitory postwar declines in the DJIA exceeded 23% over very roughly comparable timespans [Greenwald and Stein 1988]. And several declines of similar magnitude (up to 69.5%) occurred in the United Kingdom and Japan over the postwar period.

2. "The October 1987 experience illustrates that regulatory changes, derived from the one-market concept, are necessary.... [It] demonstrates that the issues which have an impact across related markets, and throughout the financial system, include clearing and credit mechanisms, margin requirements, circuit breaker mechanisms, such as price limits and trading halts, and information systems for monitoring intermarket activities....

"Moreover, the October break illustrates that difficulties in stocks and derivative market segments produce dislocations in other financial markets. These, in turn, exacerbate the problem in stocks and derivative market segments. [The newly proposed] intermarket agency must consider the interactions among a wide variety of markets encompassing stocks, stock index futures, stock options, bonds, foreign exchange and the credit and banking system, in both domestic and foreign markets" (59–60).

3. "The most fundamental requirement [of the proposed agency] is broad and deep expertise in these market sgements and instruments. However, expertise in individual instruments and market segments is not sufficient. The key requirement is expertise in the interaction of instruments and marketplaces as an integrated system....

"The critical requirement for the intermarket agency is broad expertise in the financial system as a whole because the greatest potential risk of intermarket failure is to the financial system as a whole, rather than to individual market segments" (60).

4. See, for example, "Small-Investor Brokers Lose Clients, Income In Wake of Oct. 19," *Wall Street Journal*, 26 September 1988, p. 1

5. Arrow's impossibility theorem.

6. Virtually every proposal in the Brady Report fails on cursory examination if a Paretian standard were to be selected instead.

7. Two-thirds of the fall in the DJIA between the peak on August 25, 1987 and the trough on October 20, 1987 had not been recovered by August 25, 1988.

8. Actually, the Brady Commission laments net sales by specialists that occurred either after the new equilibrium had been passed—a genuine social bad—or before the new equilibrium had been reached—a social good. The Brady Commission seems to view market specialists as some bizarre insurance mechanism that permits investors to capture the benefits of every increase in securities prices, but absorbs all the losses whenever the securities prices decline. In fact, specialists are merely inventory managers, and as such enable markets to function continuously even when buyers and sellers do not appear on the market in perfectly offsetting flows. Inventories are extremely valuable economic tools, but they are quite distinct from the mechanisms of the insurance industry.

9. There is some evidence that regulatory actions retard rather than accelerate the implementation of new technology [Macey and Haddock 1985].

10. If the regulatory action leads to a demonstrable improvement over the preexisting situation, its proponents will trumpet the success of the regulation. Such a tack ignores the proper standard of comparison, which is not inaction, but rather includes the private actions that would have occurred had they not been preempted by the regulation. Unfortunately, the counterfactual cannot be observed directly, since the regulatory mandate will insist on some other state of the world.

11. Coase [1960] shows that, though it is child's play to observe some externality-producing situations (and imagine countless others), it is all too frequently ignored that the vast majority can and will be internalized by cognizant human beings.

12. It seems to have escaped the notice of the commission members that to the extent that one of these people had found a way to withdraw at a higher price than he actually received, that would have meant that someone else would have taken a bigger loss. In other words, the complaint, is merely one that the losses were not distributed in some alternative way. The report makes much of the undeserved losses that some individuals suffered, but says little about who deserved to absorb those losses instead.

13. This is evidence that the efficient market hypothesis must be adopted in a weak enough form to embody a period for information digestion that is measured in days, even weeks, in some instances. But while such an observation has some intellectual implications, it seems to have no regulatory ones.

14. Clearly, it is desirable for the Federal Reserve system to insure that a sudden and substantial decrease in liquidity does not occur economywide. The "quantity theory of money" implies that such an impact on liquidity would be mirrored by a substantial decrease in the rate of overall economic activity. But that does not imply that infusions of liquidity need go directly to clearinghouses. Nor does it imply that the liquidity that does reach the clearinghouses through private banks should be priced at anything other than what the market dictates from other demanders of similar riskiness. In other words, the plight of the clearinghouses did not imply that they should be blessed with perferential treatment by the Federal Reserve.

15. "A security comes to be traded on an exchange in one of two ways. A company may file an application with the exchange and be accepted for listing. Alternatively, subject to SEC approval, an exchange unilaterally can trade securities not listed on that exchange, regardless of whether the issuer has applied for or even desires a listing with the exchange" [Macey and Haddock 1985, 329].

16. "[E]xchange rules, with full SEC support, make it extraordinarily difficult for a listed company to delist voluntarily. . . . The NYSE delisting guidelines, which an issuer must satisfy under section 12(d) of the 1934 [Securities Exchange] Act before applying to the SEC for deregistration, provide that two-thirds of the issuer's shareholders must vote to delist, and no more than ten percent can oppose delisting. Furthermore, the [securitles and Exchange] Commission sometimes requires a majority vote of shareholders *per capita*" [Macey and Haddock 1985, 350].

References

Arrow, Kenneth J. 1963. *Social Choice and Individual Values* New York: Wiley.

Brady Commission. 1988. *Report of the Presidential Task Force on Market Mechanisms.*

Buchanan, James M., and Stubblebine, William Craig. 1962. "Externality." *Economica* 29:371–384.

Coase, Ronald H. 1960. "The Problem of Social Cost." *Journal of Law and Economics* 3:1–44.

Dwyer, Gerald P., Jr., and Hafer. R. W. 1989. "Do Fundamentals, Bubbles, or Neither Explain Stock Prices? Evidence from Seven Countries." This volume.

Greenwald, Bruce, and Stein, Jeremy. 1988. "The Task Force Report: The Reasoning Behind the Recommendations." *Journal of Economic Perspectives* 2:3–23.

Haddock, David D. 1989. "An Economic Analysis of the Brady Report: Public Interest, Special Interest, or Rent Extraction?" Forthcoming in *Cornell Law Review*.

———, and Macey, Jonathan R. 1986. "Controlling Insider Trading in Europe and America: The Economics of the Politics." In *Law and Economics and the Economics of Legal Regulation*, ed. J. Matthias Graf, v.d. Schulenburg, and Göran Skogh. 149–167.

———. 1987. "Regulation on Demand: A Private Interest Model, with an Application to Insider Trading Regulation." *Journal of Law and Economics* 30: 311–352.

Macey, Jonathan R., and Haddock, David D. 1985. "Shirking at the SEC: The Failure of the National Market System." *University of Illinois Law Review* 315–362.

Manne, Henry G. 1966. *Insider Trading and the Stock Market.*

McChesney, Fred S. 1987. "Rent Extraction and Rent Creation in the Economic Theory of Regulation." *Journal of Legal Studies* 16:101.

Peltzman, Sam. 1976. "Toward a More General Theory of Regulation." *Journal of Law and Economics* 19:211–240.

Stigler, George J. 1971. "The Theory of Economic Regulation." *Bell Journal of Economics* 2:3–21.

Telser, Lester G. 1988. "October 1987 and the Structure of Financial Markets: An Exorcism of Demons." In *Black Monday and the Future of Financial Markets*, ed. Robert W. Kamphuis, Jr., Roger C. Kormendi, and J. W. Henry Watson. Chicago: Mid America Institute.

COMMENTARY

by Kenneth M. Lehn*

Professor Haddock provides a provocative analysis of the Brady Report,[1] a document that has played an important role in post-crash policy discussions concerning possible "reforms" of our financial markets. Professor Haddock takes a critical view of the Brady Report, suggesting that it relies too heavily on government regulation, and not enough on the private incentives of exchanges, to address possible systemic shortcomings that were revealed during October 1987.

Although I agree with most of Professor Haddock's analysis, I take a slightly different, and perhaps more sympathetic, view of the Brady Report. First, while the report's "one market" approach suffers from some weaknesses that are discussed by Professor Haddock, it does properly emphasize the importance of maintaining the linkage between the futures and stock markets, especially during periods such as October 1987. This

* Chief Economist, U.S. Securities and Exchange Commission. The views expressed here are those of the author and do not necessarily reflect the views of the Commission or the author's colleagues on the staff of the Commission.

emphasis, in part, elevates the stabilizing role played by index arbitrage, and encourages institutional arrangements that foster such arbitrage.

For example, consider the Brady Report's endorsement of coordinated trading halts in the stock and futures markets. As economists, our natural predisposition is to object to trading halts. However, in judging the potential efficacy of coordinated trading halts, it is important to recall that we had *uncoordinated* trading halts in individual stocks on October 19–20 and in the futures markets on October 20. By raising the costs of index arbitrage, these ad hoc, uncoordinated, and unpredictable trading halts contributed significantly to the uncoupling of the stock and futures markets, and diminished overall liquidity in the markets. In justifying its circuit breaker proposal, the Brady Report described the pernicious intermarket effects of uncoordinated trading halts during October 1987:

> The intermarket impact of trading halts was vividly illustrated in October. When the NYSE's automated stock order system, DOT, was rendered ineffective, index arbitrage became infeasible, robbing the index futures markets of much needed buying power. . . . Because they [trading halts] affect trading throughout the intermarket system, circuit breakers need to be coordinated from a broader intermarket perspective. . . . Closing one market segment can have a destabilizing impact throughout the market system. [p. 66]

Although practical issues concerning the design of circuit breakers exist, including the selection of appropriate triggers and procedures for reopening markets, the Brady Report's one-market approach provides a reasonable justification for having coordinated trading halts during extraordinary periods such as October 1987.

Professor Haddock criticizes the Brady Report for ignoring "the notion that adequate incentives may exist to spur private institutions such as the New York Stock Exchange (NYSE) to continue innovating and developing appropriate exchange controls." Reliance on the private incentives of exchanges is highly appropriate for many issues in securities regulation, but there is reason to be somewhat skeptical about these incentives as they pertain to intermarket issues.

For example, in response to the stock market crash, on October 20, 1987, the NYSE announced that it was indefinitely suspending the use of its DOT system, which is the automated order entry system that is used for index arbitrage trading. As the Brady Report states, "from the narrow perspective of the stock market, an inactive DOT system may have appeared beneficial, since it made program selling difficult [p. 67]." However, by raising the cost of index arbitrage, the suspension of DOT effectively removed a source of potential liquidity from the futures markets, and contributed to the persistent disparity in futures and stock prices throughout October 20.

Although the NYSE lifted the suspension of DOT in November 1987, it subsequently adopted a pilot plan that called for suspension of DOT when the Dow Jones Industrial Average (DJIA) moved 50 points or more in a single day. Evidence from April 14, 1988, the only day on which the DJIA declined 50 points or more during the pilot, vividly reveals the adverse intermarket effects of suspending DOT. On this day, index futures traded at fair value until the DJIA declined by 50 points in mid-afternoon. Almost instantaneously with the suspension of DOT, the prices of index futures went to a deep discount, and remained there for the duration of the day. Hence, it seems clear that the suspension of DOT resulted in disparate prices in the futures and stock markets, which added to price uncertainty, and likely delayed some buy orders in the equity markets. Although the NYSE subsequently announced that it would not seek SEC approval for the indefinite adoption of this plan, this example nonetheless illustrates the potential inconsistency between the private interests of exchanges and economic efficiency.[2]

Professor Haddock's analysis of the political economy of the Brady Report is insightful, but as he admits, it is too early to assess the report's importance. Already, the Brady Report has been supplanted somewhat by the creation of the Presidential Working Group on Financial Markets in March 1988.[3] On May 16, 1988, the Presidential Working Group released an Interim Report that concurred with several of the Brady Report's recommendations, including the establishment of circuit breakers, refinements in the clearance and settlement systems, and improved information flows.[4]

However, some of the Presidential Working Group's recommendations differed from the Brady Report's. For example, whereas the Brady Report recommends that the Federal Reserve Board be given authority over intermarket issues, the Working Group recommends that "cooperative efforts under the existing regulatory structure will be more effective and less disruptive than more formal, additional legislated structure."[5] Similarly, the Brady Report offers the following perspective on appropriate margin policy:

> In view of the October experience, the underlying logic of consistent margins for professional market participants in the one-market system is compelling. If from a public policy viewpoint, a given margin level for investment in stocks makes sense, should lower margins and the potential for more financial leverage and speculative investment be allowed for market participants investing in stocks via derivative investments? [p. 66]

In contrast, the Presidential Working Group presents a divided view on margin policy:

> Chairman Ruder believes that, at least as an interim measure, margins on futures and options should be increased, in order to increase investor confidence, decrease derivative market speculative activity, and reduce the illusion that the derivative markets provide sufficient liquidity to allow investors and traders to liquidate quickly large portions of their entire portfolios. Chairman Gramm, the Treasury, and Chairman Greenspan, on the other hand, do not believe that the evidence supports the conclusion that higher margins will reduce volatility. Moreover, higher margins raise transaction costs and could have a negative effect on market liquidity and efficiency, possibly increasing volatility, and risking the movement of futures trading into off-shore markets [p. 5].

Thus, while the Presidential Working Group has endorsed parts of the Brady Report, it also has qualified some of the report's major policy recommendations and rendered them less relevant.

In addition to examining the Brady Report, a complete analysis of the political economy of proposals to reform financial markets needs to examine the incentives of legislators. It is noteworthy that, one year after the crash, no significant legislation to alter the operation of financial markets has been passed. Professor Haddock suggests that this congressional inaction is consistent with the rent extraction theory, but not the special interest theory. Most likely, however, congressional inaction has resulted for several reasons that are unrelated to the rent extraction theory.

First, the institutional structure of Congress undoubtedly has had a significant effect on efforts to pass crash-related legislation. Many of the legislative proposals (For example, transferring authority over stock index futures to the SEC) have fallen within the jurisdiction of both the agricultural committees, who have jurisdiction over the futures markets, and the securities subcommittees. To the extent that these committees reflect the interests of the futures and securities industries respectively, then a political deadlock, not the rent extraction theory, may explain the congressional inaction. Second, the increased competition from foreign securities and futures markets undoubtedly has dampened legislative enthusiasm to enact legislation that may raise transaction costs in U.S. markets and induce institutions to trade abroad. Finally, as stock price volatility has declined to precrash levels, the sense of urgency that prevailed in Congress immediately after the crash has dissipated.

In sum, Professor Haddock has provided an insightful analysis of both the economics and politics of the Brady Report. In addition to accomplishing its immediate objective, Professor Haddock's article will provide a useful perspective in the future, when, after the next significant decline in stock prices, policy proposals to reform financial markets quickly resurface.

Notes

1. *Report of the Presidential Task Force on Market Mechanisms* [1988].

2. An interesting historical analogue to the NYSE's DOT policy is found in Francis L. Eames, *The New York Stock Exchange*, (New York: Thomas G. Hall), [1984]. In a chapter entitled "Use of the Telegraph," Eames writes: "The arbitrage business conducted by members of the New York Stock Exchange between New York and other American cities was formerly very large. But competition between the arbitrageurs became so extreme that some members, dealing through partners on Exchanges in other cities, often conducted their operations on these Exchanges in ways that were considered to be detrimental to the interests of the New York Stock Exchange." It was believed to be practically impossible to control a member's operations on another Exchange. Consequently, in May 1984, some of the facilities for sending instantaneous and continuous private quotations to other cities were withdrawn. Since that date the domestic arbitrage operations have been on a very reduced scale [pp. 90–91].

3. The Working Group consists of the Secretary of the Treasury, the Chairman of the Federal Reserve Board, the Chairman of the Securities and Exchange Commission, and the Chairman of the Commodity Futures Trading Commission.

4. *Interim Report of the Working Group on Financial Markets* [May 1988].

5. Ibid., p. 3.

MIX
Papier aus verantwortungsvollen Quellen
Paper from responsible sources
FSC® C105338

If you have any concerns about our products,
you can contact us on
ProductSafety@springernature.com

In case Publisher is established outside the EU,
the EU authorized representative is:
Springer Nature Customer Service Center GmbH
Europaplatz 3, 69115 Heidelberg, Germany

Printed by Libri Plureos GmbH
in Hamburg, Germany